POETRY AND THE SACRED

By the same Author

POETRY AND MORALITY

POETRY
AND THE SACRED

By

VINCENT BUCKLEY

BARNES & NOBLE, Inc.

NEW YORK

Publishers & Booksellers Since 1873

Published by
Chatto & Windus Ltd
40 William IV Street
London W.C.2

Published in the United States, 1968
by Barnes & Noble, Inc.

Printed in Great Britain

One says 'Poetry is a conservative art, that often serves revolutionary purposes'; and the other 'Poetry is a radical art, and its deepest power is its power to conserve'. There is no need to choose between these two accounts; each poet will do that for himself.

Acknowledgments

Acknowledgment is made for permission to include quotations from the following copyright material: W. H. Auden *Collected Shorter Poems* 1927–1957 (Faber and Faber Ltd and Random House Inc); T. S. Eliot *Collected Poems* 1909–1962 (Faber and Faber Ltd and Harcourt, Brace & World Inc); Gerard Manley Hopkins *Poems of Gerard Manley Hopkins* (Oxford University Press); Robert Lowell *Poems* 1938–1949 (Faber and Faber Ltd and Harcourt, Brace & World Inc); Theodore Roethke *The Far Field* (Faber and Faber Ltd and Doubleday & Co Inc); Dylan Thomas *Collected Poems* 1934–52 (J. M. Dent & Sons Ltd and New Directions Publishing Co); W. B. Yeats *Collected Poems of W. B. Yeats* (Macmillan & Co Ltd, London, and The Macmillan Company, New York).

Contents

Introductory   *page* I

1. Specifying the Sacred   4

2. Sacred into Religious   22

3. The Persistence of God   55

4. Deep-witted Wyatt   77

5. John Donne's Passion   99

6. Blake's Originality   117

7. Melville: The White Whale as Hero   144

8. W. B. Yeats and the Sacred Company   172

9. T. S. Eliot: The Growth of Vision   205

Index   239

Note on References

Readers will notice a certain discrepancy in my use of footnotes: the six essays on individual authors do not use the normal scholarly convention, while the three more general essays do. The reason is that all the six, in their original versions, were written for a critical journal whose editorial policy requires references to be kept to a minimum, and those few to be incorporated in the text. To supply full and accurate footnotes now would be a considerable labour, and one hardly justified by the result. Accordingly, I have used footnotes for these essays only in cases where a reference had to be not only identified but explained or otherwise elaborated. In the case of the three general chapters, it would be absurd to follow this practice, since there is such a range and number of works referred to. Hence the discrepancy; but I apologize for any puzzlement it may cause, or any loss of intelligibility to which it may lead.

Introductory

THERE is an unresolved problem in the very structure of this book; a problem similar to that which, in its first part, I have tried to analyse. It is not precisely the common problem of adjusting the particular example to the thesis which it exemplifies; for, in a sense, I have no thesis, or none that is not comprised by general and particular together. Rather, it is the problem of suggesting in what sense the particular analyses are 'examples' at all. One reader may think it eccentric to regard Johnson as a religious poet, while another may feel cheated by my appropriation of Wyatt; for there are many people who have an interest in keeping the term 'religious' as narrow in application as possible; on this matter, some fervent Christians see eye to eye with some militant atheists. There are other readers who, though quite happy to have the term stretched as wide as it will go, may wonder why, if I am 'really' interested in religious poetry, I show such an odd preference for Wyatt over Herbert and Hopkins, surely the two most centrally religious poets in the language. The answer to both objections is simple: The particular essays were written before the general, and are not to be taken in any simple way as examples of what is contended for there; I wrote on the people I was most interested in, not on those who would help my 'thesis'; and although I offer a definition of 'the religious' which will, I hope, cover much of the work of all the writers I deal with, I cannot offer a definition which will contain or explain them, and hence the actual applications of this word will vary, however subtly, from writer to writer.

I think, in fact, that in dealing with any group of writers, and not only religious ones, it is important to let the terms of analysis as it were vary themselves. The duty of a critic is to present the work, not to enclose it; and one's own sense of it must be so formulated as to reveal something of its *specific* life, quality, and presence. For this reason, as Yvor Winters' practice demonstrates so well, the choice of quotations is as important in its way as anything else one may do. For one thing, they are a constant challenge to find the terms which will fit the *œuvre* they represent, rather than the critic's sensibility or view of life. It is not of prime importance for anyone to bear witness to a critic's sensibility; and what the work of great poets bears witness to is not, chiefly, the sensibility represented in it.

But if it is important to serve the works, and not one's own sensibility, it is also important to place them for kind and stature in such a way as to avoid getting too involved in the ugly academic game of ranking, or the even uglier game of one-upping. As Allen Tate says, Yeats is more intelligent than any of his commentators; I feel inclined to say, than *all* his commentators. Once again, it is essential to test the works for stature in a way that will serve *them*; and once again, a certain variety of approaches seems called for.

On the other hand, I notice when I re-read these essays on particular writers that they do have something of a common structure; they are, to use the word made famous by Leavis, attempts at the 'revaluation' of writers all of whom are of great repute. Not that each essay offers a completely original reading of its subject; some may do so; it would be strange and possibly disconcerting if they all did. No doubt, too, if one had time, talent, and attention enough, something resembling a literary history would emerge from the individual assessments, as it does so remarkably in *Revaluation*. But works are apt to suffer some disadvantages when the desire to construct such a history is the primary motive of the critic. My intention takes me, indeed, away from rather than towards the construction of a literary history; for, as I have said, my intention has not been to impose, or even to elicit, a religious theme or themes, but to suggest the variety of modes and directions which the religious impulse in literature may take, and in the course of doing so, as a means to doing so, to find the terms most appropriate to the specific presence of each *œuvre* and, indeed, of each important work within it. I cannot hope to have succeeded fully, since criticism is notoriously such a personal business, and in it the personal so notoriously keeps breaking down into the subjective. I often wonder if the consciousness of this sliding movement taking place within one's own consciousness, the recurrent sense of the lapse from full attention to oblique awareness, is more responsible even than ideological fervour or the existence of so many *idées fixes* for the patterns we prematurely impose on literature. In any case, all of the writers I have been concerned with are quite capable of getting up and walking away with the nails.

CHAPTER I

Specifying the Sacred

IT is a great pity that no-one has undertaken a study of changes in the history of the word 'religious', as Raymond Williams has so valuably done with the word 'culture'. Doubtless, such a man would have an immensely harder task than Williams, whose keyword was of comparatively short provenance, and so could be approached without a great deal of discomfort. Its difficulty may be suggested by the very fact that, while Williams had a noun to work on, I feel obliged to specify an adjective. To speak of the relations between religion and poetry would be to venture on a bogland. For one thing, everyone assumes that he knows what the word 'religion' means; religion is something which you have or have not got, something that belongs to you ('what is *your* religion?') or that you would prefer to go without ('I have no time for any religion'); or it is something *to* which you belong, something by which you live, something that would remain there, unchanged, external, demanding, whether you acknowledged it or not, an institutional allegiance rather than a personal vision, and hence an institutional vision to which your relation is bound to be one of conformity rather than extension. No doubt it is these senses of the word that led Bonhoeffer to call for a 'religion-less Christianity'; though that term itself is so odd that one can never be quite sure. At any rate, religion in these senses hardly applies to poetry at all; or, if it does apply, it does so by analogy. It would be possible to go on using the noun, 'religion', with great and rigorous cheerfulness in analysing 'the issues of religious poetry', and miss the real issues entirely. But those issues are much harder to avoid when, instead of the noun, we question the adjective, 'religious', which stands at

4

the centre of a group of adjectives to suggest why they ought not to be regarded as mere synonyms or antonyms: religious, sacred, divine, supernatural, irreligious, profane, secular, natural.

Much work has of course been done on changes in religious belief and religious sensibility. There is, pre-eminently, the monumental work of Hoxie N. Fairchild, *Religious Trends in English Poetry*, which takes for its province the controversial centuries (1700–1920). There is M. M. Ross' *Poetry and Dogma*, which deals chiefly with the seventeenth century, as does Douglas Bush's *Science and English Poetry*. There is A. S. P. Woodhouse's *The Poet and His Faith*, which lives under the shadow of Fairchild's much more important work. Then there are all those works which examine the decline of a tradition or traditions. Donat O'Donnell writes of the break-up of Christendom in the modern Catholic imagination; George Steiner writes of the death of tragedy, J. B. Broadbent of the death of love poetry, J. Hillis Miller of the disappearance of God. And I have no doubt whatever that the phenomena dealt with by all these critics merge with one another in one great movement within society and the psyche. Yet it is interesting that Fairchild and Ross, for example, approach the matter in terms of the erosion of Christian dogma and, through that, the erosion of a certain symbolic or sacramental realism in the poets who were the victims of it. It is not my purpose to dispute whether such an erosion took place, or to offer an historical account alternative to theirs, but to suggest that it is time for the terms of the discussion to be widened again, to be conducted in terms of 'the religious' and 'the sacred' rather than in terms of 'the revealed' or 'the dogmatic'. My interest, in other words, will be anthropological as much as doctrinal.

If these men, with their sense of doctrinal centrality, provide a less than fully satisfying guide in my present purpose, a thinker like Arnold, with his amiable anti-dogmatism, is formalise and to render dynamic the sense of man's separation

5

equally unsatisfying on the other side. Indeed, when I think of Arnold's predilection for balancing comprehensive nouns, my preference for the adjective is strengthened. Arnold is willing to tell you not only what 'culture' is, or even what 'religion' is, but also whether this man has it or has not got it, to what extent that man approaches it or is diverted from it. However supple the play, however scrupulous the concern, the effect of this habit is to focus attention on the word rather than on the works it is apparently used to elucidate. Arnold was a most religious man, as his letters and notebooks show; but his definition of religion as 'morality touched by emotion' is singularly unhelpful.

He is not the only critic to hypostatise in this way. For Santayana, 'religion and poetry are identical in essence, and differ merely in the way in which they are attached to practical affairs. Poetry is called religion when it intervenes in life, and religion, when it merely supervenes upon life, is seen to be nothing but poetry.'[1] For A. C. Bradley, the starting-point of religion is 'the experience, on the one side, of my feared or felt separation from something conceived as beyond me, much greater than I am, superior to me in mode of existence and powerful over me; and, on the other side, the experience of the removal of that separation by my submission to, or union with, this something, a removal which gives me freedom and happiness. Or, more briefly, it is the experience of freedom from evil attained by willed union with a being which is free from evil'.[2]

As compared with Santayana, or even with Arnold, this will seem a large step in the right direction; but even here the word 'experience' tends to suggest too static and formalised a sense of that separation and that union. To take one example only: as I shall argue, the kind of redefinition of God under-taken, however implicitly, in *Moby Dick* is an attempt to de-

[1] *Poetry and Religion* (New York, 1900), p. v.
[2] Quoted by Fairchild, Vol. II, p. 280.

from and union with the forces which overshadow his life; so that we are returned to the notion of God as mysterious, active, possessing initiative, holy and terrifying—precisely the notion taken over by Christian metaphysics from the Old Testament and available, in any case, in the New. It is as though certain parts of a life's experience were discovered and declared as sacred in order to suggest that the whole of life is, in some final sense, sacred; but it also, by testifying to *God's* action and presence, makes those areas, and that God, the Holy in relation to whom men must bow down. To say as much as this is to anticipate my argument; but the fact is that we may have definitions of religion which, however generous their scope, and however consistent their terms, do a good deal less than justice to the communal experience they refer to; and I think that Bradley's definition is of this kind. So is Woodhouse's when, in speaking of religion in the West, he says, 'The minimal dogmatic requirement appears to be the recognition of a power, anterior and superior to man, which serves to explain to man himself and his universe and to give a measure of meaning and guidance to his life, and which, therefore, becomes the object of his worship . . .'[1] Whether the requirement is minimal or not, this statement of it is very flat, quite out of key with the forces it refers to. And 'explain' is surely wrong, particularly when it is great poets we are thinking of; is Donne, for example, or is Wyatt, or Coleridge, looking in poetry for an explanation of his universe?

When faced with such difficulties of definition, one does well to remember that the expert in Comparative Religion, Mircea Eliade, is more cautious in his offerings of meaning. He says, indeed, that while the element of 'the sacred' is an irreducible element in all religious experience, he sees no point in 'beginning with a definition of the religious phenomenon'.[2]

---

[1] *The Poet and His Faith* (Chicago, 1965), p. 2.

[2] *Patterns in Comparative Religion*, Meridian edition (Cleveland and New York, 1963), p. xiv.

7

The reason is clear; if he begins with a notion of what a religious phenomenon *is*, how it is shaped, what factors produce it, or how we are to account for it, he is going to miss, or to have no interest in, a large number of cases where 'the sacred' is manifested; the end result will be to confirm the truncation of a concept. I feel the same about the notion of 'religious poetry'; and, although of course I have no intention of proceeding with Eliade's far-reaching scholarly inclusiveness, I do not want to exclude any poet *a priori*.

It is interesting that, since Blake and Wordsworth, there has been a good deal of discussion about the religious nature of poetry; not about the nature of 'religious poetry', for that concept as a concept has had little effective issue since the seventeenth century, but about the religious nature, or in some cases implications, of poetry itself. In his essay 'Religion and Literature', T. S. Eliot has justly remarked that when men of our culture speak of religious poetry, they mean something which is 'a variety of *minor* poetry; the religious poet is not a poet who is treating the whole subject matter of poetry in a religious spirit, but a poet who is dealing with a confined part of this subject matter; who is leaving out what men consider their major passions, and thereby confessing his ignorance of them'.[1] That this should be so is very sad, but it is chiefly the fault of those who would claim the title of 'religious poet' for themselves. The discussion I am thinking of has taken place quite outside this charmed circle; and it is rich and varied in its expressions. Thus David Jones, D. S. Savage, and Auden all speak of poetry as itself a sacred act; and while Auden goes on to talk of it as specifying sacred occasions, Savage says that at least 'great art . . . declares the inherent structure of the universe'. That is, poetry is an act both sacred and sacralising. A. D. Hope sees it in the same terms, though he carries their implications still further. For him, poetry is

[1] *Selected Essays* (London, 1932), p. 390.

a way in which man carries out his side of the continual responsibility for maintaining the frame and order of the world, from the rising and setting of the stars, the procession of the seasons, the nature of beasts and plants and rivers and seas, the order of society and the behaviour of supernatural beings.[1]

It is hence 'an act of celebration',[2] which 'involves a sense of communion with those natures and participation in their processes. It is for the poet to feel himself to be not merely the mirror of nature or its commentator, but the voice of creation, speaking for it and as part of it.'[3] Allen Tate in his scholarly fashion and Dylan Thomas in his ebullient way suggest the same orientation for poetry.

There are many more examples, but these few will serve to illustrate both the strongly affirmative nature and the extraordinary persistence of a hope for poetry which exists against the tenor of the age. Now, it is worth remarking that most of these men are speaking precisely as poets, not as observers of poetry; that they are speaking not of religion in poetry but of poetry as a religious act; and that they are locating the religious nature of that act neither in some thesis about the autotelic status of poetry nor in some contention about the basic themes or subjects for poetry but in terms of how the poet is brought as a religious being, concerned with human life and an actor in its drama, to create works which themselves carry his religious being, fortify creation and exist as, in a sense, sacred spaces. No doubt some of them go back for their inspiration to seventeenth century or Renaissance ideas about poetry; but if they do, it is not to ideas of 'sacred' or 'divine' poetry that they are resorting, but to conceptions of the poetic venture as such. And, in any case, these conceptions had a powerful life throughout the nineteenth century; the poets I have mentioned have immediate as well as remote predecessors. Yeats of *Explorations* and *Autobiographies* stands behind them; so does the

1 *The Cave and the Spring* (Adelaide, 1965), p. 14.
2 Ibid, p. 15.   3 Ibid, p. 16.

Wordsworth of the Prefaces and Letters; so, probably, does Blake, though it is hard to be sure; so, certainly, does Coleridge, with his view of symbolism as characterized by 'the translucence of the eternal through and in the temporal'.[1] I am not for the moment concerned to specify precise influences, still less to outline the terms of any implicit debate, but to stress what I have called the strongly affirmative nature and the extraordinary persistence of this *kind* of conception of poetry. If we are to deal fruitfully with the issue of what I earlier called 'religious poetry', it may best be done by abandoning that term, at least in the short run (because there will be need for it later), and speaking of a poetry which specifies the sacred. This will be in keeping with the kinds of concern shown by the poets whom I have mentioned, and many more whom I have not. And it will enable me to work my way into my topic unburdened either by *a priori* definitions or by any suggestion (which I emphatically reject) that religious poetry is a separate and definable *genre*, or 'kind', or 'mode' of poetry.

Before, then, considering at all the vicissitudes in the concept of religious poetry over the past centuries, it is necessary to establish a meaning for two words which, though sometimes used as synonyms, cannot be usefully regarded as synonymous in any strict sense. The words are 'religious' and 'sacred'. Of the first, I propose to offer my own definition, relying as I do so both on what the adherents of a fully articulated religion might be supposed to accept and on what the 'ordinary man', who, as everyone insists, lives now in a secularised world and does not care for religion, might mean by it if he bothered with the concept at all. For the second, which is a term now used more often within studies of comparative religion than within systems or disciplines of devotion, I feel bound to rely on definitions already established within such studies, and, specifically, on the work of Mircea Eliade, who is perhaps the most influential of all the 'believing'

[1] *Political Tracts of Wordsworth, Coleridge, Shelley*, edited by R. J. White, p. 25.

contributors to the contemporary debate about the sacred and the secular, but who writes as a scientist rather than a theologian.

As I say, I cannot usefully offer a definition of 'religious poetry' for two reasons; I do not believe that it is generally useful to talk about such a *genre* or category of poetry, and it is the purpose of this whole study to suggest the great variety of ways in which poetic *œuvres* may exhibit a religious interest or impulse. But I may perhaps offer as general a definition as possible of that interest or impulse. I take it as the impulse to establish the sense of man's life and his human relationships as being connected with, or, better, bonded with forces in the universe, which have their correlations in his own psychic life and so in at least some of his chief relationsihps, but which cannot be accounted for *in terms of* his psychic life, are in some sense superior to him, in some sense govern him, are manifest to him in terms of power and presence, and in some sense require of him adoration, worship, and celebration. They may or may not involve the further concepts of a communal fall, personal sin, personal or communal salvation, and an eternal life lived either in personal or in communal terms. Therefore, they may or may not incite to attitudes of personal *devotion* of the sort which lie behind or within the 'religious' poetry characteristic of centuries up to and including the eighteenth but which have seldom been resorted to with any poetic force since the Romantic movement. They will always, however, incite to attitudes of personal submission and responsibility, even where such a spiritual movement is not very satisfyingly completed; for the forces I speak of, in whatever terms they may be conceived (and the sustained conception of them is theology) will be religious forces only so long as they are seen as having a present relevance to questions of personal identity, meaningful action, and the inner structures of feeling. In this sense, to anticipate my argument a little, a poet like Theodore Roethke or A. D. Hope may well seem to be a more 'religious' poet than many a Christian devotional poet who, however talented and serious, gives the appearance of enclosing his experience in institutional terms and conventional symbols.

It is true, however, that with the development of anthropology and comparative religion, the interest of students of religion has come to be in religious *behaviour* as a classifiable sign of this impulse and the apprehensions which it nourishes. Consequently, the word 'sacred' becomes prominent in a rather different sense from that which it had in the days when it seemed natural for poets and essayists to speak of 'sacred poetry' as though it were a separate literary *genre* representing and enclosing a psychic interest separable from the other interests of the person or the society. Whatever the large disagreements among scholars, I take them, from my limited reading in the field, to agree that the word 'sacred' is not synonymous with the word 'devotional' as a traditional Christian might even now use it, and that 'the sacred' has never been in any culture a *completely* separate category. If the latter is true of primitive cultures, it is much more true of our own, in which a concept of the sacred has for great numbers of men no overt relevance whatever. Yet it seems to be an invaluable instrument for indicating what men do when they engage in religious acts.

In one of his best known works, *The Sacred and the Profane*, Mircea Eliade begins with a reference to Rudolf Otto's famous work, *Das Heilige*, translated here as *The Sacred*. Otto, says Eliade, 'undertook to analyse the modalities of *the religious experience*',[1] which is an experience of God as *power*, the *mysterium fascinans et tremendum*. Such experiences are 'numinous', for they are 'induced by the revelation of an aspect of divine power'.[2] Speaking for himself while endorsing Otto, Eliade comments that 'the sacred always manifests itself as a reality of a wholly different order from "natural" realities'.

[1] *The Sacred and the Profane*: Harper Torchbook Edition (New York, 1961), p. 8. [2] Ibid., p. 9.

Yet he is plainly uneasy; for he goes on to insist that his own interest is not in the *irrational* aspects of religious experience but in '*the sacred in its entirety*'.[1]

It is perhaps as well that Eliade gets away from Otto's terms, for those formulations come from a particular phase of German theological thinking, and may nowadays be found misleadingly dramatic, although I do not see how they could be found completely irrelevant. Eliade's own terms may, in time, be superseded as misleadingly 'scientific' or emotionally question-begging. But there is no doubt that his venture is 'open-ended' in a heartening way, which is one of the reasons why I rely on him for my definition of 'the sacred'.

At this point of his analysis 'the sacred' refers to those forces which I spoke of earlier rather than to a mode of specifying, responding to, or participating in them:

> Man becomes aware of the sacred because it manifests itself, shows itself, as something wholly other than the profane. To designate the act of manifestation of the sacred, we have proposed the term *hierophany*.[2]

An hierophany is 'anything that manifests the sacred';[3] and so

> we must get used to the idea of recognising hierophanies absolutely everywhere, in every area of psychological, economic, spiritual and social life. Indeed, we cannot be sure that there is *anything*—object, movement, psychological function, being or even game—that has not at some time in human history been somewhere transformed into an hierophany.[4]

In each case where something is taken as an hierophany,

> We are confronted by the same mysterious act—the manifestation of something of a wholly different order, a reality that does

---

[1] Ibid., p. 10.   [2] Ibid., p. 11.
[3] *Patterns in Comparative Religion*, op. cit., p. xiv.
[4] Ibid., p. 11.

not belong to our world, in objects which are an integral part of our natural 'profane' world.[1]

And since 'the sacred is always manifested through something',[2] whether that thing is small and simple or large and complex, the recognition of an hierophany is always a break in the continuum of experience, the homogeneity of a world, which otherwise might, and to modern men often does, appear completely 'profane'. But here a certain dialectic appears in Eliade's thinking, a dialectic which at some points narrowly avoids becoming a contradiction. The designation of an hierophany is a break in the profane continuum, and so the designated or designating object seems completely other than the profane; but it also takes place in objects 'which are an integral part of our natural "profane" world', and, far from abolishing their actuality, enhances it. There is in every hierophany 'a paradoxical coming-together of sacred and profane' which 'really produces a kind of breakthrough of the various levels of experience'.[3] Therefore, while 'the sacred' is an absolute category, 'the hierophany' is not; or, to put it another way, the sacred as designating object is never completely able to manifest the sacred as that which is designated: [4]

> Obviously there are no purely religious phenomena; no phenomenon can be solely and exclusively religious.[5]

This is, of course, true in the sense that the behaviour of religious men may be of interest to people besides them, and may be analysed in terms different from those chosen by them; a sociological or juridical account, for example, may be given of it; it may be studied by people like Eliade himself. But it

---

[1] *The Sacred and the Profane*, op. cit., p. 11.

[2] *Patterns in Comparative Religion*, op. cit., p. 26.

[3] Ibid., p. 29.

[4] A distinction which Eliade himself never seems clearly to make, though his analysis requires it.

[5] *Patterns in Comparative Religion*, p. xiii.

is also true in the sense that the sacred object is never completely transformed by its sacred use; it remains within the
environment, manifestly still part of the environment, in the
whole of which it may be taken as suggesting a certain potency.
That is, it shows both a movement into the world of common
experience and a movement within the common experience to
transcend or complete itself. And it is in this second sense that
it becomes useful in the analysis of the varieties of religious
poetry: not because it establishes a category of poetry separate
from all other categories, but because it shows a movement
within the world which the poet deals with and recreates, a
movement which the poet himself might prefer to speak of in
other than religious terms. Furthermore, it is true (and here
again the relevance to poetry is obvious) that sacred things can
become 'an object of veneration or fear according to the circumstances (for the sacred usually produces this double
reaction)'.[1] We see this quality most markedly in poets like
Wordsworth and Yeats, and in a novelist like Melville.
'Veneration and fear' justly expresses the remarkable equipoise
in the recognition of superhuman forces which we find at many
crucial places in their work. But that it *is* an equipoise, and not
merely an ambivalence, is seen in the fact that 'fear' and not
'dread' is the word that commends itself to us when we think
of those passages. 'Dread' seems more appropriate to certain
passages of Coleridge and Hopkins, poets temperamentally
inclined to feel those forces as bearing down on them and even
judging them rather than as offering themselves for a complete
response. And personally I am interested to notice that, when
I think of the very diverse cases of Donne, Smart, and Blake,
I do not feel inclined to use even the word 'fear'.

Leaving such dualities, however (and I mention them at
this point to make it clear that an hierophany is not a simple
and unequivocal event in nature), I return to Eliade, who is
prepared to maintain that the acts of religious man can *never*

[1] Ibid., p. 13.

15

be fully expressed in terms of his own aspiration to self-completion but always involve the recognition of and response to forces outside him, and superior to him, which prompt to his self-completion:

> We must not forget that for religious man the supernatural is indissolubly connected with the natural, that nature always expresses something that transcends it. As we said earlier: a sacred stone is venerated because it is *sacred*, not because it is a *stone*; it is the sacrality *manifested through the mode of being of the stone* that reveals its true essence. This is why we cannot speak of naturism or of natural religion in the sense that the nineteenth century gave to those terms; for it is 'supernature' that the religious man apprehends through the natural aspects of the world.[1]

I quote these passages not because I want to use a show of someone else's 'scientific' method to support an ideology of my own, but for the following reasons: First, that since I have tried to supply a definition of 'the religious impulse in poetry' broad enough to include poets who are certainly not devotional poets, whose work does not at all lend itself to theological exegesis and does not incite either themselves or their readers to worship of an easily identifiable, traditional God, I need a further term which will enable me to both link them with and distinguish them from poets who are 'believers' in the traditional sense; and Eliade's use of 'the sacred' provides that term. Second, the works of many poets particularly since the height of the Romantic movement not only allow for but positively invite or demand analysis in terms which point to their religious quality, but avert theological or doctrinal treatment. Third, since that time, which I take to be a crucial one for my study, even the Christian poets, like Hopkins, Eliot, and Lowell, may be more helpfully approached in the broader terms than in doctrinal categories. Fourth, the more inten-

[1] *The Sacred and the Profane*, op. cit., p. 118.

sively one focusses on a quality in the poetry that one feels it
necessary to call 'religious', the more important it is that one
should provide oneself with a means of avoiding sheer subjectivity.

I confess that Eliade's language of 'the sacred' does not
satisfy me entirely; for one thing, his use of it does contain the
dialectic, verging on contradiction, to which I pointed before;
and for another, the repeated use of it is likely to suggest, and
to be misleading in suggesting, that 'the sacred' is a special and
separable category of experience. It would be a great pity if
having, through the process of historical development, got rid
of the notion of sacred or religious or divine poetry as a special
separable category of *poems*, we lapsed into the complementary
weakness of regarding it as a special, separable category of
experience or apprehension *within* a poem. I think it as important not to presume too readily on the homogeneity of the
sacred within the poet's imagination as to refuse to presume
on the profane homogeneity of the world. Yet, after all, we
need *some* language other than the jargon of 'poise', 'health',
'paradox', and so on in which to present our responses to a
poetry which has already been written and which, as it were,
opens out to be responded to in terms other than those we use
for our everyday relationships.

I do not think it tendentious to maintain that the religious
impulse, as I have broadly defined it, persists in a remarkable
and perhaps astonishing way in poetry, so that we may say
that, even in a desacralised society like our own, there are
some poets who, *as a mode of life*, concern themselves with
estimating, defining, and recreating manifestations of the
sacred. In fact, in a heavily desacralised society there may be a
few poets whose emphasis on this activity will be more inten-
sive and exclusive than it would have been in a society more
habitually open to the sacred dimensions of life. Herbert is
plainly a religious poet in a sense in which Theodore Roethke
is not; his religious poetry is a poetry doctrinal and devotional

in a way Roethke would not even aspire to; yet it would not be completely vacuous to say that Roethke's religious concerns are as intense as Herbert's; nor would it be foolish to ask if Herbert's concerns were more exclusive than Roethke's. The question certainly points to the fact that for Roethke, as for other modern poets, religious apprehensions are inseparable from poetry, or, perhaps more accurately, that for him religious apprehension, what we may even call the religious venture, is implicit in the very poetic act. It is in those terms that he participates in the world and in language. To say this is to suggest, in Eliade's terms, that he is not using poetry as a means of forming a personal religion of nature, but that he is, rather, extending and completing in language a contact with the world which is religious in its nature.

Roethke is not alone in this. In fact, we may almost specify a contemporary poetic type by using these terms; although in doing so we are not necessarily specifying a poetic category. And it is interesting that such a concern should persist and take new forms in an historical period of which the following three phenomena seem to be increasingly characteristic.

First, there is the rise of anthropology and comparative religion which, relying on all sorts of technological and procedural aids, open up to scrutiny a great number of cultures in which the similarities, often most surprising, and the dissimilarities of religious experience may be studied. In fact, among certain no doubt restricted groups of people, the evidence made available by these disciplines is sometimes taken as a new kind of proof for the existence of God or, at least, of 'the supernatural'. It is in this context, which has to do so noticeably with the continuance of poetry, and perhaps of painting, as art forms, that terms like 'the sacred' come to be used as aids to description and interpretation. If they are not yet much used in the criticism of poetry in England, that is perhaps a sign of English reluctance either to lead literary criticism outward to conclusions which might be taken as ideological ones or to meddle with forces in life which are better treated with reserve. Nevertheless, the work is being done in fields other than literary criticism, and unless poetry becomes as desacralised as society has become, it may come to be found necessary in literary criticism also.

Second, there is the remarkable and accelerating debate among Christians about the relevance of a concept of the super-natural, the misleading nature of the word 'religious' in dealing with Christianity, and the relation of the sacred with the secular. On the one hand we have Bonhoeffer's famous talk about a 'religionless Christianity', which is coming to be more and more echoed in all the Christian communions. My own habits of mind are such that I find the reference unintelligible; but at any rate the fact that the term was coined at all suggests that many people within those communions find the religious pressures of Christianity so strong that a special formula has to be used to repel them.

Then too we have attempt after attempt to dissociate Christianity from any notion of the numinous to be found in non-human nature and from any identifiable sense of the sacred. The debate about this matter is already under way, in England as elsewhere. We find books like Ronald Gregor Smith's *Secular Christianity* and Harvey E. Cox's *The Secular City*, whose tendency is clearly enough suggested by their titles, in effect opposed by Brian Wicker's *Culture and Theology*, in which the author argues for the importance of the sacred and for ways of re-establishing and recreating it not simply as a concept but as a mode of participation in the world. On the one side, the basic image of life is that of the atomised individual cleaving in faith to an absent God, or that of the modern city, not organic-seeming like (say) Florence or Dublin but so formalised and institutionalised as to seem to constitute its own world; on the other side, the basic image is that of a non-human world and a human community being remade towards some state which is seen as a final one and so as having, even in the present, a character which can only be called eschatological. Christian commentators are coming increasingly to suggest that the Incarnation has, so to speak, assimilated God to the historical process, so that there is no world outside history which can be the object of religious aspiration; but this notion, so variously approached, has not yet been subjected to the analysis which would reveal its implications. We find also the insistence, by now associated with the name of Bishop John Robinson, that to 'demythologise' Christianity involves de-supernaturalising it in accordance with the demands of a de-supernaturalised world. So there is the widespread pheno- menon of a religious faith which is wary of words like 'religion' and a Christianity which asks nothing better than to dispense with concepts of the sacred and of transcendence.

Third, arising out of the facts of the world in which they live, there are poets who wonder whether poetry is an ata- vistic survival, in certain types of psychic structure, which it would be as well to dispense with as soon as possible. A mode of life which is no more than a prolonged acting-out of a regressive syndrome is not only uncomfortable to its first victim, the poet, but confusing to its other victims, his readers. I have had the matter put to me in just these terms— by a poet, of course—and, like many other poets, I have wondered the same thing myself. Yet it is this very wondering that may be the fantasy. And poetry persists, is resorted to for a variety of purposes by an astonishing number of people in our society. Given its difficulty, its persistence is most sug- gestive. It might be thought, for example, that the very self- doubt of the poet is a testimony to, if not a proof of, his almost unwillingly persistent commitment to the writing of poetry as a sacred act and an aspiration to self-completion.

For poetry is an art and act which combines the forming of a verbal statement with the completion of a rhythmic move- ment both on the page and from within the psyche; and it usually does so by heightening imagined or observed particulars to the condition where they have a force as symbols. If this art and act are atavistic, they are also surprisingly difficult and complex. In fact, they serve something of the purpose of a sacralising act; they are resorted to in order to set aside certain experiences or places or people or memories as representatively revealing ones—in however attenuated a form, sacred ones. That some of the people for whom the making of these acts is in effect a mode of life often wonder about their efficacy is a sign not of the weakness but of the strength with which they inhabit their modes of thought and feeling. It is particularly paradoxical that this should be so during the years when the religious 'believers' are trying to 'purify' their faith of all such habits.

CHAPTER II

Sacred into Religious

THIS chapter is largely chronological in structure, but does not claim to offer a literary history, a task quite beyond its scope or my own. But, having suggested the term 'sacred' as one which may help to estimate the variety of religious poetry, I feel bound to test its relevance, and the changing emphases given it, by looking, however briefly and curtly, at some examples; for the changes will be visible not only to the philosopher or theologian or historian of cultures but to the literary critic.

Religious poetry as a *genre* exists from the earliest times and in most cultures; its prototype may be taken as the psalm and the hymn, poems written to celebrate, thank or invoke the adorable forces. And, of course, it is to be found in medieval England. But it is not with poetry which approaches this type that I am chiefly concerned, for except in rare or specialised cultural circumstances it is unlikely to express much of the deepest feelings of the culture, including its religious feelings. In my opinion, even in medieval England the most interesting expressions of religious feeling are seldom those which find ready homes in such predictable forms; and therefore throughout English poetry we are faced with the task of locating religious imaginative life in poetic forms which themselves exhibit, in Eliade's terms, sacred and profane co-existing in such a way as to break through accepted categories.

I

Professor John Peter maintains that in medieval poetry these mixed forms actually constitute an identifiable *genre*, which he calls 'Complaint'. Complaint is preaching versified; it reminds, scolds, and laments:

> To put all the examples of Complaint together—the diatribes, the lamentations, the verse homilies, the moral poems and fables, 'Mirror' and *Timor mortis* poems—is only to reconstruct, in a versified form, the thunderings of the preachers. Against what are they directed, if not against what the Catechism calls 'the pomps and vanity of this wicked world and all the sinful lusts of the flesh'?[1]

It seems to me that Professor Peter is making this kind of poetry not only a separate *genre* but the *genre* characteristic of Christian religious poetry in these centuries, a poetry used as a way of judging a world in which the means of salvation are scanted by the faithful themselves—and *out* of which salvation is to be hoped for. In other words, the implication is that, for the poets in this tradition, reminders of the world's persistent rottenness are the 'one thing needful'. It would necessarily be a poetry at once earthy and discarnational, envisaging the saving forces as existing quite outside the world of human manners and relationships.

I think it essential, even if we grant Professor Peter his category of 'Complaint', and agree, with one eye uneasily on the poetic evidence, that such poetry lasts into the sixteenth century with little change of theme or emphasis, to deny that it can be the model of Christian religious poetry, that it provides the chief religious poetry of any epoch in English, and that it is even particularly religious in the sense given by my earlier definition. Certainly it is a poetry produced by religious men, but there is a sense in which it is not religious poetry. Certainly, too, what we may call the 'Complaint tremor', the 'deep Christian pessimism', the Pascalian dark vision of human

---

[1] John Peter: *Satire and Complaint in Early English Literature* (Oxford, 1956), p. 47. Peter does not explicitly say that 'Complaint' is a *genre*, but his argument seems to me to involve such a suggestion.

finality, exists in a great deal of Christian poetry; sometimes it becomes a theme, as in Fulke Greville or Samuel Johnson, but more often it is a tremor or undertow of feeling, indicating one pole towards which the temperament is driven by the facts of living. But it exists elsewhere than in Christianity, and it is my own view that it was Eliot's perception of how decisively it led across boundaries of 'belief' that tempted him to coin the expression 'orthodoxy of sensibility'. It undoubtedly supplies one element in much Christian poetry, but by itself it does not provide the chief expression of Christian religious feeling in any poetic epoch.

We may, then, look elsewhere to find examples in early English poetry of a combination of sacred and profane; and when we find them it may be that we are not finding a *genre* at all. It is common to say that the medieval Christian world was not merely a collection of Christian societies, but a Christendom. Within the poetic order which reflected that political order there was a theoretical division of sacred and profane, but also a practical confusion between them. The *Canterbury Tales*, which is by far its greatest English product, is devoted to playing on the ironies of this very situation. But even if we leave Chaucer aside, we may find the confusion dominant in certain sorts of poetry which are, by my definition, unmistakably religious. One account of the unique cultural blend might say that the whole medieval society, in all its relationships and activities, was permeated by a religious sense; that account carries the implication that 'the profane', by being seen in such sharp focus in the context of sacred things and meanings, took on a resonance or colouring of the sacred. But another account might have it that, while that was true in theory, in so to speak cultural intention, in practice there was a tendency for the sacred to profane itself in more senses than one. Again, Chaucer offers us our most telling evidence. Of course, there are medieval hymns and carols in which we would not find any such evidence at all;

but in a good deal of other minor poetry, we would find it very readily. In much of it we get the sense that, while the whole society lived under the shadow of the divine, it did so, at certain crucial points of experience, with a feeling almost of oppression.

It thus becomes an interesting and baffling question in what sense we are to call this or that medieval poem a religious one. That they are all the products of a sacralised culture is not in question; but many poems seem to have been written in reaction against that very fact, or at least in a fascinatedly ambivalent recognition of it. To set against the pure and perfect innocence of 'I Sing of a Maiden' we have the powerful and indeed prototypical emphasis of 'Farewell, this world is but a cherry fair'; and what, for example, is the dominant feeling and interest of 'Quia Amore Langueo'?

> 'My swete spouse, will we goo play?
>   Apples ben ripe in my gardine;
> I shall clothe thee in new array,
>   Thy mete shall be milk, honye, and wine;
> Now, dere soule, latt us go dine,
>   Thy sustenance is in my scripp, loo!
> Tary not now, faire spouse mine,
>   *Quia amore langueo.*
>
> 'If thou be foule, I shall make thee clene,
>   If thou be seke, I shall thee hele;
> If thou ought morne, I shall be-mene;
>   Spouse, why will thou nought with me dele?
> Thou foundist never love so lele;
>   What wilt thou, soule, that I shall do?
> I may of unkindnes thee appele,
>   *Quia amore langueo.*'

Certainly, here as elsewhere in the poetry of Christian mysticism, secular and divine love are used as mutual analogues. But it is doubtful whether the mystical convention, which required the lower love to act as an analogue for the higher, is here filled out; the interest, while keeping both meanings in mind, may actually be of a different sort, and the set priorities of attention reversed. To say this is not to say that the sacred has succumbed to the profane, but that it is a dual force which is registered and presented in these stanzas; and so complete is the assimilation of one mode of feeling to another that it would be an impertinence to try to specify the effect more precisely. At any rate, it does not embarrass us in the way in which the erotic connotations of mystical writings often do; it is a poetry not of fantasy but of fulfilment; and its religious character consists not so much in its power to establish an allegory as in its power to present the duality of forces which I spoke of. It is worth remembering, in this context, E. K. Chambers' remark that in many of the carols, particularly the Christmas ones, it is 'the religious element that is the superadded and not the primitive one'.[1]

If we look, further, at such fine short poems as Dunbar's 'Lament for the Makers' and 'On the Resurrection of Christ' we may find both a similar difficulty of identification and an interesting dissimilarity in dramatic conception to the earlier poems. They represent a most interesting poetic personality; and, taken together, they show a dialectic of defeat and victory. It is a world in which we pass more confidently than in the so-called Complaint poems from one area of expectation to another; from

> He takis the campion in the stour,
> The capitane closit in the tour,
> The lady in bour full of beute;
> *Timor mortis conturbat me.*

to

> The grit victour agane is rissin on hicht,
> That for our querrell to the deth was woundit;

[1] *Sir Thomas Wyatt and Some Collected Studies* (London, 1933), p.

26

There is a sense in which it is a more personal poetry than 'Quia Amore Langueo'; but it is not really a personalised poetry, even in the first of the two poems. The personal situation, which there is felt very keenly, is taken as an end-example or particular focus of situations for which the paradigm, if it is to be sought at all, must be sought elsewhere.

So we get devotional elements in poems of 'complaint' and references of earthy passion in poems expressing devotion. 'Lament for the Makers' is not all defeat, not all lament; and 'On the Resurrection of Christ' shows an interest in dramatic confrontations, in 'battell', as great as that in the meaning of Christ's triumph. The concept of sacred poetry as a *genre* may remain reasonably clear, where we can find examples of it; but generally in the poetry which we continue to read, the concept of the sacred itself, while it remains the object of aspiration, in death and heaven, in practice is subordinated to the process of a life which includes devotion and decay before the eventual salvation which is hoped for. In this the medieval poets are not entirely unlike the rest of us. A further blending of perspectives can be seen in poems like those remarkable pieces, 'A Lyke-Wake Dirge' and 'To-morrow shall be my dancing day', both of them religious poems because of the nature of the forces which they acknowledge and in a sense enact, but both also escaping quite surely from categories of complaint or of the devotional. There is in both a devotion to Christ who enables man to compose his soul for a final testing, a salvation accomplished out of this world, and a compelling vision of this world as the place of specific preliminary testings. That is, the drama is not solely that of a man facing the Judgment but also that of a man preparing his life for the confrontation. One might say that, in these poems, the poet's struggle is to sacralise *himself* in and through his 'profane' activities; and both poems therefore offer a more helpful image of what religious poetry may be than the complaint poems on which Professor Peter places such emphasis.

II

Yet there *are* categories, even *genres*; I do not mean to question that, even though I have been suggesting that, if we want to speak in terms of *genres* (and personally I find other terms more helpful), we may find even in medieval poetry that there is no question of a *central genre*, to which poems may be seen as approximating, but of various *genres*, in few of which do we find many examples in a 'pure' form. For my own part, I am more interested in spirit than in *genre*. But there is no doubt that there were different categories of poems in medieval poetry, and that later poets, like Wyatt, were careful to preserve them. What I would suggest is that so fine a poet as Wyatt was not able to preserve the distinctions completely. The poems I have called his 'lutanist love-poems'[1] are just that; there is no question of finding any 'religious' interest in them. His translations of the psalms are just that; the attempt is to render in a new form precisely the piety which the psalmist expressed.

But I have argued[2] that we find an interesting link and similarity between some of the passages in his greatest 'love' poems and the finest passages in his satires and his psalms; a similarity strong enough to suggest that, at a certain level of his creative personality, Wyatt is a religious poet in the sense I have indicated. Certainly, if we took his translations of the psalms as the chief evidence for this, we would be misled; it is true that a few passages in them reinforce the sense of it got from other places in his work. If I am right in this, it is a particularly telling example of my present argument; for, as I have said, Wyatt fully intended to keep the categories separate; the language of formal prayer and devotion was not able to contain those tendencies of his being that demanded to issue in a poetry which acted out forces of a more generally religious kind. In this lies his deepest resemblance to Donne.

[1] See p. 89 ff.   [2] See p. 77 passim.

Without venturing too confidently into a century in which I have little competence, I may report my impression that, throughout a large part of the sixteenth century after Wyatt, there is little interest in religious poetry, and that, where an interest is discernible, it is an interest in a certain category of *feeling*; it is avowedly devout. Thus arose the category of the 'divine' or 'sacred' poem which persisted well into the eighteenth century. What responsibility the break-up of Christendom and the religious schisms must take for this, I cannot say. It is at least evident that 'the sacred' becomes a category, either of poem or of feeling, quite separate from others, and in a sense quite foreign to that which Eliade gives the term. But 'sacred poetry' as a completely separate category is something of a psychological monstrosity; and where are the religious poets between Wyatt and Donne? Fulke Greville, certainly, and perhaps Spenser, and arguably Sir John Davies. The first is unusual; for, whereas Wyatt was a non-sacred poet 'of Lutheran sympathies', Greville is a sacred poet of Calvinist inspiration; and that is a hard yoke for a poet to bear, not because Calvinism is of no account, but because 'Calvinist poetry' requires an unusual temperament and sets an unusual task. Greville is judged a fine poet by critics whom I admire; personally I find him interesting chiefly as a precursor of Donne. His direct language and his doom-laden ardours present a strong sense of himself as the battleground of salvation; but they do not, as Donne's poetry does, fully *create* the sense of the conflict which drives them. Again, there is a decided tremor, but it is less that of pessimism than of a fascination with the struggle and with its issue in himself; he trembles where he might adore:

> But when this life is from the body fled,
> To see it selfe in that *eternall Glasse*,
> *Where time doth end, and thoughts accuse the dead,*
> *Where all to come, is one with all that was;*

It is magnificent, but it allows little variety or development. One might say that Greville becomes trapped within the limits not only of his own temperament but also of his notion of the sacred. Davies, on the other hand, so far as 'Orchestra' represents him, strikes me as a metaphysician *manqué*; for I find his 'musical' structure creates a sense neither of sacred life nor of unusual movement so much as an incipient ideology. And when I think of Spenser as a religious poet, it is not the Spenser of 'The Shepheardes Calendar' or of the Heavenly Hymns or of the Mutability Cantos of 'The Faerie Queene', but the author of 'Epithalamion'. Quite in what sense that great work is a religious poem I cannot here argue; but it is a celebration of more than its avowed subject. Like Wyatt, but in a quite different way, Spenser is most religious when he is least concerned to be devout. And it is significant that the sense of religious forces becomes most powerful when the union to be celebrated is a sexual one. Wyatt is not the only affinity; I think, with whatever qualifications, of Donne, Hopkins, and Blake, though the differences in emphasis will no doubt be greater than the similarities.

In this connection the earlier reference to Greville may be salutary, however. For, unlike Davies and Spenser, Greville took as his aim the single-minded attainment of personal salvation and as his theme the unfitness of himself and his world; and, in so doing, he created a new expectation for religious poetry. There is no struggle, much less confusion, between sacred and profane; poetry is the statement of a wayfarer in the paths of salvation and damnation. Of course, it is a quite common view that this is the chief or 'real' subject of Christian religious poetry; not celebration, but the dialectic of salvation. To my mind, it is a most unfortunate view. It is true that Greville's poetry, for example, shows a stress in some ways reminiscent of some of the medieval poems I have mentioned: 'Farewell, this life is but a cherry fair' is an example. But there is also a marked difference. The medieval poem is concerned with a universal situation, which the 'I' formula simply presents in a dramatised form. The Tudor poem is concerned with a personal situation which reflects a general antinomy; and its emphasis is not on the process of life itself, formalised or free, but on the conflict and drama in the individual soul.

Personally I find the medieval poem sharper and more dramatic in its particularity than the later; but that is not because of the author's intentions. What is important is that the later and more *determinedly* dramatic poem became something like a paradigm for religious poetry. An age which feels that any man who actually believes in God must surely feel himself to be in conflict with Him is likely to see conflict as the inevitable centre of any Christian poem; and it would do so without anything of Greville's theological backing. This is, of course, one of the interests which Hopkins has for our time; and it is largely a false interest. After Greville, for whom it was of deathly seriousness, we get its answer and complement not in Donne but in Herbert. In him, again, drama predominates; but now it is not the evolving drama of a passionate life, as it is for Donne and even for Greville, but the drama of contrived imaginative situations. I do not suggest that Herbert did not feel the dramas he proposes in his poetry; but I do think that the dramatic forms in which he proposes them are at a large remove from his initial feeling of them. In other words, Herbert's drama is rhetorical in a way in which Greville's is not; it may be more intelligent, more cultivated, more rounded, but that is a quite different matter.

III

It does seem that, with the Metaphysicals, the attempt to set aside sacred poetry as a separate kind went with the attempt to specify as its subject the worshipper's confrontation, however ambiguous, with God; and that this concurrence, in its turn, had a marked effect on conceptions of poetic form.

The poetry was to be, on the whole, lyrical in scope, dramatic in shape. One influential view was that sacred poetry was poetry put to a sacralising use or uses; versifying the things of God, composing the soul before him, reworking psalms and parables, in other words, recreating forms already sacred. Much of it, then, was a second-order activity. It is not surprising that dramatic shapes and postures were adopted to give verisimilitude and immediacy to what was held to be an experience of conflict and reconciliation. J. B. Broadbent, indeed, claims that this was a general feature of the religious poetry which anticipates *Paradise Lost*, and he gives a more or less doctrinal reason for it:

> But English readers wanted some original expression of Christian myth in its Protestant version—revelation of the glory of God to each individual in the glorious facts of Nature; wholesome devotional nourishment; and a progressive, pragmatic view of history in which the Catholic scheme of salvation centred on the supernal drama of Incarnation, Passion, and Resurrection should be replaced by the Protestant scheme centred on the individual and more naturalistic drama of human depravity, effectual calling and imputed righteousness—involving a shift of emphasis from the crucified and risen Christ to the fallen and regenerate Adam.[1]

This account hardly applies to Crashaw or even to much of Donne, but it has a general persuasiveness. There is a sense in which much Metaphysical religious poetry is a churchy poetry, though not necessarily one carrying much feeling of communal experience. In being so, it may not precisely involve the notion of a specialised *genre*, but only of a specialised spiritual attention demanding certain forms. In fact, in so far as they concentrated on versifying psalms and parables or reworking traditional prayers, the Metaphysicals were committed to the paradoxical task of inventing poetic forms in order to reinforce

---

[1] *Some Graver Subject* (London, 1960), p. 17. The whole of his introductory chapter is relevant to my theme.

a message already declared. And, in so far as they concentrated on portraying the soul's conflicts, they were bound to rely to some extent on the stage-dramas with which they were nearly contemporary.

The venture was nevertheless surprisingly varied, and it took in a large number of poets. Even if we leave out the interesting case of Raleigh, and begin, as I think we are warranted in doing, with Greville, we have such varied poets as Greville, Southwell, Jonson (in a few not very impressive poems), Donne, Herbert, Crashaw, Marvell, King, Vaughan, and Traherne. I would not want to call every one of them a religious poet in any full sense; for, however we estimate Jonson's *gravitas* and implicit piety, his poetry is not religious in any usual sense; and, although Marvell does occasionally set his hand to 'the sacred', the results are puny by comparison with his finest work. But they do compose a *school* of religious poets; and the few 'sacred' poems of Jonson and Marvell bring them within the school. What binds all these poets together is not precisely a manner but a sufficiently similar interest in the world and in the aspiring soul caught or embattled within it. In other words, as more than one critic has said, they represent a 'brief flowering' of a religious concern *of a specific sort*, leading to a specific form or forms.

I cannot, for myself, even speculate on the 'causes' of this flowering; but critics seem generally agreed on at least four of them. First, the polemics and schisms of the preceding century had so sharpened the religious issues as to make them dramatically relevant to the daily life of the spirit; second, the very grossness of much of the polemic had led to a paradoxical purifying of devotional habits in at least some talented poets; third, the greater flowering of stage-drama had provided a dramatic habit on which the dialectic of the individual's religious life could rely, if not for models (I think that suggestion quite misguided), at any rate for stimulus and support; and, fourth, as Martz has maintained, there were available to them techniques of meditation, or of spiritual 'composition', which were themselves of a dramatic as well as a devotional cast. Doubtless there were other reasons, of a socio-economic and philosophical kind; but even those which I have mentioned are enough to suggest that many factors conspired to make their kind of poetry appropriate to the age. The question how Metaphysical poetry arose is a great deal less puzzling than the question why it declined; and to that I have seen no convincing answer at all, other than that the impulse exhausted itself with the exhaustion of its enabling conditions; which is hardly an answer.

As I have said, this school arose, and declined, during a period which begins with the greatest plays of Shakespeare and ends with the towering figure of Milton. Behind its beginnings is a great playwright, and behind its ending is a great epic. Not that I would want to see Shakespeare or Milton as a mere background to the Metaphysical exertions; God forbid. But it should now be obvious that I cannot take Shakespeare or Milton into my argument. What I think may be said is that the Metaphysicals occupy a space between Shakespeare and Milton conceived as the poles of great poetic endeavour, and that they are variously and subtly affected by both poles. This may be seen fairly clearly in the case of Donne; but the crucial case is perhaps Herbert, for the reason which I gave before, that his poetry of aspiration, conflict, and reconciliation has often been taken, and is still often taken, as a norm for Christian poetry of lyric scope, and that I think this critical tendency an unfortunate one. It is particularly unfortunate if we criticise later poets, like Wordsworth or Eliot, by comparison with Herbert's completeness, serenity and sweetness. It seems to me that Herbert's limitations as well as his strengths are both indicated in Woodhouse's comment that 'The Temple' is 'a manual of devotion: it is the seventeenth century's *Christian Year*';[1] and I personally find quite misleading

[1] *The Poet and His Faith*, op. cit., p. 73.

Eliot's suggestion that that poem gives 'a record of spiritual struggle'.[1]

The fact is that Herbert is only apparently a dramatic poet. As I have already suggested, the spiritual dramas which shape so many of his poems are actually subservient in poetic effect to a relatively simple rhetoric of exposition:

> Who would have thought my shrivel'd heart
> Could have recover'd greennesse? It was gone
>   Quite under ground; as flowers depart
> To see their mother-root, when they have blown;
>   Where they together
>   All the hard weather,
>   Dead to the world, keep house unknown.
>
> These are thy wonders, Lord of power,
> Killing and quickning, bringing down to hell
>   And up to heaven in an houre;
> Making a chiming of a passing-bell.
>   We say amisse,
>   This or that is:
>   Thy word is all, if we could spell.

It is fine, but tension is just what it lacks; and when we think of it in connection with the famous anthology pieces, 'Love' and 'The Collar', we may conclude that the attempt to import dramatic immediacy into the relationship is a misdirection of the central poetic impulse. The shaping of such poems is quite different from that of (say) 'Prayer' or 'Jordan', the first of which has for its subject and interest the mystery of things, including the call to salvation, and the second of which has its strength in being a statement, not a dramatisation. The 'I' in 'The Flower' seems to me little more than an excuse for the pattern of paradoxes which compose the poem. The poet uses a deliberately adopted stance and tone of voice, but without creating more than a minimal sense of an actual

---

[1] *George Herbert*: Writers and Their Work Series (London, 1962), p. 19.

and active self, as Donne does so often and so magnificently; and consequently the sense of relationship, of God's actual and immediate presence, which has been so ardently striven for, itself becomes weakened. The poem's speaker is caught, as it were, in silhouette, making a careful and controlled gesture to reinforce his paradoxes. One is much more aware of tactic than one is with Donne; and one remembers that one of the dangers of Metaphysical poetry, from Greville onward, is the set-piece meditation.

I can, of course, see why so many fine critics are so fond of Herbert; and I regret that I cannot be more so. He is a self-controlled poet; he has no rant or centrifugal passion. His devotion seems pure; whatever impurity of motive exists is declared, apologised for, and so in a sense transcended. His imaginative world has a reassuring solidity, partly created by the easy charm and earthiness of his language. And he actually does work out his conflicts in his poetry, or at least presents a convincing impression of doing so. Yet in that very fact lies his limitation as compared with Donne; he solves his *own* problems, he makes no demands on us. This becomes clear when we think of Herbert dealing with the image of himself as a sinner; his ease carries a good deal of self-consciousness, of a sort which suggests a man attending to the weightiness and significance of his own gestures; thus there is a recurrent (though certainly not an inevitable) tendency so to organise the drama as to magnify both sin and repentance out of proportion to the resources of his language. And when I think of Donne's passion of address to God, I find something unlikeable about the sternly playful God whom Herbert tries actually to bring into his poems as a speaking actor.

I say all this not because I want to urge a claim for Donne at Herbert's expense (that should not be necessary) but because I think it unfortunate that the dialectical principle followed in Herbert's more 'dramatic' poems should have been so widely regarded as a prototype for Christian poetry, and that it should in any case have been regarded as genuinely dramatic. For one thing, I can think of no poem by Herbert which I would prefer to King's 'Exequy'; for another, I think Blake and Wordsworth, Yeats and Hopkins and Eliot, all more tellingly dramatic than he, and not because they deal with the dramatic possibilities of the soul's confrontation with God. Like Herbert, they all set themselves at times to create a self which 'tries to speak with full awareness of a supernatural presence, one that feels the hand of the supernatural upon himself and upon all created things'.[1] But they do it with deeper and more sustained passion.

In any case, after Herbert and Vaughan, the path taken by religious poetry to its temporary end in the late Restoration period is a somewhat regressive one. To get to Dryden, we have to pass through Quarles and Cowley, the first of whom surrendered the dramatic method, and hence the sharpness of phrasing, which characterise the earlier Metaphysicals, and the second of whom, in his *Davideis*, simply by-passed the momentous humanist epic of Milton. That is, they are both sacred poets in the simple sense that their work is an adjunct to the poetry of the Scriptures; not recreating it, as Smart was later to do, but elaborating it in order to expound its meaning. Their tendency is regressive. And before noting how their brief attempt came to its dispiriting end in its opposite, it may be well to see how certain commentators have accounted for the decline.

IV

If the first half of the seventeenth century, occupied as it is by the last plays of Shakespeare, by the great figure of Milton, and by the Metaphysical poets, is a coming to fruition of religious poetry, together with the tensions implicit in that very notion, it is plainly also a turning-point in the currency of the notion itself. Several critics have maintained that,

[1] Martz, op. cit., p. 324.

during those fifty or, more accurately, seventy years, something decisive happened to the poetic sensibility, though they
do not agree on the further question whether the tendency
thus begun proved irreversible. For Eliot, what happened was
a 'dissociation of sensibility'; and this term and its implications
have been so much debated that there is no need to take them
up here. For Malcolm Mackenzie Ross, what happened was
similar, but the terminology, and indeed the interest, differs.
In his view, as soon as Protestantism came to tighten its grasp
of the literary imagination, there was a radical change in the
way in which doctrine came to issue in metaphor; an increasingly discarnational theology led to an increasingly discarnate
imagination; the 'firmament of symbol' characteristic of the
Catholic synthesis was broken and its components dispersed;
the sense of community lapsed, and the sense of the divine *in*
the natural gradually disappeared. It would seem to follow that
religious poetry in the sense in which I have been speaking of it
ceased gradually to be a real possibility, and religious poetry as
so to speak a life-long venture engaging all the faculties of man
ceased to be a compelling option for the poet:

> My argument rests on the assumption that the dogmatic sym-
> bolism of the traditional Eucharistic rite had nourished the ana-
> logical mode of poetic symbol, indeed had effected imaginatively
> a poetic knowledge of the participation (each in the other) of the
> natural, the historical, and the divine orders.
>
> The capacity of the Eucharistic symbol in poetry to function
> simultaneously at the levels of the natural, the historical, and
> the divine is threatened and eventually lost in the course of the
> seventeenth century. In poetry, 'The Blood', 'The Body', 'The
> Sacrifice', are reduced to metaphor and below metaphor, finally
> to cliché. 'Fact' and 'value' disengage and draw apart. A Chris-
> tian 'spiritism' holds itself aloof from the order of things—and
> event. The course of English poetry is therefore divided. One
> direction will be that of the utterly secular, under the sign of
> rationalism and materialism. The other will be that of the

romantic idealisms and 'psychologisms', the pseudo-sacred as against the real profane.[1]

This is a large, and largely abstract, way of treating the matter. There is no doubt a lot of truth in it; but I would want for my present purposes only to make three brief observations about it. First, the notion of a 'firmament of symbol' is one which I find myself quite unable to work with, and which is likely to prove a hindrance rather than a help in estimating the actual presence of specific poems. Second, the idea of 'the sacred' implied in his last sentence is quite different from, both narrower than and at a tangent to, the one which I have derived from Eliade. And, third, it is interesting that in his subsequent analysis, Herbert comes to bear a surprising amount of his attack. I find this strange; for though I have indicated that I find (perhaps largely for temperamental reasons) Herbert very limited by comparison with Donne, surely the quality of his poetic world which strikes one so forcibly is not simply its unity but also its solidity. It may be interesting, when we see Ross insisting that, with Herbert, 'the direction, for Anglican poetry at least, was to be away from humanism and towards mysticism', to note that many critics who appear to be very interested in humanism and not at all concerned with 'mysticism' (I think of L. C. Knights, J. B. Broadbent, and D. J. Enright) make exactly the opposite appraisal. Herbert seems for them the distinctively, and perhaps representatively, Christian religious poet.

What seems to me remarkable is not any devolution or loss of analogical vigour which happens between Donne and Herbert, but the almost total change in interest which happens between Herbert and Dryden. When we look at the complex of dates, we will be struck by the way in which the appearances of Donne's works overlap with those of Herbert's, Herbert's with Milton's, and Milton's with Dryden's. But,

[1] M. M. Ross, *Poetry and Dogma* (Rutgers University Press, 1954), p. vii.

by the time Dryden has become the great poet of the age, with
'Absalom and Achitophel' being succeeded immediately by
'Mac Flecknoe', and that by 'The Hind and the Panther', we
have a ruling poet who, for the first time in more than three-
quarters of a century, can hardly be regarded as a religious poet
at all. More accurately, we have a poet for whom religion is a
matter of *allegiance* and hence of argument, with the inevitable
creation of a new kind of satiric mode. And the tendencies
thus inaugurated carry on for a century more. Pope is a very
great poet, but he is not a religious one; for, if he is much
more intensely aware than Dryden of forces to which man's
life is subject, he sees them as forces threatening civilisation
and the unity of the individual psyche, not as forces requiring
in any sense adoration or even awe.[1]

The same is true of Swift as a poet, of Thomson and even of
Johnson. The last is, of course, a paradoxical case; for if in
one sense he is a deeply religious poet, in another he is almost
an anti-religious poet. His gravity is governed by a sometimes
desperate pessimism which seems to derive both from Roman
and Old Testament examplars; the forces which he writes
of in 'The Vanity of Human Wishes' are forces which prompt
to despair rather than to adoration; and any awe which he
feels in contemplating them is a 'tragic' one invoked by
their inevitability; what devotional resources he can muster are
mustered by a promise of escape from them, not by any hope
of transcending or transforming them. Not until Smart do we

[1] Of course, Pope has a much greater claim on our attention than my
remarks suggest. It may be held that his poetry registers a very strong
religious impulse, but gives it a negative or ambivalent cast; that in register-
ing it he is responding to precisely those forces which his age rejected; that
where sacred dimensions are seen in his experience, they are seen chiefly
under their destructive or awful aspect. I think there would be a good deal
in these claims, but I still would not want to speak of him as a religious
poet; one of his central differences from Wordsworth lies in the fact that
Wordsworth liberates in his poetry the forces Pope could not keep out
of his.

find religious poetry of any force emerging again; and Smart, though 'Augustan' in certain of his interests and procedures, in some ways predicts the great Romantics, with their quite new sense of the sacred forces in life and of how they may be re-created or created in poetry.

It is interesting, quite by the way, that if religious poetry lapses with Dryden, so does love poetry, and so does any poetic habit in which tragedy, in either the Shakespearean or the Marlovian sense, can be written. One is tempted to speculate that the fate of religious poetry is bound up with those of love poetry and of tragic awareness.[1] Hoxie N. Fairchild gives a different account from this; like Ross, he sees poetic failure as coming in a quite discernible way from doctrinal inadequacy; but he places the point of breakage some decades later than Ross does; for one thing, he completely accepts Herbert. His massive five-volume work, *Religious Trends in English Poetry*, begins at 1700. He shows how widespread, not only in the post-Restoration decades but also in the early eighteenth century, the irreligious spirit was; Deism came gradually to replace Christianity as the effective motive-power of poetry, scepticism came to be as strong a component as faith in that motive-power, and many poets held very strongly either to a scepticism about *any* purpose in the universe or to an explicit dislike of Christianity and its practices. That is, Fairchild finds ambivalence almost everywhere, and not least in those bodies of minor poetry which their authors would by then continue to call 'sacred', 'divine', or 'religious'.

It is true that John Peter maintains that, a hundred years earlier, there was a widespread ambiguity in moral attitudes; but then Christianity was neither explicitly despaired of nor overtly mocked. At the opening of the eighteenth century, scepticism was strong, faith enfeebled. 'Religious poetry',

[1] See, for example, the odd distribution of erotic poems in *The Body of Love*, D. Stanford, ed. (London, 1966). It supports my thesis surprisingly well.

what there was of it, tried once more to become a separate *genre*, and an intolerantly narrow one, which would admit very little of the poet's life-process. When we find Fairchild cataloguing 'divine poetry' of the eighteenth century, what he is actually dealing with is poems addressed directly to God, most of them 'hymns', and many of them designed for congregational singing; not a religious poetry at all, in any of the various senses in which I have been using the term, but a sort of defiant anti-poetry. Even in the most important of them, Isaac Watts, 'God and nature have nothing in common except in the sense that nature bears witness to the divine power'.[1] Not too strong a witness; more a hectoring reference than a way of life.

As for other poets, like James Thomson, religious poetry is no more than an ego-centred reflection on or 'survey of the works of Nature'.[2] Those works are used to testify to an absent God by testifying to no more than the poet's own reflective powers. In the first forty years of the eighteenth century, the tendency of poetry may be expressed in the formula: 'In short, irreligion goes down; orthodox Christianity goes down; sentimentalism comes up.'[3] After 1740, both religion and rationalism become increasingly swamped by empiricism, scepticism, and sentimentalism. It is true that, partly as a reaction to all this, the Evangelical revival in mid-century produced its own poetry; but Fairchild maintains that this is, in my own term, an anti-poetry, a body of proto-hymn and proto-apologetic, of which the aim is not to express a full sense of life, but to enthuse or to expound on received grounds.

I cannot offer to follow Fairchild's analysis further. Personally I would agree with it as it affects the period up to the beginnings of the Romantic movement. At that point we part company. For his whole account of Blake and Wordsworth

[1] Fairchild, op. cit., Vol. I, p. 124.
[2] Ibid., p. 517. [3] Ibid., Vol. II, p. 5.

rests on the contention that they compounded these vices and corrupted doctrine still further. My own view of the use of 'doctrine' in such an analysis will, I hope, be seen in the following pages. Of Blake I have already written.[1] But Wordsworth is, in any case, the crucial example; and Fairchild takes him as such. For him, Wordsworth is the *opposite* of Donne, Crashaw, and Herbert. Unless men acknowledge their dependence on God's initiatives in saving them personally, they will confuse their own feelings of goodness and strength with God's grace, and treat as a possession what is more properly a need:

> Grace becomes not something that human nature needs, but something that human nature possesses. Different as they are in many respects, Donne, Crashaw, and Herbert are almost wholly free from this confusion. Since they are children of the Church their strong religious inwardness never becomes independent of outward grace, the gift of a transcendent God who has stooped to immanence. In no essential respect do they foretoken the romantic Wordsworth.[2]

If one thinks in doctrinal terms divorced from what is actually going on in the poetry, this is true—or nearly true. But there is a great danger when following this 'historical' impetus to take Wordsworth as simply an example, however 'great', of the debasement of the Protestant sensibility. His greatness is in his originality and his representativeness; and so it virtually excludes the use of him as an 'example' of a tendency; he re-presents a great deal more than he represents. In fact, if he is influenced by what Fairchild calls 'sentimentalism', he also to an astonishing degree reverses the trend of conventional sentiment by so royally creating in his poetry objects adequate to define it; and, to the extent that he does *that*, he also enlarges the feeling so as not merely to personalise it and make it his own but also to give it a scope, an inner

[1] See pp. 117-43.   [2] Ibid., Vol. I, p. 567.

tension and amplitude, which make it inappropriate for us to discuss it in terms of 'sentimentalism' at all.

From one angle, he *may* be an example of Protestant sentimentalism at its melting end; but that is not the most revealing angle, for it both diminishes and distorts. From another angle, or from *within* the poetry so to speak, he is a man who, experiencing the presence of God, does not merely tell us so, but sets out on the immense task of defining that experience and its object in such a way as to re-create them both. There is naturally a danger of subjectivism in this; but, leaving aside the reflection that that may be a danger for all poetry, one cannot in all justice saddle him with a sense of immanence as a substitute for a sense of transcendence. The opposition is, in fact, misconceived when it is so great a poet who is in question. Wordsworth's effort was to re-define God's action in the world by re-creating his personal experiences of forces which make available to him an 'opening toward the transcendent'. This is something Thomson never began to do.

So, if Wordsworth is in some sense the 'heir' of Thomson, or of any tendencies represented by Thomson, he brings the inheritance to so new a definition that it is expanded beyond recognition in any easy terms. He transforms what he inherits. Admittedly, one does not get from his great poetry any but ambiguous and momentary apprehensions of a personal God in the traditional Christian sense. But one feels going on, and in the greatest passages going on most intensely, a struggle not to exclude any relevant intimation either of immortality or of mortality. If the result does not accord with our images of God, it may be that our images of God have been got too easily. Fairchild is right to see the Romantic effort as involving a 'self-expansion';[1] but in Wordsworth's case it is an expansion of the self to meet and answer the force which elicits it. The tension between Wordsworth and (say) Herbert may establish them as the poles of poetic feeling; but that tension is a

[1] Ibid., Vol. III, p. 3.

salutary one in the history of religious poetry. So Herbert
writes, in 'Man',

> My God, I heard this day,
> That none doth build a stately habitation,
> But he that means to dwell therein.
> What house more stately hath there been,
> Or can be, then is Man? to whose creation
> All things are in decay.
>
> For Man is ev'ry thing
> And more: He is a tree, yet bears more fruit;
> A beast, yet is, or should be more:
> Reason and speech we onely bring.
> Parrats may thank us, if they are not mute,
> They go upon the score.
>
> Man is all symettrie,
> Full of proportions, one limbe to another,
> And all to all the world besides:
> Each part may call the furthest, brother:
> For head with foot hath private amitie.
> And both with moons and tides.

And Wordsworth writes, in 'The Simplon Pass',

> Brook and road
> Were fellow-travellers in this gloomy Pass,
> And with them did we journey several hours
> At a slow step. The immeasurable height
> Of woods decaying, never to be decayed,
> The stationary blasts of waterfalls,
> And in the narrow rent, at every turn,
> Winds thwarting winds bewildered and forlorn,
> The torrents shooting from the clear blue sky,
> The rocks that muttered close upon our ears,
> Black drizzling crags that spake by the wayside
> As if a voice were in them, the sick sight
> And giddy prospect of the raving stream,

The unfettered clouds and region of the heavens,
Tumult and peace, the darkness and the light—
Were all like workings of one mind, the features
Of the same face, blossoms upon one tree,
Characters of the great Apocalypse,
The types and symbols of Eternity,
Of first and last, and midst, and without end.

I know the differences are extreme, but I cannot agree that
either is a more 'religious' passage than the other, or religious
in a more satisfying sense; and Fairchild's account would seem
to require that Wordsworth's is not only markedly less satisfying than Herbert's but actually manifests so clear a perversion
of sensibility as to make it anti-religious in the fully Christian
sense. Certainly, the *notions* of what religious poetry may be
differ widely; the passages are polarised in tone, in form, in
decorum; where Herbert dares primness, Wordsworth risks
hecticness. Herbert's sense of the world's process arises
within a doctrinal frame, and a very tight one, as the shape of
the stanzas itself suggests; Wordsworth completely ignores the
question of any such frame, as the run of *his* lines testifies.
Herbert meditates an awareness in the context of an address,
to a known God; Wordsworth creates an awareness in such a
way as to create also an address, but to an indefinite God.
What seems to me interesting is that, while both poets are
aware of process, and both use remarkably different analogical
habits to assign it a meaning, Herbert is re-defining the
world in the presence of a known God, while Wordsworth
is re-defining God by making the world present to himself in certain terms. And in both cases, they are sacred
terms.

Of course, Wordsworth at no point leads outward to the
possibility of a devotional stance; but in poetry the devotional
stance has its own dangers; and, because his 'God' is an unknown one, it is self-transcendence which is his chief concern.
But self-transcendence is not merely self-expansion; and in

this poem what we get is the possibility of the person's transcending himself by creating in language the sense (at once
possibility and paradoxical fact) of the world's being brought
to a state of self-transcendence. For it is noticeable that
Wordsworth is concerned with process as the testimony to a
spiritual state. If, for example, one asked oneself which of the
two passages was the more sacramental in a traditional
Christian sense, one might very well answer 'Wordsworth's'.
Wordsworth is not submerging himself in sensation, any
more than Herbert is. Nor, of course, is Herbert concerned
with a state to the exclusion of a sense of process. Whatever
the great differences between them, differences which I
have done no more than touch on, they at least share this
paradox: that poetry can treat process as manifesting the
state to which it aspires; in very different senses, that state
is in each case a sacred one; the perception of it is in each
case itself a sacred awareness; in both cases religious poetry
is being used not as a *reminder* of what is already known, but
as a way of establishing a sense of the sacred which, without such a use of language, could not be established at
all.

V

It seems to me that it is more fruitful to regard Wordsworth
(and Blake and Coleridge) in some such light than as theological degenerates. And it is important that we become clear
about the most appropriate light for seeing them. The problem
is not so much how to use earlier poets as a norm against which
to assess them, but how to use *them* as a source of concepts
with which to analyse the nature and direction of poetry from
Tennyson to the present: all of which is, from one obvious
point of view, post-Romantic poetry. If the lack of doctrinal
clarity gives a certain vagueness to the Romantic aims, the
great and ambitious vigour of Blake and Wordsworth cancels
out the debilitated and debilitating 'sacred' poetry which

precedes them, and so helps to complete the redundancy of that concept of the 'sacred'. It is a great poetic energy which can once more connect apprehensions of transcendence with the 'organic' feelings which it shows arising both in extraordinary and in the most ordinary situations. And, since we really cannot hope to disentangle doctrine from feeling even in the work of the Metaphysicals, we may see the Romantics as creating a body of religious poetry which does not encourage but discourages the forming of irrelevant categories and the making of false distinctions. Christian critics do no service to religious poetry by applying to our literary traditions concepts which would see *The Prelude* as a perversion of the religious life or as assimilable to modes of sensibility already established by far lesser men. While poets like Collins, Gray, and Chatterton may be regarded as 'harbingers of the Romantic Movement', they emphatically do *not*, any more than Thomson does, provide a set of terms in which Blake and Wordsworth can be profitably assessed. It is relevant, and important, that it was Gray whom Wordsworth attacked for his 'gaudy and inane phraseology'. In one way, these poets are even anti-Wordsworthians, because they rely on, rest in, those sentiments which it became Wordsworth's task to transcend and transform. Similarly, while it is true that Blake always despised what he regarded as Wordsworth's 'naturalism', for the purposes of my present account he can be more profitably joined with than opposed to Wordsworth.

I think we have at this point to make up our minds which poets we are to call religious ones, and in what contrasting or complementary senses we are to call them so. For my part, I can see no point at all in using this language of Gray, Burns, Keats, or Byron, to say nothing of a great horde of lesser subsequent poets. As to Shelley, it may be possible to call his impulse 'religious'; but if I were forced to do so myself, it would be in a sense damaging to his whole *œuvre*. Pound is another ambiguous case; for it is possible to argue that among

the first twenty Cantos there are several which give with
power and beauty a re-creation of classical pagan religious
awareness, but one is never sure to what extent his re-creation
of this awareness is a curiosity of his personal mental museum.
For these reasons, I think it appropriate to say that their
interest for us has little to do with any religious impulse or
awareness. Arnold and Tennyson again make me pause. As
Arnold's Notebooks show, he was a sincere Christian, but in
his poetry he can hardly find the capacity even to raise the
religious *issue*. And I agree with Eliot in finding the religious-
poetic interest of 'In Memoriam' to exist in its quality of doubt
rather than of faith.

If we exclude such poets, I would contend that, since the
beginnings of the Romantic movement, we can see two lines
of religious poetry. They are not precisely lines of influence;
perhaps they are lines of concern. And they do not steadily
diverge; at some points and in some ways they converge; but
they may be regarded as separate. The first is that which runs
through Blake, Wordsworth, Coleridge, Whitman, Yeats,
Lawrence, Dylan Thomas, and Roethke, and whose motive-
power is to re-define God's action in the world in such a way
as to create a quite new sense of God and of man's relation
with him. The second is that which runs through Smart,
Hopkins, Eliot, the later Auden, and the earlier Robert
Lowell, and of which the motive-power is, generally, to
re-create God's action in the world in such a way as to reinforce
a sense of its presence and urgency. The first seeks to create a
tradition, the second to redefine one. The first records the
action of God, and its feelings are those of amazement, inadequacy, a need to speak, even to expound; the second prac-
tises the presence of God, and its feelings are those of worship,
sinfulness, a need to address and be heard. Undoubtedly the
doctrinal is one way of expressing the difference; but it is
not the only way; and, for example, I have suggested[1] that

[1] See p. 205 ff.

Eliot's venture in *Four Quartets* has something in common with Wordsworth's in *The Prelude*. But in all cases there is a concern for the sacred and for poetry as sacred speech or form, since it is the language in which the sacred is not only expressed but approached. And because I think it dangerous to become stuck in contrasting formulae I find it useful at this point to say that if, for example, we take Roethke as the extreme of one kind and the later Auden as the extreme of the other, we may still find them having a surprising amount in common.

Roethke, I suppose it will be agreed, is a non-denominational poet, a poet of the purely immanent God, if of any; Auden is 'obedient to Canterbury', and his later poetry would generally be thought over-refined in attitude and over-abstract in its reflective procedures. In fact, a different sense of each poet may be got when one notices in what a tone Roethke utters the word 'God', and what effects are got by Auden in following 'Prime' with 'In Praise of Limestone' at the beginning of *Nones*, and in closing his most recent collection, *About the House*, with 'Whitsunday in Kirchstetten', whose last line is 'if there when Grace dances, I should dance'. There is not much of Whitman behind this potentially very melancholy celebrant of an individual salvation; behind Roethke Whitman looms, and is acknowledged; 'Be with me, Whitman, maker of catalogues'; and the life of natural things is named, evoked, mimed, to bring out the process of the living human self:

> How can I dream except beyond this life?
> Can I outleap the sea—
> The edge of all the land, the final sea?
> I envy the tendrils, their eyeless seeking,
> The child's hand reaching into the coiled smilax,
> And I obey the wind at my back
> Bringing me home from the twilight fishing.
>
> In this, my half-rest
> Knowing slows for a moment,

And not-knowing enters, silent,
Bearing being itself,
And the fire dances
To the stream's
Flowing.

Do we move towards God, or merely another condition?
By the salt waves I hear a river's undersong,
In a place of mottled clouds, a thin mist morning and evening

I rock between dark and dark,
My soul nearly my own,
My dead selves singing.
And I embrace this calm—
Such quiet under the small leaves!
Near the stem, whiter at root,
A luminous stillness.   "The Abyss"

Plainly, it is not only Whitman who stands behind such poetry,
but Wordsworth too: the rhythm of the feeling is of the
systole and diastole: a luminous stillness is sensed in moving
things, and things are apprehended in movement towards their
own stillness. This is not in Roethke the vacuous paradox it is in
many poets; for it is precisely the *hierophanic* quality of things
which Roethke is trying to define by this method; one might
say that in the very paradox of movement-in-stillness, stillness-
in-movement, lies the hierophany. The result is in one sense a
pantheism, and Roethke might say that his hierophanies did
not merely manifest or declare God but revealed him. But
behind the accumulative energy and interest is the basic
interest which Roethke shares with Auden: the selfhood of the
observer-participant in natural processes, selving himself by
his awareness of other selves, feeling in his very nervous system
the stress which he regards as being from God, gathering his
nervous system to respond by naming God.

   In taking up Auden it is tempting to quote from 'Prime',
but to quote any of that remarkable poem is to be drawn into
quoting it all. Perhaps I can make the point by quoting the

end of 'In Praise of Limestone':

> Not to lose time, not to get caught,
>   Not to be left behind, not, please! to resemble
> The beasts who repeat themselves, or a thing like water
>   Or stone whose conduct can be predicted, these
> Are our Common Prayer, whose greatest comfort is music
>   Which can be made anywhere, is invisible,
> And does not smell. Insofar as we have to look forward
>   To death as a fact, no doubt we are right; But if
> Sins can be forgiven, if bodies rise from the dead,
>   These modifications of matter into
> Innocent athletes and gesticulating fountains,
>   Made solely for pleasure, make a further point;
> The blessed will not care what angle they are regarded from,
>   Having nothing to hide. Dear, I know nothing of
> Either, but when I try to imagine a faultless love
>   Or the life to come, what I hear is the murmur
> Of underground streams, what I see is a limestone landscape.

Auden's method is as much an accumulative one as Roethke's, but in nothing like the same way; where the latter 'catalogues', accumulates names, movements, evocations, images, the former works through an accumulation of epigrams and tones. One of the great critical problems in dealing with Auden's later poetry is to estimate its tone, which has so obvious a dominance in the poetic economy that it, so to speak, generates images and rhythms rather than proceeding from them. His immensely varied good-humour, sometimes wry, sometimes with an undertow of melancholy, occasionally random, often witty, seems to be his central stance for observing the religious world while it is still in its secular seeming. It is a most ambiguous and dangerous method of dealing with the emotions and the issues; but in this passage it is significant how the emphasis falls: there are preferred, chosen processes and land-scapes, which alone can admit the sacred to full definition; the loves of 'the natural man' are inescapably the matrix for a sense of 'the blessed', it is through 'the murmur/Of underground streams' and the 'limestone landscape' that God draws the soul and becomes established there. The natural may be an hierophany; and nothing but the natural can be.

I think this comparison instructive, for it has a wider application. It is pointless taking an Either/Or approach to the question of religious poetry, demanding or rejecting orthodoxy, wincing from or joying in its opposite, crying for a poetic line that marches indefatigably on to God or for one that lollops around him. There is a sense in which all religious poetry is doctrinal, but there is also a sense in which the actual shape a doctrine takes is a matter of temperament. In Roethke and Auden we have separable doctrines, I have no doubt; but we have also separate temperaments; and it is not necessarily Auden who is the more rigorist either in doctrine or temperament. A similar effect, of confrontation and contrast leading to a sense of complementary forces at work, would be got if we compared any poet of the one kind with any poet of the other; indeed, the same effect would be got if poets from within the one group were contrasted, Wordsworth with Whitman, for example, or Blake with Dylan Thomas. What we are concerned with is a phenomenon of divergence and convergence at once; and this fact makes it much less easy than my formula would suggest to distinguish one tendency from another.

Poets like Whitman and Dylan Thomas, for example, will inevitably be disputed cases. As to the first of them, I would not insist on the word 'religious' in speaking of him; but could anyone who held (say) Dowson and Lionel Johnson to be religious poets seriously argue that Whitman is not? Certainly, he has had an impressively religious issue. In fact, he seems to me a poet who urgently demands revaluation. Here if anywhere in poetry (so the conventional assessment runs) is a poet who undiscriminatingly notes a succession of particulars without assigning a meaning to any of them beyond the fact that he is noting them: a joyful yet barbarian victim of the *datum*. Indeed, it is his very openness to the world *as given* which makes the word 'religious' appropriate. He notes not only things, but things in a continuum of the created; for it is the sliding shine of 'the other' on the things which he notes that makes his response to them something much more than a catalogue or set of notations. Perhaps I am carrying paradox too far. But when I think of Emily Dickinson and her fine and intense concern to question the meaning of everything I cannot help feeling that, as compared with Whitman, the final weight of her feeling comes to de-sacralise life; while Whitman, with his famous lack of discrimination but his innocent sense of the world as present and demanding, sacralises everything.

> Passage to India!
> Lo, soul, seest thou not God's purpose from the first?
> The earth to be spanned, connected by network,
> The races, neighbors, to marry and be given in marriage,
> The oceans to be cross'd, the distant brought near,
> The lands to be welded together.
>
> A worship new I sing,
> You captains, voyagers, explorers, yours,
> You engineers, you architects, machinists, yours,
> You, not for trade or transportation only,
> But in God's name and for thy sake O soul.

It is not only physical 'explorers' who are addressed in this affirmation, but poets and artists.

CHAPTER III

The Persistence of God

I T may be thought that the tendencies of which I have just been speaking are a nineteenth-century phenomenon, and that all of the post-Romantic poets I have mentioned are remarkable chiefly for their refusal to accept an industrialised and technological society; that is, they remain 'religious poets' by keeping their imaginations outside history. Increasingly the case has come to be argued that the great modern poets, Yeats and Eliot, are not really opponents of Romanticism but its heirs: revisionists at most. One critical opinion has it that they return poetry to the central impulse of the great Romantics after the Victorian inter-regnum. Another suggests that they have little in common with Wordsworth and Coleridge but continue the diversion of the Romantic impulse which Tennyson inherited from Keats. Yeats' views of Blake and Shelley are well known, but how much they affected his poetry is quite another matter. My own view is that neither of the two opinions is particularly helpful. It seems to me that Yeats and Eliot had a liberating effect on poetry similar in kind and scope to that of the great Romantics, and that they bear a relation to 'Victorian' or late-Romantic poetry very similar to that which Wordsworth and Coleridge had to the late Augustans. In each case there is a body of debilitated poetry which lies behind theirs as a kind of hinterland, and which it is precisely the purpose of their renewing venture to transcend and transform. This is, of course, a quite conventional view; but I do not see how it is shaken by the discovery that Eliot is, 'after all', surprisingly like Tennyson. Critics are often more surprising than poets.

But the renewal of poetry was in each case the renewal of

basic forces in the psyche which had been both weakened by the poetic practice of the preceding decades and threatened by new social tendencies with which that practice was quite incompetent to deal. If Blake, Wordsworth, and Coleridge had to overcome scepticism, sentimentalism, and deism, they had also to face the new facts of industrialism from which the sentimental poetry of their immediate predecessors offered an unsteady escape. The weakness of the immediate poetic conventions was complicated by social change. Yeats and Eliot found themselves in a very similar position. Yeats has described at length in *Autobiographies* how he was affected by the poets and thinkers of his youth: he had not only to transcend the imaginative world represented by Johnson and Dowson on the one hand, Henley on the other, but also to cope with the threat to his inmost aspirations represented by Huxley and Tyndall. In a sense, all these men were the history from which he was trying to awake; and the new Ireland of the 'shop-keepers', the new Europe of revolutionary violence, were the history through which his renewed and waking self had to bear him. For Eliot, the stresses and interests were very different, but the task of accommodation and of transformation —in short, of 'waking'—was very similar. And as with Wordsworth and his peers, the renewal had to involve an experimental renewal of poetic forms.

At the same time, the modern pioneers had to face something which the Romantics had not, at least in the same form. By the time Yeats was coming into his strength and Eliot was beginning to publish, Nietzsche's 'God is dead' had gone deep into the individual consciousness and was already permeating the culture. If the conventional religion in which the Romantics grew up did not answer to their deepest needs, the conventional scepticism or humanism in which Yeats and Eliot were separately educated did not answer to theirs. It is true that one further similarity with the Romantics emerges, that implicit in the renewing of poetry was a renewing of the religious impulse: a renewing and re-definition. But they were less seemingly central to their culture than the Romantics had been; so by renewing the religious awareness they ran the risk of also sharpening the sense of its irrelevance in the culture, at any rate to more than a few people.

Of course, it is a commonplace that something resembling a religious *feeling* or feelings has survived into the present century, but that in many of its expressions it has survived by becoming attached to 'non-religious' objects. On the one hand, there is the astounding growth in our century of what are in fact competing eschatologies: Marxism, liberal scientism, cosmonautism, and that project for the Reich which was to last a thousand years. The millenarian spirit reared itself in the midst of carnage. On the other hand, there has been something resembling a cosmic despair growing under the shadow of that millenialism; for if there are many who regard the millennium as a promise, there are many more who regard it as a threat. The pressure of these conflicting forces has increased rather than lessened as the century has progressed. In the 'thirties, it was possible for a poet to write 'Who live under the shadow of a war, What can I do that matters?' But things are more daunting now. Men live, and poets work, under the shadow of the nuclear bomb (the disappearance of mankind in fire) and of world over-population (the burial of humanity under the weight of mankind). Consequently, perhaps the most usual note in the lesser poetry of the present is a sense of fatedness not very far removed from the more philosophical Roman sense of fate; and going together with it are attitudes not far removed from those Professor Peter groups under the heading of 'Complaint', although now these generally exist without any placing or compensating hope of release into heaven, unless it be the temporary heaven of some past or imagined personal relationship, the personal-sacred, in Mircea Eliade's terms.

God being dead, religion becomes dispersed, attenuated, or

inverted. Over the period in question, indeed over the past hundred years, J. Hillis Miller claims to detect a widespread phenomenon which he calls the 'disappearance of God'. This is a particularly interesting concept, similar to that of the *deus otiosus*, but differing in that it is as though one could discern through a whole period a movement or initiative on God's part to remove himself from human awareness. Eliade maintains that something similar has happened in many cultures, and that there is a recurrent tendency for God conceived as a source, guide and end of human life to be submerged in a sense of God-as-process.[1] George Santayana maintains that modern religion has followed the exact devolution observable in Greek religion, so that 'what an age of imagination had intuited as truth, an age of reflection could preserve only as fable; and as fable, accordingly, the religion of the ancients survived throughout the Christian ages'.[2] The result is that 'irreligion for the many and Stoicism for the few is the end of natural religion in the modern world as it was in the ancient'.[3] This view fits in startlingly well with certain élitish implications in the work of all the great Modern poets, but it is depressing nevertheless; for if Santayana is right, we are deep in the trough of an unimaginative age, and it is not only *belief* that has been impaired but certain central capacities of the psyche. Santayana's view is noticeably more extreme and disheartened than that of Eliade, to whom the modern condition exhibits not a complete failure of religion but a shift from the transcendent to the immanent, from person to process, in specifying the sacred. This has certainly happened in our society. And in such a world, if it is strange that poetry survives, it is still stranger that poets should find in themselves the impulse and strength to go on defining their experience in such a way as to redefine God-acting-in-the-world: what we may even call the reappearance of God. This was Hopkins' constant theme:

[1] *Patterns in Comparative Religion*, op. cit.
[2] Santayana, op. cit., p. 56.   [3] Ibid., p. 64.

I am soft sift
In an hourglass—at the wall
Fast, but mined with a motion, a drift,
And it crowds and it combs to the fall;
I steady as a water in a well, to a poise, to a pane,
But roped with, always, all the way down from the tall
Fells or flanks of the voel, a vein
Of the gospel proffer, a pressure, a principle, Christ's gift.

It is not that there is anything tentative about the poet's
sense that God does act in the world; but there is something
provisional, not to be counted on or explained, in the soul's
meetings with him as he acts; the meetings are accomplished
in sensuous terms; it is, so to speak, a sensuous initiative that
God takes towards us in and through his world; and the soul,
in responding, 'selves itself' and praises that very initiative.
What is interesting is that, if this was Hopkins' theme always,
it was also at times that of Dylan Thomas; but in Thomas, while
the Christian universe of reference remains, it is so transformed by the poet's sensibility that all trace of the devotional
disappears, to be subsumed in an individual celebration of the
analogues themselves:

Under and around him go
Flounders, gulls, on their cold, dying trails,
Doing what they are told,
Curlews aloud in the congered waves
Work at their ways to death,
And the rhymer in the long tongued room,
Who tolls his birthday bell,
Toils towards the ambush of his wounds;
Herons, steeple stemmed, bless.

In the thistledown fall,
He sings towards anguish; finches fly
In the claw tracks of hawks
On a seizing sky; small fishes glide
Through wynds and shells of drowned

Ship towns to pastures of otters.   He
In his slant, racking house
And the hewn coils of his trade perceives
Herons walk in their shroud. . . .

The God invoked here is the God of a more primitive, biological resurrection than the God of Hopkins. What was in Hopkins a God to be addressed and a God initiating the address from beyond his worshipper has become in Thomas a God emblematised by the sensate beings that act his life (hierophanies in a quite primitive sense) and sensed (but no more than sensed) in the very fact that those beings are part of a self-renewing process. Where Hopkins combined a certain separateness from God with an awareness of him as a personal presence, Thomas' emphasis is almost on calling him back into existence by naming his creatures as active beings; unity is the dominant aim and feeling, celebration replaces address in determining the mode and interest. Yet it is interesting, quite by the way, that Thomas shares with Hopkins, as also with Donne, Herbert, and Smart, a concern with a markedly shaped stanza-form which is often a feature of the more intense kinds of religious poetry.

It is also interesting that the 'biological' concern, the cumulative method of progress, the patterned effect of the stanza, and the primitive quality of the hierophanies, do not exclude a propensity for conceits, and for sheer surface play. Hopkins has much less of this quality; his attention is clenched always on *significance*, abiding meanings, to which the interest in stanza-pattern seems a corollary. Thomas, in fact, goes near to exemplifying Eliade's dictum that a whole world may be perceived as an hierophany; and while the fluidity of his movement within his stanza-form is no doubt the result of such a perception, the relative tightness of that form may be the result of a sense of the dangers latent in it; where everything is sacred, nothing really matters. There can be no doubt that Eliade's reminder (it is offered as that) needs to be offset by other reminders. One might say, for example, that it is possible to see the whole as an hierophany only if certain objects, persons, actions, areas of experience have previously been seen as hierophanies within it and designated as sacred events in a man's life-process; alternatively, one might say that, while it is possible to *conceive* of the whole as an hierophany, it is not possible, given the actual situation of men, to *perceive* it as such. Both of these reminders are among those which the poets in one of the two chief post-Romantic religious traditions are in danger of forgetting. I mean that represented among others by Whitman, Lawrence, Thomas, and Roethke. But while I think Whitman the greatest of these four poets, and the most uncomplicatedly religious of them, I also think him the most in need of such reminders. His failure to distinguish (if that is what it was) was so energetic and uninhibited that it makes as much sense to treat him as a fully secular poet as to treat him in the religious terms which I have chosen. The same is not quite true of Roethke, although on a lesser scale he offers a similar case to that of Whitman. The cases of Thomas and Lawrence are perhaps more interesting, because offering greater ambiguity. Lawrence, for example, seems to me an unmistakably religious poet no matter what definition of the term is used; he certainly does not attempt the Whitmanian task of, as it were, creating from a secular continuum a total hierophany; on the contrary, he places enormous emphasis on defining the full weight of particular presences, on shaping actions, movements, appearances to make them momentarily central to a world, so that they may become hierophanies within it. But his problem is created by the violent, and often apparently unmotivated way in which he swings from such a shaping presentation to ejaculatory abstractions which seem to have no sensible link with the issue at all. He oscillates between the earth's weight and the weightlessness of space; there is a centrifugal principle at work in his poetry. So there is in Thomas, but, by comparison with the other poets I have mentioned, Thomas resorts so eagerly to Christian references, images, and significances, that I think we may say he is a Christian poet. In a sense; in a sense, at any rate, in which they are not:

> And freely he goes lost
> In the unknown, famous light of great
>   And fabulous, dear God.
> Dark is a way and light is a place,
>   Heaven that never was
> Nor will be ever is always true,
>   And, in that brambled void,
> Plenty as blackberries in the woods
>   The dead grow for His joy.

If one gets over the faint traces of sentimentality in the breathless paradoxes, one is forced to realise that this is resurrection imagery. Thomas is concerned, as the others are, to re-define God's action in the world; but his re-definition is attempted, as theirs on the whole is not, in the frame of the Christian myth. That is, in his poetry the elements of the Christian imaginative universe bear to one another something like their traditional relations; it is their separate meanings that have, in some cases, changed. G. S. Fraser has somewhere called Thomas a religious poet who approximates to a Catholic 'kind'; I think there is some truth in this; or, rather, he might be described as a somewhat heterodox pre-Catholic poet.

What, of course, all these poets are doing, and the declared Christians refuse even to try to do, is using their imagistic power to suggest that the world may after all be, *au fond*, innocent; hence the ambience or radiance of innocence which tends to surround their images, and to infuriate readers of a less optimistic cast of mind. Actually, no deception is being practised; there is no pretence that, if only you say the world is innocent, it will become so. Rather, there is something mid-way between sympathetic magic and a quite sophisticated sacramental view of the representative nature of language: in other words, the implicit supposition is that if a world of innocence can be created in poetry, it may come to reveal something which corresponds to it in the 'real' world, and the existence of which has not been fully appreciated. The stress is put on the capacity of poetry at once to represent and to reveal qualities in experience which are not apprehensible except by its means. So the 'golden age' to which Marvell and his contemporaries looked back becomes the golden depth of the ordinary to which our contemporaries search down. It is a specifically, and hearteningly, Romantic trait. Wordsworth, if not Coleridge, stands behind it; but then so does Blake, so indeed does Smart. The difficulty of the task to which it prompts is suggested by the fact that Wordsworth and Blake finally compounded their innocence in verbosity, and that Smart wrote out of a sort of madness. But, then, there were always dark places in the imaginations of Blake and Words- worth, and it is precisely in their greatest poems or passages that these places come to definition of a most vibrant sort. Whitman had no such darknesses in his temperament; he had plangency, regret, a capacity for sorrow, but nothing deeper; such relative insensitivity is a great preservative of a poet's gift. As for Lawrence, *his* darkness was too easily transformed into anger, indignation, or scorn ever to produce the sheer luminous dread on which part of the Romantic spirit nourished itself. Lawrence would *choose* his numinous moments, *make* them happen, and in the doing both express and circumscribe their numinousness; again, a weighty gift, leading to some magnificent passages, and a great self-preservative, but leading also to an odd combination of over-elaborateness and lack of creative ambition, at least in poetry. He could have learnt more from Wordsworth, as Thomas could have learnt more from Smart.

The Christian religious poets are not involved in this ven- ture; and the reason is in each case partly temperamental, partly doctrinal. They do not believe that poems can be

innocent worlds representative and revealing of a basic innocence in the common world, because they see the existence
of innocence as part of a complex in which depravity is precisely the opposite term. Of course each of them has moments
of superb innocence; I have argued[1] that Eliot's poetry involves
a spontaneity that tends towards the recreation of the world;
Hopkins writes of a world charged with the grandeur of God,
and greatly values innocence, quiet, modesty, service; Auden's
vision of Eden as arising in a limestone landscape has something
touchingly innocent and vulnerable about it. But none of them
is content either to celebrate or to work by a process of
cataloguing; God's world already has a shape, the shape of its
salvation, is not just a continuum of *facts*, however radiant;
the poet's task is to discover that shape, not merely to praise
that salvation.

I repeat that I do not want to be absolutist about the
existence of two 'tendencies', particularly if it gives the impression that there are two definable groups or schools of
poets who may be defined by their allegiances. There are not;
there are merely tendencies which, in a vague and general way,
diverge. But if we can say even so much as that, we can say
something of the differences between them. And it *is* true, as
certain Christian critics more rigorist than myself would say,
that the differences are in a sense doctrinal, and that a doctrinal
account could be given of them. The trouble is, it would not
take us very far, and would very likely leave the poets stranded
somewhere on the near side of identity. There are always
limits to the value of doctrinal terms of reference in estimating
poetic quality or even poetic kind. For example, Vaughan is
often regarded as a pre-Wordsworthian, believing something
like what Wordsworth believed, interested in the numinous
quality of childhood, having access to 'spots of time', and so
on. That is, a similarity both temperamental and doctrinal is
discovered between them. Personally, I do not believe that

[1] See p. 236.

the similarity exists. Vaughan's

> They are all gone into the world of light

or

> I saw Eternity the other night

is as far as removed from Wordsworth's response to nature as is Herbert's

> Church-bels beyond the starres heard, the souls bloud,
> The land of spices; something understood.

The difference is that, for the Metaphysicals, instantaneous individual vision has to be made sense of in doctrinal terms, placed in a world whose terms of reference are those provided by a Christianity which is a revealed and practised religion; that is to say, in a *common* vision. To put it another way, both Vaughan and Herbert believe in wholes, complexes of meaning in nature and history which the individual perceptions testify or point to. The modern non-affiliated religious poets who derive ultimately from Wordsworth do not believe in any whole except that of unending process, and so do not believe in any *interpretative* frame at all. If we ask whether they are therefore pantheists, the answer must be both yes and no. They do not necessarily believe that the process which they perceive and of which they are part is the all, but they do write as though it were the only whole in terms of which they can think; the hierophanies may provide 'an opening toward the transcendent', but they do not indicate a God who is to be worshipped. At moments a God may be addressed, but the address goes, as it were, into the process, implicitly demanding a revelation that has not yet been granted.

When an ordinary man is in this position, the relevant question is what he thinks of Christ, and what, if anything, he makes of the incarnation. For a modern poet it is not quite so simple, if simple is the word. And the reason has to do with Christianity as a myth and so a source of images. With Dryden, as I have said, religious issues began to be raised in terms of religious allegiance and argument; and since Wordsworth they have, for most poets, been raised outside the terms of Christianity entirely. There are still Christian artists; but in prose, for some reason (if not in poetry) they present a phenomenon which would have been unimaginable even to Donne, with his passionate self-questioning and his doubts about his allegiance; the phenomenon in which so many professedly Christian artists create a world truncated, or peripheral to the real world, or perverse in its values, or rejoicing, however glumly, in its infidelity to its supposed inspiration.[1] What was once a drama of salvation has tended to become a drama of unfaithfulness. And as to the non-Christian artists, one hesitates to use Christian terminology at all, because one suspects that they would repudiate it as making a claim on them under the pretence of characterising their work. The fact is that, insofar as Christian terms of reference imply a basic iconography, they have become a liability to poetry. Auden has gone so far as to maintain that the incarnation has made a free play of the imagination impossible.[2] I do not believe this, for if it were true for Auden it would have to be true also for Dante, Chaucer, and Donne. But it *is* true that, the further we go historically from the condition known as Christendom, the more the Christian poet has to create his own iconography; and it may not seem at first sight a Christian one at all. At various times both Eliot and Auden have done this; their task in the creation of images has not been less arduous than that of Yeats.

It is clear, then, that even among the poets I persist in calling religious, professedly Christian poets are now in a minority. Of the non-professing poets, I have named only a few, those who come, it seems to me, from Wordsworth and/or Whitman. There are, of course, others, who find their precursor in Coleridge or Blake, just as there are Christian poets like

---

[1] See Donat O'Donnell: *Maria Cross*, (London, 1954).

[2] W. H. Auden: *The Dyer's Hand* (London, 1963).

Muir, Campbell, Edith Sitwell, Allen, Tate, Ransom, R. S. Thomas, and James K. Baxter, whom I have not so far mentioned. But I stick to the line I have been dealing with for the simple reason that it is both identifiable and remarkably resilient; and it raises an issue which can be treated under formal, doctrinal, psychological, and anthropological aspects. The poets in it tend, first, to work by accumulation, and to use that accumulation both to celebrate life and to reveal some special quality (the hierophanic) in life. It is impossible in most cases to tell if they believe in a personal God, since the object (if any) of worshipful attention never becomes defined, though he may sometimes be addressed. D. H. Lawrence has said that since 1851, the year of *Moby Dick*, artists have been concerned with 'post-mortem effects'. That is one way of looking at it. But the poets do not all acknowledge the death. Psychologically all of them rely on the 'I' as perceiver and maker, but not in a Wordsworthian way; for the aim is not to define or place the 'I', much less to treat its history as a kind of providential progress, as in *The Prelude*, but to use the 'I' as an angle from which to celebrate the world in which it moves and so, by extension, to celebrate *it* as the celebrant. It is a priestly role, in other words, and it is not surprising that a dark note of human fatedness persists under the celebration or that the fatedness is seldom fully declared. It is an art exacting and solitary, confident yet spasmodic, speaking on behalf of a mankind whom it hardly dares, in the ordinary sense, to represent. So it is a markedly anthropological poetry, one which is always tempting primitivism; it makes large gestures, as in Whitman, defines man in biological terms, as in the early Thomas, sees him lambent in a green universe, as in Roethke, tries to shape sensate beings in all their mysterious presence as in Lawrence. There is a reliance on immediate perception, a return to childhood, dreams, or sexual love[1] to find representatively sacred areas and develop sacralising images. There

1 All of them generally recognised as foci for apprehensions of the sacred.

67

is an odd combination, especially in Thomas and Roethke, of the sense of recurrence with that of the gratuitous, the not-to-be-anticipated; yet in both of them the combination is very different from what we find in Yeats, who is often taken as the exemplar of this paradox.

It must be said that a strong case has been made out, by Professor Frank Kermode, in criticism of these very qualities of which I have been speaking. Kermode is not thinking of religious poetry, but of what he considers a main strand in modern literature: this literature, he thinks, is primitivist, even in its seemingly sophisticated symbolist modes, myth-making, intuitionist, anti-rational, drawn to magic as an alternative science, and given to dreams of apocalypse. Without necessarily intending to, it may generate destructive tendencies:

> It appears, in fact, that modernist radicalism in art—the breaking down of pseudo-traditions, the making new of a true understanding of the nature of the elements of art—this radicalism involves the creation of fictions which may be dangerous in the dispositions they breed towards the world.[1]

Some of those fictions are fictions of apocalypse, and they 'turn easily into myths; people will live by that which was designed only to know by'.[2] The point, I take it, is that constant harping on a cosmic threat turns it into a sort of promise. Elsewhere, Kermode speaks of the same tendency in more general terms, and suggests that it is so common among literary intellectuals as to be one of their defining characteristics as a group. A 'scholarly primitivism', the 'anti-intellectualism of the modern intellectual', produces personal religions by ransacking the deposits of old mythologies:

> The development of intellect is [seen as] the true Fall of Man. This is the basic Romantic primitivism: the high valuation of

[1] Frank Kermode: 'The New Apocalyptists': Partisan Review, Summer, 1966, p. 351. [2] Ibid., p. 353.

primitive image-making powers. Under imagistic primitivism would be included all modern doctrines of symbol, image, ideogram, *figura*, and type.[1]

Such habits produce also historical or pseudo-historical theories about dissociation:

> Why do people who think along these lines almost always take up with the occult? Because it has been since the Romantic movement (what it was for a time in the seventeenth century) the seductively obvious alternative to Science. It is an inexhaustible study, full of fascinating analogies and sudden confirmations, and very congenial to the generally syncretic cast of the literary mind.[2]

It is unfortunate in some ways that Kermode's attention should fall so heavily on Yeats under these rubrics; for, by comparison with most modern poets, I consider Yeats eminently rational. Still, there is no doubt that the tendency of which Kermode speaks exists and is influential, even though I am not completely happy with his account of the relations between the different elements in it. As for the word 'primitivism', social anthropologists now seem chary of using it at all. So Godfrey Lienhardt says, in his *Social Anthropology*, 'Though certain psychological and physiological differences, like social differences, may well exist between different human groups, the study of them even now is not enough to warrant any generalized statement contrasting "primitive" with "civilized" man. Even the word "primitive" as now used is merely a matter of literary convenience.'[3] If we do use it of poetry, we must, I feel, distinguish a real primitivism from an ideational one; and while Roethke represents the first, I personally think Yeats an example of the second. However, these may be no more than semantic differences. Whether or not Kermode's

1 Frank Kermode: *Puzzles and Epiphanies* (London, 1962), p. 32.
2 Ibid., p. 147. See also the important long paragraph on p. 110.
3 London, 1966, p. 21.

account is adequate, certainly, so far as the religious poets I am dealing with are concerned, there is a self-yielding, if not to God, at least to the sacralising power of one's own perceptions and to *its* capacity to utter the transcendent. The odd thing is that Robert Lowell, an avowedly Christian poet, often shows the same tendency; it may be said that, whatever his doctrine, he has his own primitivism; and in certain of the early poems we find the remarkable blend of self-yielding to individual perceptions with an over-assertive patterning of experience which apparently has the purpose of establishing the reality of his struggle with God but actually serves to point up the arbitrariness and violence of those perceptions. In other words, Lowell's struggle is often with his own spontaneity, as we can see if the splendid 'Mr. Edwards and the Spider' is compared with certain passages from 'The Quaker Graveyard in Nantucket'. I will not quote from the first, which needs to be seen as a whole; but I do feel that, however apparently 'satirical' its tone, a sense of concern for salvation emerges very powerfully —and very calmly—from its dramatisation of an obsessional concern with damnation. Lowell projects his inner conflict on to a sinister, and faintly absurd, historical figure; and in doing so he manages to frame and distance his own deepest impulses. But in the latter poem, which proceeds from a personally felt situation, we get the opposite of calm and poetic authority; it would hardly be unfair to say that we get religion as myth and myth as ejaculation:

> In the great ash-pit of Jehoshaphat
> The bones cry for the blood of the white whale,
> The fat flukes arch and whack about its ears,
> The death-lance churns into the sanctuary, tears
> The gun-blue swingle, heaving like a flail,
> And hacks the coiling life out: it works and drags
> And rips the sperm-whale's midriff into rags,
> Gobbets of blubber spill to wind and weather,
> Sailor, and gulls go round the stoven timbers

Where the morning stars sing out together
And thunder shakes the white surf and dismembers
The red flag hammered in the mast-head. Hide,
Our steel, Jonas Messias, in Thy side.

In what sense, one asks, is this a *Christian* poetry by com-comparison with Lawrence or Thomas or (God help us) Wordsworth? Part VI, which follows the passage just quoted, is both lovely and devout, but it is also muted. And when one looks at the rest, one wonders if Lowell has fallen into the trap so adroitly avoided by Auden in 'In Praise of Limestone', triumphantly leaped by Hopkins in 'The Wreck of the Deutschland', and authoritatively opened by Eliot in 'Little Gidding'; has he imparted an iconography to give a passing significance or a flimsy frame to a psychic conflict which has arisen quite independent of it and of what it represents? I do not know; but there is *something* wrong with this as religious poetry. The Donne of an equal violence, of 'Good Friday, Riding Westward', would hardly regard it as an equivalent violence; he might be inclined to say that a truly Christian religious man worries less about the contours of his feelings than about the relationship to which his feelings testify. The results of Lowell's procedure in most of this poem, and in many other well-known poems from his early books, is that confusion *becomes* his meaning, and the cries to God become desperate appeals for release from a tangle of horrors and boredoms which, in a sense, he has created himself. The relation between cerebration and passion in Donne is very different.

If, as I have said, it is important to distinguish a real primitivism from an ideational one, and not to assume that definiteness of 'doctrine' will unfailingly save a poet from either of them, it is also important to question how wide, and indeed how recent, a range of literary works is covered by Kermode's broad and complex formula. I think that, however persuasive his case, we must resist the temptation to approach modern literature as a whole in terms of it. Most of our contemporary poets, I suspect, would simply not know what one was up to if one approached their work in terms of 'primitivism', 'apocalypticism', the occult, alternative sciences, and so on. It is not that the terms do not apply somewhere in their immediate literary ancestry, but that the poets would not recognise them as applying to *them*. As recently as 1961, Professor William Empson said that the revival of Christianity among critics had rather taken him by surprise.[1] Surely the surprise is fifteen years out of date. Personally, I notice few religious presuppositions, Christian or otherwise, in the contemporary literary criticism I read; nor do I notice many in contemporary poetry; indeed it is worth hazarding the guess that the critics and poets who show any real *interest* in religion are, in fact, a minority. Everywhere one senses that religious valuations, religious frames of reference, are not, or are ceasing to be, an issue. Questions even of interpretation which would once have *required* a religious terminology now get by with at best a 'metaphysical' one (though it is my own conviction, born of experience, that they do not really get by at all which has provided one motive for the writing of this book). Many teachers are not concerned to establish even a working meaning for words like 'supernatural' or 'redemption' where the poems would seem to require them. Taking, then, a broad and casual look around the literary scene, one might conclude that poetry as a venture has been secularised, or is at least a long way along the path to complete secularisation. I do not think this impression is accurate. In addition to the minority of religious poets, Christians and others, there are somewhat nervous signs of a preoccupation with the Christian myth. Was it, for example, anything more than a psychological oddity that led the Beat poets to call the record of their Albert Hall recital *Wholly Communion*? If it was a joke, it was a joke as revealing as it was bad. And I note with interest that in its first

[1] *Milton's God* (London, 1961), p. 9.

two issues *The Review*, perhaps the most stringently honest small magazine in Britain, raised not so much the religious question as the question of the inevitability of the religious question. So Donald Davie says, in a discussion with A. Alvarez, that he too is 'pretty much' an atheist but goes on to reflect:

> Of course, in the history of poetry down the centuries, however much it may embarrass us in fact, the grounds for poetry have frequently been religious or—this is a new word I've lately learned (I'm not quite sure what it means)—ontological. It does seem to me increasingly—though it's embarrassing for me to admit it because of my own agnosticism—we may be selling the pass on poetry from the start when we don't allow that it may have metaphysical or religious sanctions. This is what I meant by respecting the otherness, the being of a tree, a stone wall, a landscape.[1]

This is engagingly wistful; but what is interesting in it is not the fact that Davie worries himself by wondering about such possibilities, but the reason he gives for wondering. He is concerned not with the likelihood, however 'embarrassing', that Christianity may be true, but with the possibility that the very art of poetry *implies* a religious view of the world; his concern is not doctrinal but phenomenological. And I suggest that, in expressing it, he is articulating a concern which many other poets have while hardly knowing that they have it: the concern which led to the remark I quoted in Chapter I, that possibly poetry was an atavistic habit of the psyche.

In any case, taking up a similar theme in the second issue of *The Review*, Colin Falck suggests[2] that the contemporary anxiety about communication is a *direct* consequence of the fact that we are in a 'crisis of belief'. This, of course, is an issue so familiar as to be banal; but Falck makes something interesting of it, for it is only recently, he says, that 'This worry has become highly explicit and all-pervasive and any

[1] *The Review*, No. 1 April/May 1962, p. 19.
[2] *The Review*, No. 2 June/July 1962, p. 5.

poetry whatever has seemed to lie under some kind of meta-physical threat'. Some kind of metaphysical threat: the phrasing is significant. What Falck is facing, and what Davie was facing in the previous issue, is the oppressiveness of a poetry denied by its own procedures an 'opening toward the transcendent', and so bemused by this failure that the anxiety becomes expressed in a further involution of procedures. The result is that, in lacking belief, the poet lacks a subject-matter: 'This gives a clue, of course, to today's apparent problem about subject-matter; the difficulty in finding subject-matter is really an honest half-way stage to seeing that it is the idea of subject-matter itself which is now problematic.'[1]

I have simplified Falck's argument at the risk of distorting it; but I do think that the questions asked by him and Davie show a valuable concern with the fullness and freedom of poetry. For much of the poetry of which Kermode spoke in terms of 'primitivism' is not merely offering a primitivistic reading of human experience, it is engaged in an imaginative enquiry into the phenomena of that experience, and so can itself be esti-mated in phenomenological terms. When we attempt this estimate, we will not approach the poets in doctrinal terms either by pointing out, as some Christian critics would, how they fail to measure up to the Christian revelation, or by reminding them, as Kermode has a tendency to do, that they are resorting to occult primitivist doctrines and that their poetry exemplifies such doctrines. On the contrary, we may see them as tentatively opening up areas of a personal world to see how they may admit or lead to a wider significance. Here a quotation from Eliade is pertinent:

> Yet this experience of profane space still includes values that to
> to some extent recall the nonhomogeneity peculiar to the
> religious experience of space. There are, for example, privileged
> places, qualitatively different from all others—a man's birth-
> place, or the scenes of his first love, or certain places in the first

[1] *The Review*, No. 2 June/July, 1962, p. 8.

foreign city he visited in youth. Even for the most frankly non-religious man, all these places still retain an exceptional, a unique quality; they are the 'holy places' of his private universe, as if it were in such spots that he had received the revelation of a reality *other* than that in which he participates through his ordinary daily life.[1]

In some ways this is simply a statement of observable facts; the question is what to make of them. Here the 'as if' becomes important. For poets who would regard themselves as religious it is a guide; for poets who would not it is a problem and a challenge. That is, all of these poets possess such 'places'; and each of them must ask himself, however implicitly, in what sense they are 'holy', what, if anything, they signify, whether they help to seal up a private universe or whether, on the contrary, they open it up to a wider world of meaning. For the majority of poets of today, the creative task is to *test* those privileged places—and privileged persons, moments, and events as well—for sacredness: *do* they offer an opening towards the transcendent? Will the testing of their specific feeling, the exploring of their possible significance, open them up towards the transcendent, or will it merely return the poet to the involuted rounds of his own consciousness? I do not know that words like 'primitivism' help very much in these matters. I do know that too ready or complete a 'religious' terminology is likely to obscure the actual experience in the case of many poets, although it very obviously applies in the case of many others. Of course, in a civilisation still permeated by Christianity, albeit by a Christianity which is generally experienced only as an ethical expectation, a prolonged and serious investigation of a life-process to see on to what dimensions of meaning its chief phases open would be bound to confront the poet with the question of Christianity as a revealed religion; he would be bound to ask himself, however implicitly, whether the claim to a revelation might be

[1] *The Sacred and the Profane*, op. cit., p. 24.

what was needed to complete his own self-questioning; given the oddities of the Christian presence in his society, God knows what answer he would give himself.

In any case, the degree to which he can open up personal experience, generalise and re-create the 'holy places of his private universe', is still the measure of any poet's greatness. When they are opened up to a common universe recognised as in any sense holy, the result is poetry which we call religious. But they may open on to a universe in which blankness, or stoicism, or the pragmatic need for human kindliness seems the dominant feature; and then we would probably not call the resulting poetry religious. As the American poet Anne Sexton has said, 'Need is not quite belief'. No; nor is aspiration the same as expectation, or moments of brightness a total faith. But if we may see religious poetry in our day as proceeding *either* from a practice of the presence of God as a person *or* from the attempt to define the action of God as force, we must also remind ourselves that either/or approaches to arts such as poetry inevitably end up with a trancated art. It is legitimate to hope for a poetry of the future in which both qualities are active; if we get it, we shall be seeing again what we have seen often enough before, creative artists leading theologians out of their conceptual dilemmas.

CHAPTER IV

Deep-witted Wyatt

I

IT would be idle to ask what is the present state of the 'Wyatt debate'; there is no debate.[1] In fact, so far as I can see, there is very little interest at all among critics in catching Wyatt's unique flavour or in estimating how closely, and in what poems, it approaches greatness. This cannot be because he is inherently uninteresting; for in my own experience the best undergraduates are quick to see his interest and to locate it in the poems where it is most fully manifest. Nor can it be because critics have in the past reached such agreement that there is nothing left to debate; on the contrary, that collection of potted estimates which, no doubt with a touch of bitter irony, Professor Kenneth Muir prints at the beginning of his *Muses Library* edition of the poems is so full of contradictory views and almost wilful misestimates that one is forced, with equal irony, to the conclusion that H. A. Mason is right when

[1] There is, however, a fairly regular succession of commentaries, which could be taken as amounting to a Wyatt industry, albeit a backyard one. The names of Hallet Smith, Kenneth Muir, and H. A. Mason have now been joined by those of John Stevens, Patricia Thomson, and Raymond Southall. Some of this work is most illuminating; but much of it shows a critical timidity which is bound to be depressing, especially when it is combined with a marked tendency to quote, echo, duplicate one another's labours in a way that does not sharpen but blurs the critical issues. In such a closed critical circle, it is not always clear what precisely any of these later critics thinks of the chief theses of the critics whom he quotes so liberally. In particular, there is a general failure to grasp the nettle of 'They flee from me. . . .' Disagreements exist, of course, but the onus is too often put on the reader of deducing that they are. No wonder there is no Wyatt debate.

he says, 'I think that Wyatt has never been looked at'. In the sixteenth century he was thought at any rate the equal of Surrey; Warton in the eighteenth century judged him very much Surrey's inferior; and after that the critical enterprise, most limply conducted as it is, has been directed to finding what of his work and reputation could be salvaged from his own alleged misuse of English measures or his alleged over-use of Continental ones. Generally, the salvage was conducted in terms of his 'lyricism', of Wyatt as Tudor *trouvère*; and even Muir, who has done, and is apparently still doing, such valuable work as an editor, thinks that his 'greatest poems are not his translations, but the lyrics for which no direct source has been discovered. . . .'

It is true that Mason takes a position directly opposed to that; and I shall consider his views later, for it seems to me that they offer the most fruitful occasion both for agreement and for disagreement. What I want to do for the moment is to stress how sad it is that so fine a passion should generally have had so cold and uncomprehending a response; so that, if Surrey could write on his death,

> Wyatt resteth here, that quick could never rest,
> Whose heavenly gifts encreased by disdayn,

a twentieth-century critic like Berdan can come to the almost unimaginable judgment:

> The important thing is that in his work the early Tudor found examples of a large variety of verse forms, coldly but carefully worked out. It must be granted that a poet whose primary interest is in form, rather than in content, is not great. Poetic technique, clever phrase, witty conceit go a little way, but only a little way. On the other hand, the great emotions that have aroused poets from the beginning are not present in Wyatt's work. The nature in his poems is of the lion-and-tiger sort drawn from books; beauty apparently makes little appeal; and his love serves merely as the occasion to make far-fetched

comparisons. This lack of emotion is apparently one of the reasons why critics call him 'virile'! . . . But the most successful are those written to be sung.

The undergraduates whom I mentioned as being quick to locate Wyatt's interest and to respond to his feeling are not, of course, thinking of the poems to which Berdan gives such tepid praise. And in the face of his kind of malestimate; in the face of a general lack of critical interest; in the face of those conventional estimates which are still current and which give Wyatt pallid acknowledgment as a skilful sonneteer, or an accomplished lutanist, or a gracious eclectic among verse-forms, perhaps the first thing which a contemporary critic ought to do is to draw up a personal list of poems, dividing them into groups and specifying the kind of interest which may be expected from each. Such a list is bound to be very personal, and the groupings certainly cannot be held to be absolute; yet drawing it up may well be a service to many readers who have not yet been taught to 'read' Wyatt and who are bemused by the conflicting opinions of the anthologists.

First, there are the poems which are great, are great throughout, and are great by virtue of the passion they actually present and define: 'Whoso list to hunt . . .', 'They flee from me . . ., 'Stand whoso list . . .', and Satire One.

Second, there are the poems which, although uneven or less fully 'charged with meaning', are nevertheless clearly the work of a great poet, works which testify to a greatness they do not wholly prove; poems such as: 'My galley chargèd with forget-fulness', 'Where shall I have at mine own will', 'In eternum', 'What rage is this?', 'The pillar perished is', Satire Three, Psalms 51, 130 and 143. To these may be tentatively added 'If thou wilt mighty be', and 'The flaming sighs', although the first shows some banality of diction and the second has a melodramatic beginning.

Third, there are poems which, although generally weak,

have some powerful phrasing: 'I have sought long', 'The restful place', 'So unwarely', 'Lux, my fair falcon', 'Like as the bird', and Penitential Psalm I.

In the next three groups the interest is of a different, and to my mind generally inferior kind.

Fourth, there are the poems which, although conforming to a song convention which they cannot transcend or much advance, are so gracefully *achieved* as to seem original even when we know they are not: 'Madame, withouten many words', 'Patience though I have not', 'My lute, awake' (regarded by some critics as his finest poem), 'And wilt thou leave me thus?', 'Forget not yet . . .', 'The joy so short', 'Pass forth my wonted cries'.

Fifth, there are poems, a good number, which, though they do not go any distance towards establishing even an illusion of intimacy or originality, have a decided technical interest in that they show Wyatt mastering often quite complicated verse forms. Among these we may list: 'It may be good', 'Ever my hap', 'Such hap as I am happed in', 'Ye know my heart', 'If chance assigned', 'All heavy minds', 'Is it possible', 'Blame not my lute', 'I abide and abide'.

Sixth, there are poems which, without possessing a more than momentary distinction as poetry, have an historical interest, in that they refer definitely, and at times with a transferred poignancy, to Wyatt's known condition at the time of their writing: 'Some time I fled', 'He is not dead', 'Tagus, farewell', 'That time that mirth', 'Sighs are my food'.

Of course, it would be absurd to offer any definitive categories by which to assess so interesting, repetitive, yet protean a poet as Wyatt; it could put one in the position of a man solemnly deciding among dogs at a cat-show. And I readily confess that even the groups I have listed run this danger: For example, it is easy to imagine someone arguing that 'My lute, awake', which I have just put in the fourth group, is in fact superior to 'Where shall I have at my own will', which I have put in the second. It is just as easy to imagine someone else arguing that they are poems of the same *kind*, and should go into the same group. The difference between them in kind and quality may not be striking, but my own conviction is that there *is* one. And, as more than one critic has pointed out, Wyatt presents so unusual a challenge to the twentieth century reader that it is useful to make a preliminary decision about what the poems are on which his greatness depends, and then to talk about them in such a way as to offer a body of work to readers who have been for the most part so badly served by anthologists and critics. The important thing is not to pretend that the divisions are barriers. And I want to stress my conviction that if the only poems we had available to us were those listed here in the third, fifth, and sixth groups, we would have no warrant for considering Wyatt a distinctive and distinguished poet; and that if we added to those the poems in the fourth group, we would still have no warrant for calling him a great one. His greatness is seen primarily in the poems in the first two groups; and if the poems in the fourth group become relevant to that question of greatness, it is partly because they show the opposing strains in his attitude to poetic statement, partly because they grace what in the other poems has been more starkly established, and partly because they show, with a certain fineness of their own, the tendencies he had to transcend. It may be relevant to add that Tillyard, in printing a select anthology consisting of sixty poems of the more than two hundred available, does not include 'Whoso list to hunt' or 'Stand whoso list' at all, and prints only the closing movement of Satire One. This fact shows quite graphically what resistance there is to the notion of Wyatt's distinctiveness and greatness represented by my first two groups.

II

Surrey's testimonies in verse to Wyatt's power may themselves have been written within a convention; but we do know that, despite his being a much younger man and having Catholic sympathies where Wyatt's were Lutheran, he was unusually affected by the older poet's death. We may therefore pay him some attention when he claims that he 'knew what harboured in that head' and that he knew Wyatt as a man subject to dread and worry, yet courteous, various and a lover of virtue. Tottel for his part referred to 'the weightiness of the deep-witted Sir Thomas Wyatt'. And we know that others of his contemporaries regarded Wyatt as anything but an emotional and intellectual lightweight. It therefore will not seem surprising when, four hundred years later, H. A. Mason takes up these themes of praise, and treats Wyatt as a Christian Humanist in the new line of, and sharing the concerns of, More and Erasmus. Certainly, he was a 'court poet' in more than one sense; if he sang for the court, he also used its song-forms to express the weight of court life on his spirit.

Certain of the facts of his life reinforce this sense that one gets from his poetry. He was barely twenty when his marriage ended because of his wife's infidelity. He was thirty-three when he was imprisoned for several weeks and forced to watch from his prison window the execution of Anne Boleyn and her alleged 'paramours'; and when we reflect that she had possibly been his mistress and they had certainly been his friends, we may understand the dragging force of the verses which he wrote about their executions:

> A time thou haddest above thy poor degree,
> The fall whereof thy friends may well bemoan.
> A rotten twig upon so high a tree
> Hath slipped thy hold and thou art dead and gone.

Shortly after these events, which some critics argue left him
clearly and radically a changed man, he was given a succession
of diplomatic jobs, some of them baffling in the complexity of
the tactical interests to be served; and in 1540, when he was
thirty-seven, he was again forced to watch an execution, this
time of his patron Thomas Cromwell. Contemporary accounts
make it clear that he was extremely affected by Cromwell's
death, and whatever iron was already in his soul went deeper
and bit more sharply. 'The pillar perished is' dates from this
event and refers to it, and it is likely that 'Stand whoso list'
does also. The Penitential Psalms seem to date from 1540 or
1541, and the Satires from the years between the two executions; but the chronology is uncertain, and is the subject of
scholarly argument (or, at the least, conjecture). At any rate,
the poems which I consider give him his claim to greatness all
seem to exist within the frame of these downfalls, their
shockingness, the weight of intermediate duties, many of them
uncongenial to him personally, and the general sense which was
developing its sharpness in him, the sense of life as a continuum under constant threat of arbitrary power and offering
no or only brief retreats for the threatened spirit. Henry VIII
seems to have had a highly paradoxical sense of fitness in the
uses of violent death, and especially in the Court uses of a
poet forced to witness some of them. Wyatt, in his turn,
developed a sense of the death itself, as well as of the courtly
impermanence to which it gave salutary witness. Poets benefit
in peculiar ways from the graces of despots; it may be that
Henry, and the whole order which he stood for and above,
converted a jongleur into a poet, and song into deeply felt
meditation:

> Stond who so list vpon the Slipper toppe
>   Of courtes estates, and lett me heare reioyce;
> And vse me quyet without lett or stoppe,
>   Vnknowen in courte, that hath suche brackishe ioyes:
>   In hidden place, so lett my dayes forthe passe,

> That when my yeares be done, withouten noyse,
> I may dye aged after the common trace.
> For hym death greep'the right hard by the croppe
> That is moche knowen of other; and of him self alas,
> Doth dye vnknowen, dazed with dreadfull face.

So direct is the syntax, and so economical the statement, that it would be easy to miss the play (a play almost of wit) on the words 'known' and 'unknown' that runs through this fine poem, giving the prevailing dread its edge of self-mocking bitterness. For if the statement is direct, the feeling which accompanies it varies in a compelling manner. The 'forthe passe' and 'withouten noyse' add to the bitterness of 'brackishe ioyes' a peculiar trailing tenderness of accent, which is given greater force or presence by the suggestion, however faint, of a rhyme in the four successive endings ('ioyes . . . passe . . . noyse . . . trace'); and that trailing quality leads to an equally original feeling of content and satisfaction in 'I may dye aged after the common trace'; which leads in turn to a dramatically satisfying clenching rhythm in the next line, 'For hym death greep'the right hard by the croppe'. 'Dazed with dreadfull face' is the precisely right, and precisely shocking consummation of such a process in the poem.

The quality so completely expressed in this poem moves back, as it were, into our reading of lighter poems, even where these are of no great significance. We have, after all, a puzzle in accounting for a certain solemnity or bitterness beneath the 'lover's' feigning; we note a use of something like an unpremeditated double bluff: lightly the poet feigns bitterness, but in such a way as to let something of a real bitterness come through and be established by the feigning. It is hard to distinguish this quality in separate love-poems, but it does seem to me to be a feature of his work as a whole, even if we exclude the half-dozen unmistakably great poems, in which of course there is little or no feigning. His stance of desolation (as a 'lover') does seem to answer to something not only in the literary conventions (which, as Mason pertinently argues, were debilitating ones) but also in the historical facts which gave its peculiar tone to the courtier's life at that time. It is as though the courtly hollowness with which the 'lover's' alleged bitterness is declared did not rob that bitterness of all its authentic sting, but showed it deriving less from a love-relationship than from a relationship with the realities of political power, and, specifically, from the impotence experienced against those realities. In the hollowness of the verse, with its endless plaints, it is *that* hollowness which is echoed, the hollowness which comes inwardly from the occupancy of the 'Slipper toppe'.[1] So it will be no surprise that, in translating Alamanni for his first Satire, Wyatt, writing in temporary retirement, completely changes the quality and tone of his model in order to express a splendid freedom of spirit. To be at home 'in Kent and Christendome' was such an unexpected bonus for a man of Wyatt's responsibilities and cares that the verse jets out with a remarkable eagerness and assurance:

> This maketh me at home to hounte and to hawke
> And in fowle weder at my booke to sitt.
> In frost and snowe then with my bow to stawke,
> No man doeth marke whereso I ride or goo;
> In lusty lees at libertie I walke.
> And of these newes I fele nor wele nor woo,
> Sauf that a clogg doeth hang yet at my hele:
> No force for that for it is ordered so,
> That I may lepe boeth hedge and dike full well.
> I ame not now in Ffraunce to judge the wyne,
> With saffry sauce the delicates to fele;
> Nor yet in Spaigne where oon must him inclyne
> Rather then to be, owtewerdly to seme.
> I meddill not with wittes that be so fyne,

---

[1] A point something like this has been made more than once before, but I have never seen it suggested that any considerable feeling gets into Wyatt's poetry under cover of a feint which itself involves a pretence to feeling.

Nor Fflaunders chiere letteth not my sight to deme
  Of black and white, nor taketh my wit awaye
  With bestlynes, they beeste do so esteme;
Nor I ame not where Christe is geven in pray
  For mony, poison and traison at Rome,
  A commune practise vsed nyght and daie:
But here I ame in Kent and Christendome
  Emong the muses where I rede and ryme;
  Where if thou list, my Poynz, for to come,
Thou shalt be judge how I do spend my tyme.

If, indeed, there is a point in regarding Wyatt's poetry as that of a 'Christian Humanist', it is in this passage, above all, that we may hear the accent of that humanism. The concerns of the poem as a whole are no doubt satirical, but everywhere in the earlier and more satirical sections we find the promise of the personal liberation so splendidly celebrated in this closing passage. It is a freedom which quite transcends the usual contentment experienced by the jaded courtier in retirement; it is, in fact, a lusty joy, which hardly knows how to sing itself. Not that the rhythmic freedom of the lines can account fully for the presence of this quality; there is also a tang and sharpness of particularity in the detail, a keenness of perception at once manly and fresh, quite unlike the plaintiveness which faintly enters Herbert's poems of retirement or the consumer's avidity with which Jonson, in 'To Penshurst', takes for images of his satisfaction whatever comes to hand from Penshurst's heavy board. In Wyatt there is an altogether more compelling sense of fulfilment, and it does not depend on the mere cataloguing of satisfactions. The sense of physical renders the sense of spiritual freedom; and the happy stride of the lines renders *that*. It is interesting, for example, that the tercets which immediately precede the passage I have quoted are much more clogged in movement, and much more difficult to read aloud with any sharpness of definition. The extraordinary liberation is a liberation from the slipper top, whose

tyranny we have felt elsewhere in his verse. But it is also a
liberation from certain rhetorical habits of his own.

And both freedom and constriction, promise and threat, are
felt, in their own terms, in the greatest of the 'love poems'. I
use inverted commas both because they are metaphysical
poems as much as love ones, and because they are as far in
spirit and formal firmness from the works of the amatory
lutanist as they can be. What distinguishes 'Whoso list to
hunt' and 'They flee from me', and makes them unmistakably
greater than even such poems as 'My galley chargèd with for-
getfulness', is not merely the fact that the stance of the
rejected *lover* is so convincingly established but the establishment under or within it of the man for whom *all* experience
has a mysteriously threatening quality. That quality demands
to be expressed not only in terms of dread but in terms of an
invitation to the contemplation of its mysteriousness; and it is
the greatness of both poems that they do so triumphantly
create the mystery which they contemplate. They are all the
greater as *love* poems for that.

The more obvious case to take is 'Whoso list to hunt', for
it is arguably about Anne Boleyn; but it is also the less satisfying, and for reasons connected with the *nature* of its mysteriousness. It has a quality both of the allegorical and the esoteric,
where 'They flee from me' has neither. Not that its images are
merely decorative; on the contrary, their grace and lightness
are the index of their power to sustain and define their
emotion:

> Yet may I by no meanes my weried mynde
>> Drawe from the Diere: but as she fleeth afore,
> Faynting I folowe. I leve of therefore,
>> Sins in a nett I seke to hold the wynde.
> Who list her hount, I put him owte of dowbte,
>> As well as I may spend his tyme in vain:
>> And, graven with Diamonds, in letters plain
> There is written her faier neck rounde abowte:

Noli me tangere, for Cesars I ame;
And wylde for to hold, though I seme tame.

The glancing yet precise stress on 'drawe' and 'faynting' indicates the kind of quality I mean.

Professor Muir has shown that, if other men's poems were sometimes merely the occasions for Wyatt's 'translations', he did sometimes set out to translate Petrarch and others in the ordinary sense. He was not temperamentally averse, as T. S. Eliot and Robert Lowell are not, to following another man's ordering of experience; quite the contrary. Therefore, when he departs most markedly from his model, as he does here, we may take account of the fact as a testimony to the force and originality of the feelings for the shaping of which the original provided not so much the mould as the incentive. 'Whoso list to hunt' is quite cut off from its Italian root, and the reference to Caesar has precisely the opposite effect to that gained by Petrarch. Muir quotes another critic as saying that Wyatt 'converts Petrarch's contemplation of the hind into a prolonged account of hunting'. This is true, but it may leave a misleading stress; for the emotional movement of the opening lines follows the weariness of the hunter, not the exhilaration or hopefulness of the hunt, which the jaunty good-fellowship of 'Whoso list to hount, I knowe where is an hynde' seemed to promise. And the emotional feeling of the poem as a whole has a quality of haunted and haunting suspension, as though Wyatt's creative effort (and that, possibly, an exhausting one) had gone not only into charting a physical movement with its emotional concomitant, and bringing *that* into juxtaposition with a bitter recognition of Caesar's 'rights', but also into establishing a total awareness which does deserve the title 'contemplative'. It is a commonplace that two distinct reasons are given for his abandonment of the hunt: she is too fast and tiring for Wyatt, and she belongs to Caesar. But this is not a discovery by the critics, it is a revelation, indeed an insistence, by the poet. The movement of the hunt (though it strikes us, really, as being something more mysterious and impalpable than that) and of the hunt's ceasing comes to rest on something that has the effect of a confrontation.

> And, graven with Diamonds, in letters plain
> There is written her faier neck rounde abowt. . . .

Here we see, in a change of emphasis indicated by that paradoxical use of the connective, 'and', both a sudden humanising of the hind and an almost mystical apotheosis of the forces which she represents. That 'faier neck' is unmistakably human, yet the diamond letters are a sort of sacralising talisman. And in the paradox created by seeing in so small a space two such differing aspects of the 'hynde', one does indeed get a sense that pursuing her is equivalent to seeking to hold the wind in a net: a hunt which, if persisted in, will lead to some more than ordinary distraughtness.

Caesar in this poem may not have much of a specifically political weight. But these great love poems do vibrate at points with a feeling similar to the really good poems of fate.

> The piller pearisht is whearto I lent

and

> They fle from me that sometyme did me seke

have a similar accent and a similar seriousness, although of course the poems which these lines introduce are quite dissimilar. What I do think needs insisting on is that the feeling of the lutanist love-poems (if I may call them that)[1] is still more remote from either. 'The pillar perished is' does not strike me as a fully successful poem; but what is interesting about it is not the quality of its poetic realisation, which is

---

[1] I am not suggesting that even these minor poems were written to be sung to the lute; in fact I find Dr. John Stevens's argument on this point quite convincing. See *Music and Poetry in the Early Tudor Court* (London, 1961), especially Part Two. The more important thing is that such poems pretend as it were that they are written for singing; the greater poems do not.

truncated, nor the sensational quality of its occasion, which is the execution of Thomas Cromwell, but the heavy, dragging prose quality of its *feeling*, a poignancy as far as possible from the professional poignancy of the lutanist love-poems. So far is it from *pretending* to feelings that, in its middle section, it hardly even becomes poetry. The numbness felt there may be a creative fault, but it *is* an index to the authentic numbness of its author. And, despite this dragging prose quality, a quality antithetical to song, the sonnet in fact ends with four fine lines which markedly echo, while they plainly transcend, the language and manner of several of the lesser love-poems:

> My penne in playnt, my voyce in carefull crye,
> My mynde in woe, my bodye full of smart,
> And I my self, my self alwayes to hate,
> Til dreadfull death do ease my dolefull state?

The fact is that a language, a manner, a style of pretending, adopted for the purposes of conventional avowals have been turned into a technique of self-utterance, available when some worthwhile self and some genuine 'woe' become available to utter. It is interesting, incidentally, that while this sonnet is a translation from Petrarch, the last lines are quite original; and they are burdened with a feeling as direct as it is relevant. One cannot fail to notice how they echo and transcend their precursors among the 'love' poems:

> Ys yt possyble
> So cruell intent,
> So hasty hete and so sone spent,
> Ffrom love to hate, and thens ffor to Relent?
> Is it possyble?

My own preferences among these poems are not for those in which the fact of desolation is woefully hymned, but for those in which any pretence to a 'real' passion is disdained, and the songs come forth from the lover's stance to exist in their own right as songs. In the best of these we are conscious of the song as a moment or move in a sophisticated *debate*; the narcissistic quality tends to be subdued, and in the occasional sharpness of the phrasing one gets a tremor of the passion which is not pretended to, either seriously or in feigning. 'And wilt thou leave me thus?' is lovely in just this way:

> And wylt thow leve me thus?
> Say nay, say nay, ffor shame,
> To save the from the Blame
> Of all my greffe and grame;
> And wylt thow leve me thus?
> Say nay, Say nay!

But it is lovely because the pretence of a 'real' stance has so disappeared as to make it completely a song, and no more than a song. As for that stronger lyric, 'Madame, withouten many words', the pretence of a stance has so fully disappeared as to give it the sharpness of a beautifully formed debating point:

> Yf it be yea I shalbe fayne;
> If it be nay, frendes as before;
> Ye shall an othre man obtain,
> And I myn owne and yours no more.

But however much one may like some of these songs, and whatever one's preferences among them, the personal anthology one constructs from them must be a small one, otherwise the sheer monotony of repetition will kill them off for us; and one could not give any of them any but a low place in one's scale of values. I would not dismiss them so sweepingly as H. A. Mason does,[1] but I agree with him that the great majority of them are pseudo-poems, and that the whole issue which they raise should be shifted to one side in order that finer poems may be brought more centrally into view, and the issues raised by *them* focussed more clearly.

[1] See also Stevens, op. cit.

III

Mason's dismissal of the 'love' lyrics (though it must be remembered that for this purpose he is thinking only of the poems in the *Devonshire* MSS.) is based partly on the perception that Wyatt is not on the whole an *original* lyrist, so that the more one insists on his reputation as a lyrist the more subtly one is undermining his reputation as a poet; and partly on the contention that Wyatt 'abandoned' the lyrical modes to take up translation. He speaks of 'They flee from me' and 'What rage is this?' and says they are

> fine poems, and if you wish, you may call them lyrics. But they are not in any sense continuous with the 'Devonshire' poems. They belong to Wyatt's real activity as a poet. For Wyatt did not become a poet in the full sense until he abandoned the courtly lyric for something I should like to describe as translation.

'They flee from me' is not translation in any sense, and it is perhaps for that reason that Mason shows some eagerness to get it out of the discussion (I think it myself Wyatt's greatest poem); but, leaving that aside, one still has the difficulties with Mason's formulation: that, since there is no certain chronology for Wyatt's poems, we cannot know when he 'abandoned' one thing and took to another; and that, given the facts about their affinities with their originals, there is something paradoxical in stressing that these poems are 'translations'. As I have mentioned, Satire One, 'Whoso list to hunt', and 'The pillar perished is' are all in some sense translations; but the freest and most moving section of the first departs very significantly from its original, the central paradox of the second entirely reverses the point made in *its* original, and the most moving lines of the third are not in the original at all.

Yet I do think that Mason is basically right, and that it is important for a revaluing of Wyatt that we recognise his rightness. If we shrug at the word translation, we may still see great good sense in the judgments that 'Wyatt turned to creative translation when he had some urgent personal matter to "distance"'; and he 'used his original as a Mask or Persona, as a means of finding and creating himself'. The body of work so affected includes the Satires, the Psalms, the poems I have mentioned individually, and a few others; it does not include 'They flee from me'. And whether those critics are right who say that his three Satires are the first genuine satires in English, whether it is true that his translations of the Psalms are the best metrical translations of them in the language, it does seem plain that in both kinds he was using an objectively existing mode or model and an objective 'impersonal' task to 'distance . . . some urgent personal matter'. What I have said about the freedom attained by Satire One suggests this pretty clearly in the case of the Satires; and, as Surrey was no doubt the first to point out, the Psalms which Wyatt translated had to do with the lusts, the weaknesses, and the repentances of a man in high places. Quite how much either is a 'translation' is open to question. But it is interesting that, at the moments of deepest intensity (I put it this way because both groups, but the Psalms especially, have dull passages), there is a marked similarity between Satire and Psalm. This lively, piercing gravity comes most rewardingly at the end of poems. So Satire Two ends:

Hens fourth, my Poynz. this shalbe all and some:
   These wretched fooles shall have nought els of me
   But to the great god and to his high dome
None othre pain pray I for theim to be
   But when the rage doeth led them from the right
   That lowking backwards vertue they may se
Evyn as she is so goodly fayre and bright,
   And whilst they claspe their lustes in armes a crosse,
   Graunt theim, goode lorde, as thou maist of thy myght
   To frete inwards for losing suche a losse.

And Psalm 51 ends:

> Low hert in humble wyse
> Thow dost accept, O god, for plesant host.
> Make Syon, Lord, accordyng to thy will,
> Inward Syon, the Syon of the ghost:
> Off hertes Hierusalem strength the walles still.
> Then shalt thou take for good thes vttward dedes,
> As sacryfice thy plesure to fullfyll.
> Off the alone thus all our good procedes.

The similarity of spirit in these passages, the moral intensity of the first preparing for the religious intensity of the second, should make it clear that, over quite large stretches of his poetry, Wyatt was no mere lute-addicted amorist but precisely the 'deep-witted' humanist he has been praised for being. Nor are the gravity, the blend of sadness and ardour, the originality of accent, found in both kinds of poem the marks of a poet for whom 'translation' was a work of filling up a mould made by another poet. It should be stressed that he is both distancing an urgent personal feeling and using a mask to discover and create himself. But these very facts also make me wonder whether there is any more than a legalistic rightness in using the words 'translation' and 'translator' at all.

No Psalms are reprinted in the *Silver Poets* selection from Wyatt; but the Psalms are integral, though not necessarily central, to his achievement as a poet. That achievement, so I have argued, is not the achievement of a 'love-poet' in any conventional sense; but nor is it the achievement of a 'translator', whatever force a critic like Mason gives to the world. 'They flee from me' is not a translation in any conceivable sense (though it is very likely influenced by Ovid), and it is above all a love poem. Any argument about Wyatt has to take account of these two facts.

I do so without uneasiness, though with a sense of inadequacy. The feeling of the poem comes more direct and more

pondered, though much less insistent, than the feeling of a
good poem like 'What rage is this?' Yet it lives in a poetry both
more dramatic and more lambent than such a poem as 'Lux,
my fair falcon'. Where the latter says, with a too bitter
emphasis of understatement.

> But they that somtyme lykt my companye,
> Like lyse awaye from ded bodies thei crall:
> Loe, what a profe in light adversytie!

the finer poem sings

> They fle from me that sometyme did me seke
> With naked fote stalking in my chambre.
> I have sene theim gentill tame and meke
> That nowe are wyld and do not remembre
> That sometyme they put theimself in daunger
> To take bred at my hand; and nowe they raunge
> Besely seking with a continuell chaunge.

The difference is one of scope and spiritedness. 'Lux, my fair
falcon' has a convincing bitterness; 'They flee from me' has an
extraordinary resilience. And that quality, which is a quality
of basic spirit, of what expectations a man's deepest feelings
entertain of life, leads to a greater activity in the poetry; these
who flee used not merely to 'lyk my companye', they 'some-
tyme did me seke', and that 'With naked fote stalking in my
chambre'.

The sense of purposive yet mysterious activity created in
this opening stanza is also a matter of its sensuousness (so
splendidly established by the delicate checks and irregularities
of the rhythm), and hence is an index to the *kind* of passion it
has: a passion as unlike Donne's as it is unlike that of Shakespeare's sonnets. The critical problem is to define this activity,
this sensuousness, this passion; it is not to identify the kind of
animal suggested in the analogy. I have heard deer, birds, and
mice proposed for this purpose; my own preference is for

racehorses, but it is as irrelevant as any other. It is far more important to identify their action than to identify *them*. And their action, so subtly paradoxical, does provide the sensuousness which I spoke of. They were gentle, yet they stalked; they are now wild, yet it was when they were tame that they 'put theimself in daunger'; yet that was only to 'take bred', and now, one supposes, their 'raunging' brings them not only greater freedom but into greater danger. I am not, I hope, being literal-minded; I am chiefly trying to point out how extraordinary is the alternation—or, better still, the succeeding metamorphoses—of feelings and perspectives, given as they are with so unfaltering a sense of direction. When we attend sensitively to that rhythm within the poem's movement of feeling, we will not worry much about identifying either the analogical beasts or the 'daunger' to which they exposed themselves. But we may note that their very anonymity makes the whole action of the poem mysterious, and gives the sensousness its peculiar cast. The passion is not, as it is in the greatest of Donne's poems, a matter of utterance made *revelation*, not a matter of 'utterance' in that sense at all, but a tremor of undeclared feeling in the rhythmically established sensuousness.

The second stanza, in which the object of the poet-lover's attention, formerly presented by analogy, is strikingly humanised, is one of the few great passages in our poetry creating the sense of a fulfilled and satisfying sexual love. Yet it is the purpose of the poem to say that that love is in the past, that the fulfilment it brought was temporary, and that it ended in 'a straunge fasshion of forsaking':

> It was no dreme: I lay brode waking.
>> But all is torned thorough my gentilnes
> Into a straunge fasshion of forsaking;
>> And I have leve to goo of her goodenes,
>> And she also to vse new fangilnes.
> But syns that I so kyndely ame serued,
> I would fain knowe what she hath deserued.

One might suppose that here a poem which began in meditation ends in bitterness. That, I think, would be too naïve a
response. There *is* a note of celebration in all three stanzas;
the second begins, after all, 'Thancked be fortune', a blessing
heartily recalled even in a seemingly bitter retrospect; and,
however mysterious the love celebrated ('she me *caught* . . .'),
the third stanza again begins, 'It was no dreme; I lay brode
waking'. There is a play in this stanza between two perceptions, if not two orders, of reality: the sense that the fulfilment
which *might* have been a dream was in fact a waking, and the
sense that the strange fashion of forsaking, though a recalling
of the mystery of such a meeting, was also a mutual release of
obligations, to be wryly commented on. The precise tone of
the last two lines evades me, as it has evaded many critics;
though their meaning is clear enough, in its devious way.
Wyatt is certainly not setting up a standard stoic position in
the face of sexual fulfilment and loss; he is trying to keep
several differing nuances in mind; and his means of doing so
is his strangely sensuous rhythm, so effective in establishing
the mysteriousness (though not, perhaps, the power) of
passion.

It would be absurd to say that this was not a love poem; and
perhaps it sounds priggish to say that it is not *just* a love poem,
as if there were something wrong with a poem which couldn't
do better than *that*. But in fact the poem's feeling is not simply
a feeling of love's fulfilment, or of its loss, or of the two in
juxtaposition; it is a feeling of the manifold lights and shadings
of life, in which, at its most intense and astonishing moments,
awareness and dream, animal and woman, friendliness and
recoil, ecstasy and tenderness, acceptance and bitterness, are
equal possibilities. To say that it has something 'metaphysical'
about it is not, however, to say that it anticipates Donne. It
may have more in common with Donne than with the Shakespeare of the Sonnets; and it is, in my opinion, the finest poem
of a poet who is one of the four great love poets in the

language. But it surprises us less as coming from the Wyatt of the Satires and the Psalms than as coming from the Wyatt of 'Is it possible' and 'Me list no more to sing'. It is filled with mortality: but it is filled as delicately, indeed as religiously, as any poem I know.

CHAPTER V

John Donne's Passion

The intricacies and subtleties of his imagination are the length and depth of the furrow made by his passion. His pedantry and his obscenities—the rock and the loam of his Eden—but make us the more certain that one who is but a man like us all has seen God.—
W. B. Yeats

I

DONNE has been unusually well served by his critics. Yet the best of them have paid little explicit attention to that quality which I think is the most obvious and remarkable one in his poetry—his passion. I mean his *poetic* passion, through which he serves and acts out those life-passions whose existence in him gives him his subjects and whose intermittent presence to his understanding gives him, often, his themes. It is this that most needs definition; yet his finest critics have seldom embarked on it. It is not that which constituted his interest for Johnson or Coleridge; rather, they seem amazed, and perturbed, by his *intellectual* energy, and, in Johnson's case, by the poetic anomalies to which it seemed to lead. Dryden's remarks about him, if we took them seriously, would amount to a complaint that he had no passion, or the wrong sort. And the most famous modern essays—those by Eliot, Grierson, Leavis and James Smith—are, ostensibly at least, concerned with quite other problems in the assessment of him. Perhaps, for most of these, the matter is too obvious to need discussion. Yet I think it does; for a number of lesser critics have noticed it at some length, and in such terms as to suggest that it baffled them.

It is no accident that Donne's enduring strength lies in his shorter poems; the 'Anniversaries', with their fervour of transition from one kind of interest in life to another, are certainly exceptions, but very few of the satires or epistles or epithalamions, few even of the elegies, could provide a firm base for his greatness. The reason surely has to do with the quality I am speaking of. And it is necessary to use a word like 'passion' to define that; for I am doing something more than noting the presence in or behind the poetry of intense 'emotions'—a word which in our loose modern usage perhaps suggests something merely endured, stored up, or released, while 'passion' suggests a kind of action, of acting out the personality's deepest powers in terms of explicit feeling. If we fasten on this quality, we are forced to raise the question of the part which it characteristically takes in the economy of the poem.

No doubt the part will differ from poem to poem, but in ways which allow a significant similarity to emerge. We have, for example, the conclusion to 'The Second Anniversary'; and we have the way in which the first stanza of 'The Good-Morrow' rises into the second. The first of these is a clear case of what I mean.

> Could any Saint provoke that appetite,
> Thou here should'st make me a French convertite.
> But thou would'st not; nor would'st thou be content,
> To take this, for my second yeares true Rent,
> Did this Coine beare any other stampe, then his,
> That gave thee power to doe, me, to say this.
> Since his will is, that to posteritie,
> Thou should'st for life, and death, a patterne bee,
> And that the world should notice have of this,
> The purpose, and th' authoritie is his;
> Thou art the Proclamation; and I am
> The Trumpet, at whose voyce the people came.

The second may seem less clear a case, and it is only by attending very closely to the detail, both of reference and rhythm, that the reader may see whether or not it justifies my contention. Yet it seems to me, also, a more important and rewarding example than the first.

> I wonder by my troth, what thou, and I
> Did, till we lov'd? were we not wean'd till then?
> But suck'd on countrey pleasures, childishly?
> Or snorted we in the seaven sleepers den?
> T'was so; But this, all pleasures fancies bee.
> If ever any beauty I did see,
> Which I desir'd, and got, t'was but a dreame of thee.
>
> And now good morrow to our waking soules,
> Which watch not one another out of feare;
> For love, all love of other sights controules,
> And makes one little roome, an every where.
> Let sea-discoverers to new worlds have gone,
> Let Maps to other, worlds on worlds have showne,
> Let us possesse one world, each hath one, and is one.

In both passages, a movement of ratiocination or of rhetorical embellishment becomes suddenly a moment of passionate affirmation: of an affirmation of the passion underlying and motivating the reasoning. The first is the closing movement of a long poem which, however fascinating, was in danger of relying on central conceits so exaggerated as to make the whole inaccessible to us. I think we see this exaggeration, even eccentricity, is to be found in all the lines quoted, except the last two; we note in the earlier lines something like a determination to push and strain mental complexity towards the limits of the imagination's capacity; yet that extraordinary closing *coup* (which at first sight may appear the most exaggerated of all) has an effect of a different and more compelling kind. It is, as it were, an ultimate intensity of affirmation of the sacred and of the poet's right to affirm it. But that effect, though wonderful, is only momentary, and it is an effect merely of declaration, declamation, a sudden trumpeting of function and authority. The passion is of the voice, and the authority is in and of the passion.

The second case is different. 'The Good-Morrow' is throughout a passionate affirmation of a passionate state, which is one of mutual recognition and completion. The first stanza is even vehement in its insistence on the feeling which is both its motive-power and its subject. Yet it has also, I think, something of that almost manipulative cerebral quality which is as often a weakness as it is a strength in Donne. It is exaggerated, hyperbolic; and while it does not conceal, but reveals and presents a strong emotion, it does so in a slightly lopsided manner, so that by the end of the stanza one is not sure what attitude one is being invited to take. Is there, in fact, something even whimsical in the 'T'was so . . .'? Yet the second stanza resolves all doubts. It is at once an opening-out and a concentration of the emotion. There is a slight but discernible change in pitch, a greater directness in the language, and a wonderful free-striding rhythm, in which the mutuality of the recognition ('*our* waking soules': the selves are felt as waking with and towards each other) can be established. What has happened is that the second stanza has become not simply a development of the emotion presented in the first but a quite new revelation of its nature and scope, to the point where it is transmuted, and can no longer be accounted for simply as '*an* emotion'. It is a moment of *passion*; and its effect is *revelation*. One feels that it would have been impossible without the logical or rhetorical preparation of the first stanza: as though what was declared there is revealed here.

'Twicknam Garden' shows yet a third way:

> Blasted with sighs, and surrounded with teares,
>   Hither I come to seeke the spring,
>   And at mine eyes, and at mine eares,
> Receive such balmes, as else cure everything. . . .

It does not close with, or mount towards, but begins with the moment of passion (which here has an apocalyptic ring); and the poem then develops as an 'explanation' of what has been declared. The basic conceit of the poem (which has its own difficulty) is, given this opening, used in a quite direct way to provide a retrospective context for the apocalyptic utterance, the speech which comes as though unbidden.

'The Extasie', that well-loved and much-anthologised oddity, has its moment of revelatory passion coming at the end to reveal something the previous terms of which have been drawing the imagination in a quite different direction. 'Else a great Prince in prison lies' is, in terms of what it states, the consummation of an argument; but it is also, in the elevated directness of its tone, the *end* of the arguing process as such: in terms of sensibility, a stop and even a reversal. And I cannot help feeling conscious of the passionate moment being forced from Donne by the sheer unsatisfactoriness of his previous procedures. There is a disproportion and a disjunction between the economy of the poem as a whole, with its involved wit, and the deeply resonant feeling achieved in that closing passage, which seems, for all its logical aptness, to come from an artistic motivation not accessible to the poet during the rest of the poem. Then, there are poems like 'The Blossome' and 'The Flea', which, though very distinguished in the Donne fashion, are little more than feignings of passion: that is, whatever force is declared in them is declared in the sense that it is merely talked about or recorded, and does not find its *poetic* equivalent and witness in the movement of the poem. The language in these poems is 'artificial' in a way of which not even 'The Extasie', much as I dislike that poem, is guilty.

The curious quality whose varied and contrasting presences I have pointed to has been noted by other critics; but many have given too simple an account of it, and several have taken it as a vice rather than a virtue. In the 'Twentieth Century Views' *John Donne* (edited by Helen Gardner) we find several examples of this. Saintsbury's view is similar to my own, and I heartily agree with him when he says that 'no poet has gone nearer (than Donne) to the hinting and adumbration of this infinite quality of passion, and of the relapses and reactions from passion'; yet such a statement does not take us very far into the question of poetic kind and quality. C. S. Lewis, on the other hand, groping eloquently away from the challenge of a poet whom in this respect he seems not to understand at all, thinks that Donne writes 'not only *about*, but *in*, a chaos of passions': a view which makes redundant all questions about the relation of the passionate moments to the economy of their poems, and which, happily, is quite remote from our experience of Donne's best work. And another contributor, Professor Crofts, finds (if I may give Helen Gardner's summary of his position)

> Donne's 'love-sick fancies, twaddle upon twaddle', effective only in 'giving us a sense of difficulty overcome' when at last we arrive at 'a passionate outcry'.

This does seem to get the issue back to front. For that 'passionate outcry' is not merely outcry, even in 'The Extasie', and the quality of passionate revelation does not merely 'overcome' the 'difficulty' but consummates it; and the 'difficulty' does not merely stand, or even twist, there waiting to be overcome, but aids in its own overcoming, if indeed that is the word. Poetry for Donne is not a laxative for the emotions. Arduous (and, I might add, passionate) thought is his poetic medium; the so-called passionate outcry is not a release from thinking but a recognition of the profound meaning and object of the thought. And what is revealed in it, at its best, is the sense of relationship. It brings present, by a new resonance, a change in pitch or tone or movement, the imagined object of feeling, whether that object be a woman or God or Donne's other self.

I think we may do more than merely point to these qualities in Donne; they can be demonstrated, as nearly as anything of this order can be. I think, for example, of that extraordinary passage at the end of 'Elegie XVI: On His Mistris':

When I am gone, dreame me some happinesse,
Nor let thy lookes our long hid love confesse,
Nor praise, nor dispraise me, nor blesse nor curse
Openly loves force, nor in bed fright thy Nurse
With midnights startings, crying out, oh, oh
Nurse, o my love is slaine, I saw him goe
O'r the white Alpes alone; I saw him I,
Assail'd, fight, taken, stabb'd, bleed, fall, and die.
Augure me better chance, except dread *Jove*
Thinke it enough for me to'have had thy love.

Now, we have here something which might certainly be
called a 'passionate outcry'; but it is essential to note that it is
managed dramatically and with a sense of its paradox. The
voice of the poet or of his *persona* gradually rises until it
becomes the voice of his mistress imagined as imagining his
death. That is, the poem at this point has two *personae* rather
than one; and the movement between them is both rapid and
abrupt. Their relationship would be hard to define; and no
doubt there is something gratuitous, even arbitrary, in the use
of such a rhetorical device. But the powerfully flexible
rhythms, the peculiar tone ('oh, oh/Nurse, o . . .'), the
mounting and almost cascading pitch, have the effect not only
of dramatising, and that in the most idiomatic sense, Donne's
perception of some mysterious quality in a sexual relationship
but also of suggesting, in a mode seemingly quite alien to the
mental and emotional mode of his male *persona*, *his own* fears
of journeying, of death, of destiny. To say that there is a
substratum of humour in this joining and mingling of voices
is to get somewhere, but not very far. The declaration, the
passionate utterance, the *revelation*, is accomplished, but by
means which are as dramatically oblique as they are daring.
And such an unusual depth and quality of control (for that is
what it is) shows clearly that Donne is not just addicted to
emotional outbursts when the wit runs out or otherwise forces
them on him. On the contrary, he is unobtrusively controlling

the drama of a relationship (between himself and his mistress, his two selves, himself and his destiny) to the point where its burden of mutual terror is apocalyptically disclosed. If one judges that such a poetic habit shows some affinity with drama, it is not to go on and see, with Patrick Cruttwell, the stanzas or phases of a Donne poem developing by analogy with the acts of a play. Personally, I should use the fact to point to Donne's unique clearsightedness, which is of a sort best accommodated by a lyric form.

II

The passion that is no mere outcry, but a revelation; the poetic logic that is no mere 'tactic' of elaboration but a straining towards revelation: we find them not only in the poems I have mentioned, but in others, in 'The Canonization', for example, 'The Anniversarie', and 'The Sunne Rising'. In this last poem we become most strikingly aware of them at that moment at the end of the second and the start of the third stanza where the kings and lovers who formerly were seen as opposites are now seen to be the same; and not merely declared to be the same but, by a deepening of the feeling carried by a deepening of the poetic resonance, revealed as the same. The word 'tactic' is inadequate to define such a quality of instantaneous recognition.

We are not surprised to find this happening in a love poem; but we find it also in Donne's religious poetry and, indeed, in his prose, at certain magnificent moments in his sermons and devotions. It happens, too, in poems whose kind we are hard put to indicate; for *what*, exactly, are we to call 'A Nocturnall Upon S. Lucies Day'? Is it a love poem? a religious meditation? a lament? a metaphysical speculation? Or all these, and more? Here there are no intimations of mortality without intimations of immortality, no deprivations without the sense of an immediate and compelling presence. It is a poem which, by postulating impossibilities, creates expanding possibilities:

Study me then, you who shall lovers bee
At the next world, that is, at the next Spring. . . .

If this is a shock, it is again a shock of revelation; and it both
extends and reverses the logic of the poem which contains it.

And if we take 'Elegie XIX: On His Mistris Going to Bed',
perhaps the most erotic poem in the language, we may consider that even here we find a poetry revealing dimensions,
possibilities, other than those its logic insists on. In the passage
effectively beginning, 'O my America! my new-found-land',
there is an extraordinary emotional and rhythmic freedom, yet
the exotic overtones carry a suggestion of a quite radical and
expansive adventurousness, of a geographical and metaphysical
adventure which finds its expression in and through the moment
of sexual exploration. This is play yet more than play. And if
we return to 'And now good morrow to our waking soules',
we see more clearly that, in its boldness of tone and movement,
it does not have anything of the quality of outcry, or outburst.
This is no Lear on the heath, or Antony crying of inconstancy,
or Othello railing and declaiming. What it reveals, in revealing
the meaning which the logic of its poem has, is the presence of
another person, who is there, in the poem, not to be persuaded
or assailed, but to become part of the vision of mutuality. It
may be true, as so many critics have complained, that no
woman would like to be addressed in such terms; but it is
unlikely that she would fail to recognise that she was there,
and being addressed. In other words, here and elsewhere
Donne has accomplished by lyric means what one might have
supposed could be accomplished only by the exchanges of high
drama.

What is true of the best of the *Songs and Sonets* is true also of
the best of the religious poems. Here, too, the *end* of the poetic
process is not simply to address God or the poet's soul but to
create a sense of a relationship already existing but now,
through the moment or moments of revelation, expanding in
possibility. The patent difficulty of the attempt should not

blind us to the occasional depth of the achievement. The trouble is that, except in one case, the achievement is so imperfect. We know the dangers: the set-piece meditation, which can go so far in the direction of imitating its biblical models as to produce glosses on or translations of psalm, parable, or saying of Christ, and so raises for us the question of its own redundance; and the deliberate construction of rhetorical paradoxes so strong that they convert the religious dialogue (between self and God, or body and soul) into a game. These are as much dangers for Donne as for Herbert, or for Crashaw, who came near to succumbing to them entirely. Therefore it may be worth approaching his greatest achievement, 'A Hymne to God my God, in my Sickness', by way of his most celebrated near-success, 'A Hymne to God the Father'.

This poem is certainly a highly distinguished and taking performance; yet it exemplifies both Donne's danger and the characteristic economy of his poetic passion. It is significant, for one thing, that the word 'performance' should suggest itself at all. I cannot avoid the conclusion that God is being invited to take part in a very subjective game; there is something unpleasantly self-congratulatory, suggested by the tone and reinforced by the rhyming, which gives an unusual and surely inappropriate smoothness to the rhythms. The famous pun on Donne's surname is made not only in the last stanza (where it has the effect of clinching a deeply-felt paradox) but in all three; and, because of that, we find at the end of the first and second stanzas a curious note of furtive triumph, rather than of the genuine self-accusation and regret which the poem pretends to. Only in the last stanza does the note of deep personal involvement come clear, and the lines act what the whole poem proclaims:

> I have a sinne of feare, that when I have spunne
> My last thred, I shall perish on the shore;
> Sweare by thy selfe, that at my death thy sonne

Shall shine as he shines now, and heretofore;
And, having done that, Thou haste done,
I feare no more.

The invocation to God to 'Sweare by thy selfe' is both enormously audacious and suitably desperate; it presents an unusual personal stance very clearly, but at the same time suggests the presence in it of undeclared depths, a suggestion reinforced by 'I *have* a sinne of feare', with its implication that the sin is not a single act but a continuous state of being. Here Donne is using, however briefly, a fully poetic language to create shifting perspectives on the religious relationship. The fact is, that the economy of the poem does *not* work towards the revelation *in intenso* of its own form and meaning, but leaves two attitudes working against each other to a mutual but oblique enlightenment.

But if Donne is a poet of religious conflict, and of death, he is also a poet of the resurrection. At this point I may refer again to Professor Crofts, because he presents in one paragraph an unwitting summary of most of the (vulgar) prejudices and misconceptions which linger on:

. . . the sentence begins with the pronoun 'I'. And for Donne everything did so begin, and end. Throughout his life he was a man self-haunted, unable to escape from his own drama, unable to find any window that would not give him back the image of himself. Even the mistress of his most passionate love-verses, who must (one supposes) have been a real person, remains for him a mere abstraction of sex: a thing given. He cannot see her —does not apparently want to see her; for it is not of her that he writes, but of his relation to her; not of love, but of himself loving. And so in later life, though the stuff of his meditation changes, this inability to lose himself remains. It is not of God that he thinks so often or so deeply as of his relation to God; of the torturing drama of his sin and its expiation, the sowing and the reaping, the wheat and the tares. The great commonplace of his sermons, it has been said, is death; but in truth it is not death that inspires his frightful eloquence so much as the image of himself dying.

In my opinion, every sentence in this is wrong—in part grossly, in part subtly. I have already expressed my conviction that, both in love poetry and in religious poetry, Donne so intensely and so fully creates the sense of relationship that he brings present, by suggestion, his partner in it; and I have indicated the nature of the evidence. As for death, he *is* preoccupied with it, and he is preoccupied also with his own imagined dying, but he is also preoccupied with the resurrection. His interest is therefore neither so partial nor so self-concerned as Crofts says. In sermons and in poetry, he sees resurrection as implicit in death; and he shows that the expectation of resurrection can be traced in the acts of dying. It is the peculiar triumph of 'A Hymne to God my God' that it dramatises this, in such a way as to go beyond the expression of emotion, even beyond the creation of a revelatory passion, to the attainment of a serene ecstasy.

Donne's feeling for death, and dying, is of a unique cast; and in this poem it contains neither posturing nor play. The poem creates what is indicated so eloquently at so many places in the prose works: a sense that the hope of resurrection is not held out as a frenzied compensation for death, but is the end of an imaginative perception that earth and heaven are constantly in a dramatic relationship, so that living, dying, death, and resurrection may be felt as stages in the one process *carried on in the one place*. It is unnecessary to produce prose quotations in evidence; but they are numerous. Still, the *dramatic* nature of the process, as it appeared to Donne, may be seen in one passage:

> Man is but earth; Tis true; but earth is the center. That man who dwels upon himself, who is alwaies conversant in himself, rests in his true earth. Man is a celestial creature too, a heavenly creature; and that man that dwels upon himselfe, that hath his conversation in himselfe, hath his conversation in heaven.

It is obvious that Donne's prose and his poetry are much more of a piece than those of most poets; and it is obvious that so constant a weighing and feeling of the paradox would be likely to issue in at least one great, unimpaired poem. Yet none of this could have prepared us for, though it might have led us to hope for, the unique shapeliness and resonance of the 'Hymne', a height and purity of emotion created, and shaped, by the depth and purity of decorum.

The fineness of the poem is that it is deathly serious, yet full of intimations of life; most intense, yet beautifully controlled and modulated. It has nothing of the 'almost histrionic note' which Helen Gardner perceptively hears in the *Holy Sonnets*, and which she attributes 'partly to the meditation's deliberate stimulation of emotion'. In it we find no 'overdramatising of the spiritual life'. In fact, the 'spiritual life' (that unpleasant and misleading term) is not in the poem at all as an object of overt attention; Donne has gone beyond any tendency to present his 'spiritual life' as an example for our inspection, or even for his own. The poem is immensely self-aware, yet at no point self-conscious. His meditation emerges as the speech of his whole being, conscious, concentrated, shaped, yet oddly relaxed, as in the tone (half-musing, half-exultant) of the opening:

> Since I am comming to that Holy roome,
> > Where, with thy Quire of Saints for evermore,
> I shall be made thy Musique; As I come
> > I tune the Instrument here at the dore,
> > And what I must doe then, thinke here before.

The tone may even be called that of a composed astonishment, and the finely variant rhythm perfectly renders it in all its emotional complexity, meditative, hopeful, wry, sober, joyful.

The next two stanzas develop images which occur in other places in Donne's *œuvre*, and establish that curiously serene decorum. About them I would note only two things: First, the fact that 'discoverie' is rhymed with 'die', as the rhythms of their two lines are played off against each other,

> That this is my South-west discoverie
> *Per fretum febris*, by these streights to die . . .

and, second, the way in which the note of resigned acceptance ('die') is no sooner sounded than it is succeeded by 'I joy', which, with the repetition of 'straits', gives a new, more exultant, and instantaneously accepted perspective on dying. In stanza 4, Donne's habit of hyperbole comes out in a movement of heightened questioning; but it is in the wonderful two last stanzas that the seemingly opposed energies of the poem, which hitherto have worked against each other in a surprisingly decorous way, are blended in the moment of complete triumph:

> We thinke that *Paradise* and *Calvarie*,
>   *Christs* Crosse, and *Adams* tree, stood in one place;
> Looke Lord, and finde both *Adams* met in me;
>   As the first *Adams* sweat surrounds my face,
>   May the last *Adams* blood my soule embrace.
>
> So, in his purple wrapp'd receive mee Lord,
>   By these his thornes give me his other Crowne;
> And as to others soules I preach'd thy word,
>   Be this my Text, my Sermon to mine owne,
>   Therfore that he may raise the Lord throws down.

I hope I will be understood if I say that, here, the poet's voice takes on ('So, in his purple wrapp'd . . .') a surprisingly deep, even sombre resonance while extending that decorum and enhancing that ecstatic serenity. The strength and urgency of 'Looke Lord' quite avoids abruptness or over-emphasis. And the parallel structure of the last two lines of stanza 5 goes with the overtly personal reference in the last three lines of the poem to make the final movement at once heart-breaking and exultant. One remembers 'the Trumpet, at whose voyce the people came'.

Everything in this poem delights me; and it seems to me one of the glories of our literature. To call it 'revelatory' in the sense I have formerly used would doubtless be misleading; its note is nowhere apocalyptic, and it does not work towards any revelation. Yet one might say that it is itself a revelation, even an apocalypse. The relaxation of tone is, in a sense, the passion's atmosphere, and the condition of the ecstasy's growth. We have here no merely didactic certainty, and no tactic of persuasion; we have, rather, a passionate composure whose emotional roots go as deep as the imagination can conceive.

Compared with the 'Hymne', even so unusual a poem as 'Good Friday . . .Riding Westward' has roughnesses and fluctuations of tone and even those occasionally magnificent productions, the *Holy Sonnets*, have either a certain hollowness of accent or a certain wilfulness of imagery. There is something subtly wrong with the pitch:

> Oh my blacke Soule! now thou art summoned
> By sicknesse, deaths herald, and champion;
> Thou art like a pilgrim, which abroad hath done
> Treason, and durst not turne to whence hee is fled. . . .

The voice, in short, represents a convention, which is one of highly rhetorical self-reproach; and the imagined personal stance from which the voice issues is also one made familiar not only in poetry but in sermons, homilies, and prose meditations; the speaker engages in self-analysis and self-reproach on behalf of other people who may be expected to be familiar with its terms; and the very formalised urgency is a way of insisting on the representativeness. This is why I think Helen Gardner is right to point to 'an almost histrionic note' and 'a deliberate stimulation of emotion'; and it is also why I find the *Holy Sonnets*, though resoundingly impressive, not quite so distinctive as one might have expected, and not entirely satisfactory in suggesting the super-natural dimensions of the dialogue. God is a dangerous interlocutor for poetry, even when it is Donne who addresses Him.

'Batter my Heart' is, of course, distinctive in its erotic analogies; and 'Death be not Proud' has its magnificent moments; but both are histrionic. The splendid exception is 'At the round earths imagined corners'; and it is worth reflecting that this too is a poem of resurrection rather than self-accusation or self-reproach. It tempts the poet to violent affirmation, but not to histrionics:

> At the round earths imagin'd corners, blow
> Your trumpets, Angells, and arise, arise
> From death, you numberlesse infinities
> Of soules, and to your scattred bodies goe,
> All whom the flood did, and fire shall o'erthrow,
> All whom warre, dearth, age, agues, tyrannies,
> Despaire, law, chance, hath slaine, and you whose eyes,
> Shall behold God, and never tast deaths woe.
> But let them sleepe, Lord, and mee mourne a space,
> For, if above all these, my sinnes abound,
> 'Tis late to aske abundance of thy grace,
> When wee are there; here on this lowly ground,
> Teach mee how to repent; for that's as good
> As if thou'hadst seal'd my pardon, with thy blood.

As in the 'Hymne', we have presented here not only the unique quality of Donne's passion but the finest paradox of that apparently contentious subject, 'religious poetry'. It is no doubt hard for any man in our cultural circumstances, tempted by so many intimations of despair and limitation, to imagine that a poet could write a poem like the 'Hymne', which vibrates with the promise of the resurrection, or one like the Sonnet, which offers to dramatise the fact of it. Yet Donne's greatness as a religious poet comes largely from precisely these poems. His sensibility is apocalyptic in a quite unusual way, and the dialectical habit of reasoning which is native to it is a splendid medium in which that sensibility can be brought into play. The rhetorical magnificence of this sonnet of course activates the perception of '. . . warre, dearth, age, agues, tyrannies/Despaire, law, chance . . .'—in fact, all the means of dying, and, by using *them* as the emotional pivot on which the poem turns, shows the movement towards resurrection in terms of a whole world brought into sudden paradoxical movement rhrough its death-agonies. That is, the emotional insistence on the ways of dying helps to establish the paradox which the biblical notion of the resurrection of the body inevitably contains, and so presents it as imaginatively real. What is surprising is that there is not a single note of cheapness. And the final effect is, as elsewhere, one not of persuasion but of revelation.

III

It would be otiose to multiply terms and distinctions; I realise that already I may have begged certain questions. Donne is a most difficult case, not simply because of the frequent sensuality of his religious poetry and the metaphysical questionings involved in his love poetry, but because of the way in which his expository method, which is one of concentration, creates an imaginative world whose chief feature is its expansiveness. I would say, while being fully conscious of the paradox, that Donne's ingenuity is both more obvious than Marvell's and less pervasive. Marvell's unique suppleness, indeed, his creative energy as such, seems to go towards enclosing the experience within the poem, and enclosing the poem within a pattern of paradoxes arising out of the experience; it is a poetry which reflects itself as in a set of mirrors. Donne's energy and subtlety, on the other hand, work towards opening up the experience so that, at a certain point of the poem's logic, its dimensions may be fully revealed; the chief feature of his poetry is its openness, an openness not only to a common world but to the range of its author's own passions. Marvell usually creates the sense of an enormously subtle thinking self without using, and certainly without stressing, the first personal pronoun at all; the emotional grammar of his poems does not usually depend on a formal grammar of the 'I'. But Donne characteristically uses both the formal and the emotional grammar of 'I' and 'we' and 'thou'. So we become less conscious of Donne manœuvring a *persona* throughout the poem than of his creating that powerful sense of situation and relationship in and of which the created speaking-voice speaks, and which the shifts in its tone reveal at depth. His poems are dramatic in a way in which Marvell's are not.

In all the poems I have mentioned, we are perhaps more conscious of the growing self-awareness of passion than of anything else. And, except in special cases, we should, I think, be careful in our use of the word '*persona*'. We are conscious that he is revealing his deepest self; we are not conscious of his being 'outside' his self in any of the usual ways. The poet writing his poem and the speaker speaking it from within are, in his work, barely if at all distinguishable. It is interesting, for example, that a very good book on the development of the idea of the *persona* in English poetry should barely mention Donne, although he is often held to be the most self-centred poet in the language. Whatever his 'metaphysical' procedures may suggest to the contrary, he does not so much explore the self as uncover and reveal it, and then in terms of situation and relationship. What he does explore is the concepts and analogies through which the revelation is made. But that is a different matter.

CHAPTER VI

Blake's Originality

BLAKE has been perhaps too readily accepted, and so too easily misrepresented: first by the taste sponsored by nineteenth-century anthologists with their penchant for 'clothing of delight' and 'England's green and pleasant land', which is simply the taste of the determinedly non-poetic; second, and even more cripplingly, by the taste of those who see him as bringing to the explanation of human existence a neglected and esoteric doctrine which is valuable in itself and from which the poetry gets its depth of implication. A mixture of sentimentality and mystagogy has made people unable to discriminate his considerable from his inconsiderable work, the great from the minuscule. Where everything is 'interesting', poetry, *poetic* value, becomes an irrelevance or a burden.

It needs to be said that Blake's greatness lies not in the easy sentiments he touches, or in the 'traditions' he represents or recreates, but in the amazing originality with which he perceives and creates the actual world. The paradox is unavoidable; for if his originality is a matter of *vision*, it is not a vision 'seen' as in a crystal ball and reproduced in charmingly translucent images; he reveals the depths of human life; and if his revelation has an emotional accent, it is the accent not of a fey and inevitably detached innocence, but of an exulting in the powers of life—and in the powers of art, which reveals life at depth. He does not merely reproduce a vision, he creates one.

Often, indeed, Blake seems explicitly to aim at something both greater and less than he actually achieves: greater, in the sense that what he aims at is beyond human powers altogether; less, in that his poetry is more *creative*, more incarnational, earthy, instinct with emotion, than his prose writings suggest.

As Eliot has pointed out, Blake's originality was achieved at the cost of a certain psychic isolation from other artists, like Wordsworth and Coleridge, as seminal as himself; and we may find in that isolation the explanation of the fact that his poetic modes, though capable of a unique intensity, are also lacking in expansiveness. At the same time, the originality is evident from the start. His juvenilia (I think of the best of the 'Songs' from *Poetical Sketches*) are unlike, say, Yeats' in having a buoyancy of accent and movement which enables them to transcend the conventional quality of their images and makes us think, not of Gray or Collins, but of Shakespeare.

Yet they do not prepare us fully for the liberation of creative energy found in the greatest songs of *Experience*. Nor do his prose explanations, which, on the contrary, have the effect of subtly misrepresenting his mature achievement. We remember his famous declaration, 'I must create a system, or be enslaved by another man's. I will not reason and compare; my business is to create', and notice that, as he grew older, he became less interested in poetry than in system-building, or, rather, the impulse to 'create' became ruinously identified with the concern for systems. In a sense, there is too much *prose* in Blake's total *œuvre*, too much eccentric and self-justifying statement; and it is this, rather than his poetic practice, which has led so many commentators into speaking as though the poetry existed for the sake of the system that is thought to support it, as though the verse served chiefly to validate the prose.

For example, his prose writings give some support to the predilections held by critics like Kathleen Raine and Witcutt. In them he lays claim to the esoteric status which his best poems ignore or transcend. 'I know of no other Christianity and of no other Gospel than the liberty of both body and mind to exercise the Divine Arts of Imagination, Imagination, the real and eternal world of which this vegetable universe is but a faint shadow, and in which we shall live in our eternal or imaginative bodies when these vegetable mortal bodies are no more. The Apostles knew no other Gospel. . . .'

If a traditional doctrine lies behind this, its name is gnosticism; and Bronowski, for example, sees Blake as a propounder of 'the Manichaean heresy'. The implications of the doctrine for his art are unmistakable. As he says elsewhere,

> The Last Judgment is an overwhelming of bad art and science. Mental things are alone real; what is called corporeal, nobody knows of its dwelling-place; it is in fallacy and its existence an imposture. . . . I assert for myself that I do not behold the outward Creation and that to me it is hindrance and not action; it is as the dirt upon my feet, no part of me. 'What', it will be questioned, 'When the sun rises, do you not see a round disk of fire something like a guinea?' O no, no, I see an innumerable company of the Heavenly host crying 'Holy Holy Holy is the Lord God Almighty!' I question not my corporeal or vegetative eye any more than I would question a window concerning a sight. I look through it and not with it. . . .

The consequences which this profoundly anti-incarnational view has for his art are to be seen under one aspect in the *Songs of Innocence*, under another in the later *Prophetic Books*. In both, we find a poetry striving for the condition where it shall be the direct expression of a direct vision, a vision of the holiness of existence concealed by fleshly life and capable of shining through fleshly life to a man who looks through but not with his fleshly eyes; a direct vision of essences. The wonder is that he gets so close to achieving the impossible; but the artistic dogmatism such a view tends towards is seen as much in the abstracted limpidity of *Innocence* as in the insistent convolutions of the *Prophetic Books*; both conditions nullify the effect of revelation which is aimed at. It is chiefly in the finest poems of *Experience* that Blake's exalted ambition is *poetically* realised, and by poetic means almost antithetical to those which his gnostic philosophy promises. He becomes a great poet by virtually contradicting himself. And we get in *Experience* a poetry not transparent but in a sense realistic, in a sense dramatic, sagely pondered, and urgent to the point of exultation.

What Blake wanted, and what his earlier lyrics attempted to supply, in accordance with the gnostic insistence of his 'doctrine', was a poetry of clear transparent images, of simple repetitive rhythms, and of hard clear formal outlines. Yet the greatness of his finest poetry cannot be accounted for by invoking such qualities. His creative impulse goes deeper than that.

II

Innocence was published in 1789, *Experience* in 1794. As we have them, they are clearly collections which complement and in a way answer each other. They are usually taken as documenting, analysing, and presenting the 'two contrary states of the human soul' of which their joint title-page speaks. And it is interesting to note that, for some commentators, the difference between them seems to represent a change in Blake's attitude towards the world, a change which can be located and understood if we go to his biography: the difference between the two books is a difference between the two Blakes.

That is one way of looking at it. Another is to see them as two sets of poems written deliberately to illustrate Blake's thesis about the two contrary states of the human soul, to give large-scale poetic shape to a carefully integrated philosophy and its 'traditional' symbology. To see them this way is to see them as extremely schematic and calculated; it is to shift the stress from biographical to philosophical considerations.

Both views seem to me misleading. The first is plainly naïve as an account of the development of a great poet, and the second seems to miss the most obvious truths about Blake as a creative artist. He was, at his rare best, an artist of direct perceptions, not of formulae and schematic constructions; his moral and philosophical interest in what he saw around him

was not divorced from the act of seeing. He perceived significance in the same act as he perceived actualities; he created
as he gazed. This is one meaning for the phrase T. S. Eliot has
used of him: 'A peculiar honesty, which, in a world too
frightened to be honest, is peculiarly terrifying. . . . Blake's
poetry has the unpleasantness of great poetry'.

It is obvious, in any case, that the two collections are of very
different poetic value. The lyrics in *Innocence* may be necessary
to point up those of *Experience*, but taken by themselves they
are a fragile and unimportant body of poems. If Blake had
written nothing else, he would be remembered only as a
pleasant minor oddity of our literature. They are often
applauded as the product of a perfectly child-like vision of
reality, but that is a dubious compliment; for the purposes of
creative art the child's vision of reality is very limited, and if
Blake is a great poet it is precisely because his imagination is
adult. Despite their thematic importance in his work as a
whole, most of these poems have the texture, the resonance,
the immediacy only of rather thin folk-songs or of rather
primitive hymns. Whatever their philosophical sources, their
poetic sources seem to lie in Watts' *Divine and Moral Songs*.
Generally, the details of their poetic working are unadven-
turous. 'Exuberance is Beauty' says one of the proverbs in the
Marriage. Most of the poems in *Innocence* may speak of a condition of exuberance, but they are not themselves exuberant;
the poetry lacks the vitality which it speaks of. We get an
impression of subdued creative life, as though Blake were
writing at quarter-pressure, refusing to let his creative energy
loose in the details of the verse, and, in his search for
child-likeness, indulging a poetic habit distanced from adult
pressures.

The two 'Nurse's Songs' give a hint of a deeper motivation;
taken together, they make a surprisingly complete statement of
what is implied, psychologically and morally, in the difference
between the two spiritual states. The difference is total, and

it is accentuated by the close similarity in the wording of the poems.

> When the voices of children are heard on the green
> And laughing is heard on the hill,
> My heart is at rest within my breast
> And everything else is still.
>
> 'Then come home, my children, the sun is gone down
> And the dews of night arise;
> Come, come, leave off play, and let us away
> Till the morning appears in the skies.'
>
> 'No, no, let us play, for it is yet day
> And we cannot go to sleep;
> Besides, in the sky the little birds fly
> And the hills are all cover'd with sheep.'
>
> 'Well, well, go and play till the light fades away
> And then go home to bed.'
> The little ones leapèd and shoutèd and laugh'd
> And all the hills echoèd.

The movement of this has a sweep and confidence that are missing from many of the other songs; one feels that Blake is more engaged in this situation than he is in poems like 'The Blossom'. It is a situation of harmony: harmony among the children, between the children and the nurse, and between all of them and the processes of nature. Neither the words of the nurse nor the coming of night are felt as a threat; and the remonstrances of the children are not felt as an impertinence. The harmony is so complete that children and adult share one mind and one set of values; and we feel that the human beings live so sympathetically with the processes of nature as to be hardly distinguishable from them. Children, birds, and animals are united in a common play, all spontaneously following their individual natures. There is harmony because there is spontaneity; things consent to one another because they are all free. And the texture of the verse gives us this sense quite adequately; the verse moves lightly, and attempts very little; but it has a joyous leap about it, and an echo of living things. We find in it at least the accent of exuberance.

The 'Nurse's Song' in *Experience* presents the opposite picture and feeling.

> When the voices of children are heard on the green
> And whisp'rings are in the dale,
> The days of my youth rise fresh in my mind,
> My face turns green and pale.

> Then come home, my children, the sun is gone down,
> And the dews of night arise;
> Your spring and your day are wasted in play,
> And your winter and night in disguise.

It is only half as long, because there is and there can be no free dialogue between nurse and children. They can have no answer to her sad sense of waste, precisely because they share it. The nurse identifies her own authority with the coming of night, and there is now a note of threat in the way she speaks of it. The children play not on a hill but in the dale, not with laughter but in whispers; their play is as furtive and unwholesome as the thoughts that rise in the nurse's mind. Here there is no harmony, but a profound and final alienation. Even the world of non-human nature, presented as empty of living creatures, is merely a sinister echo-chamber for the heart's cynicism.

The structure of each poem, and even more of the pair, suggests that Blake's method is one of something like allegory; and it is significant that his finest poems transcend allegorical considerations completely. While he devotes his poetry to illustrating a thesis, however aptly, his vision remains, as it were, half-created, and his deepest springs of creative power barely touched. So, although the first 'Nurse's Song' and 'The Little Black Boy' do have a fascination for us, it comes as much, perhaps, from the meanings they point to or allegorise as from

the meanings they realise poetically; and only one poem in
Innocence seems to me unequivocally to invite an interest in it
for its achieved poetry as well as for its 'theme'; that is 'Holy
Thursday'. It is interesting that this poem has a colourfulness,
a degree of open feeling, a majesty of movement, and a density
of texture, lacking in most of the others. If, in reading it, one
thinks of an eighteenth-century visionary like Smart, one thinks
also, oddly enough, of Chaucer:

> 'Twas on a Holy Thursday, their innocent faces clean,
> The children walking two and two, in red and blue and green,
> Grey-headed beadles walk'd before, with wands as white as snow,
> Till into the high dome of Paul's they like Thames' waters flow.
>
> O what a multitude they seem'd, these flowers of London town!
> Seated in companies they sit with radiance all their own.
> The hum of multitudes was there, but multitudes of lambs,
> Thousands of little boys and girls raising their innocent hands.
>
> Now like a mighty wind they raise to Heaven the voice of song,
> Or like harmonious thunderings the seats of Heaven among.
> Beneath them sit the agèd men, wise guardians of the poor;
> Then cherish pity, lest you drive an angel from your door.

The verse-form is that of the eighteenth-century street-
ballad; but the simple conventional form is quite transformed
by the subtle changes in rhythm and the richness of texture.
The result is that a sense of spontaneous activity both combines
with and presses against a measured, almost ritual movement.
The apparent naivety of phrasing goes with a considerable
economy in the control of a more vital situation than most of
the other *Songs of Innocence* have. Worship in a city church is
made to appear like a ritual movement of natural processes:
'wands as white as snow', 'they like Thames' waters flow',
'flowers of London town', 'The hum of multitudes was there,
but multitudes of lambs', 'a mighty wind . . . harmonious
thunderings'. Perhaps it is from this rather more measured and
complex blending of the natural and the human that the poem

gets its power; it is one of the few cases in *Innocence* where the poetic energy is allowed to flow freely and channel out the verse-form.

Even so, 'Holy Thursday' lacks the more radical power of the best poems in *Experience*, because it lacks their almost frightening degree of compression. There are forces in society and in the poet's own psyche which he has yet to elicit and confront; he confronts them fully in certain poems of *Experience*; and the confrontation enjoins on him an intensity of realisation which the conventions he adopts in *Innocence* will not admit.

> O Rose, thou art sick!
> The invisible worm
> That flies in the night,
> In the howling storm,
>
> Has found out thy bed
> Of crimson joy,
> And his dark secret love
> Does thy life destroy.

Here is the force, the intensity, I speak of; and when one has felt its impact I do not see how one can offer to 'interpret' it in the highly schematic way which Kathleen Raine affects. Its poetic power comes from a dramatic confrontation, and the poem itself is the reverse of schematic. Where 'Holy Thursday' marched out in the loosely processional rhythms of the ballad convention, 'The Sick Rose' leaps or strikes out from the void to assume its own compact and challenging life. So instantaneous does the poet's creative act appear that the objects and their relationships are created poetically in the same action which perceives them. So we have a remarkable intensity of vision, of uncluttered seeing and feeling, in which things and their relationships are seen in the one fierce act; and we have, too, a remarkable sense created of the mysteriousness of the energies which establish that relationship. To ask if the rose is good, and the worm bad, seems just as cheapening and irrelevant as to ask how their poetic use illuminates old myths of Cupid and Psyche. What it creates it transforms, beyond recognition in those terms; and what we notice is a strange energy which, through its very exuberance of living, destroys: a unique co-presence of values, affirming and destroying in the one movement. The worm is certainly sinister, and not least in the way in which the elements seem to guide him in and to his work of destruction; yet the poem closes with a note of savage exultation, an exultant finality which persuades us not to ask about 'good' and 'bad', or about symbolic references, whether simple or esoteric. The second last line, with its heavy accumulation of three equal stresses culminating in 'love', launches us into the last line, which is rapid and somehow conclusive in its very rapidity. We cannot doubt that, in reading this poem, we are privileged to share in a creative process which is not only uniquely compressed but also uniquely manifests some radical ambivalence of the human spirit, which finds in its very ambivalence the strength to create symbols of it. The deepest and most mysterious psychic powers are made accessible to and in it; and the *creative* miracle is that they should be made accessible so cleanly, so starkly, so free of any impulse to polemic or schematisation.

III

It is in *Experience* that Blake is at his greatest, and it is there that he is most directly concerned with revealing at depth the dilemmas of human life. Not that he is any the less a 'symbolist' poet, but he is so in a different and more satisfying sense; and it is not that he abandons his sense of life's holiness, but he expresses it less naively; the unmistakable access of power which we feel in the best of these lyrics comes from the centrality of their concern with what actually makes (and un-makes) a fully human existence. The heights of life's possibilities are now perceived in the depths of its actual condition; the symbols shine more fiercely the more they illuminate a world of facts; aspiration fights through rage and scorn to become, not wishful thinking, but an energy of affirmation; holiness is mirrored by repression. And we are reminded of Yeats' vision of

> . . . that William Blake
> Who beat upon the wall
> Till Truth obeyed his call.

Yet more than one commentator has gone to some trouble to avoid recognising this obvious quality of the poetry; some apply to his philosophic, others to his psychic 'sources'. The lovers of the esoteric speak as though, because Blake's symbology has been derived from Porphyry and Plotinus, the concerns of his poetry simply echo the themes of their philosophy. Others are still more knowing.

Even F. W. Bateson, whose commentary is generally thoughtful and helpful, gives so categorical an account of the genesis of the imagery in the two groups of poems that we are conscious of psychology (and rather *ad hoc* and amateur psychology at that) encroaching on the poetry to categorise where it should illuminate. Mona Wilson sees *Experience* as a product of the period of pain and disillusionment which Blake passed through in his development as a mystic; they are the product, she says, of his passing through the 'Purgative Way'. There is probably some truth in this; for the finest of the songs have an authentic pain in them as well as an authentic rage or joy or exultation, and we do sense the presence of purgation. But again it is not a satisfying explanation; like Bateson's comment, it is too merely biophysical; it does not adequately define the state or the word, but merely indicates in general terms the area in which a cause could most usefully be sought, if one considered such a search worthwhile.

In addition, Blake's achievement is much more varied, less monolithic, than such 'explanations' would suggest. Even in *Experience* there is a variety so marked that it almost entitles us to speak of different *kinds* of poem.

Of these, the poems which deal most directly with the psychological consequences of repression seem to me the simplest; and, although the best of them have an undeniable poetic force, a large part of their interest lies in the psychological insight or the psychological thesis which they contain. In them, Blake comes very close, as he did in some poems of *Innocence*, to being a didactic poet, and the sense one gets of his imagination is very far from any direct, immediate perception of essences. 'A Poison Tree', for example, is a poem of rather limited creative aims, which escapes in the end from the limitations of the convention it establishes:

> I was angry with my friend:
> I told my wrath, my wrath did end.
> I was angry with my foe:
> I told it not, my wrath did grow.
>
> And I water'd it in fears,
> Night and morning with my tears;
> And I sunnèd it with smiles,
> And with soft deceitful wiles.
>
> And it grew both day and night
> Till it bore an apple bright;
> And my foe beheld it shine,
> And he knew that it was mine,
>
> And into my garden stole
> When the night had veil'd the pole:
> In the morning glad I see
> My foe outstretch'd beneath the tree.

The simple symbolism is as much a device for enabling Blake to construct a neatly effective parable as something that comes into the poem through the deeper pressures of creative energy. The poem is, in fact, a sort of gnostic parable; it has a brisk forward movement and a surface glitter, but the symbols are not deployed with any great energy. If they were, the poem might have become too complex for Blake's purposes, and the parable would probably have become lost or confused. As it is, the poem in its simple anecdotal structure drives Blake's insight home, recurrently sharpening its point.

Not that it is simply a didactic poem; it seems, in fact, to result from the tension of at least two distinguishable impulses. Its onward-driving energy is evident from the first line; and there is an authentic suggestiveness about the key images that helps not merely to state a moral but to create a poetic world. But this suggestiveness begins only in the third stanza, and it represents a tendency of Blake's imagination to transcend the allegories it takes to with such eagerness. By the third stanza, it is becoming almost impossible to continue the allegorical account of the poem which the first two stanzas positively enjoined on us. The apple, allegorical symbol though it plainly is, partly escapes from the field of formulable meanings and shines there mysteriously in the verse; and it quickly becomes associated with those mysterious, primal forces signified by the words 'garden' and 'pole'. Here again is a temporary release of creative power similar to that in 'The Sick Rose'; and again it carries a note or resonance of exultation, in the rhythmic stress on 'glad' and 'outstretch'd', which the allegory itself does not seem entirely to warrant. This exultation, so hard to define, much less to account for, is a feature of Blake's unique poetic world. Yet, in this poem, that world remains only half-created. There is suggestiveness, resonance, in the poem, but it is of a limited range.

'Infant Sorrow' is a product of the same interest to which 'A Poison Tree' testifies, yet it is quite free of any concern that we might call allegorical. As a result, it is both a more cryptic and a more suggestive account of the way people infect one another with their own fears and suspicions.

> My mother groan'd! my father wept.
> Into the dangerous world I leapt;

Helpless, naked, piping loud:
Like a fiend hid in a cloud.

Struggling in my father's hands,
Striving against my swaddling-bands,
Bound and weary I thought best
To sulk upon my mother's breast.

The poem resists analysis and, as we can see more clearly when we compare this version with the much longer one in the Rossetti MS., its power is altogether more original and revolutionary than the more simply parabolic power of 'A Poison Tree'. Its compression is extreme, almost defiant; and its remarkable economy makes it a cryptic and ambivalent utterance, whose meaning it is impossible to paraphrase. Yet the psychological climate of a whole world is suggested in its hard, terse, repetitive rhythm and unselfconsciously daring imagery; one notices that the parents' fear (nothing less than a fear of life, of the 'dangerous world' itself) infects the baby at the very moment of his birth—and perhaps earlier, perhaps at the very moment of his conception. It is true that the poem itself does not explicitly mention fear; but it seems to me unmistakably to suggest a fear of a very primitive kind, together with the concomitant notion of one man's fear infecting others. If this reading is not taken, the poem will lack any convincing causality, the lines will simply record unrelated particulars of behaviour, and what seemed an intense economy may well become a symptom of alienation or psychic displacement in the author. I feel justified, on the contrary, in taking it to have so direct a causality, and so strong an economy, that it leads us to speak of a communion of sinners as well as a communion of saints: a common disharmony as well as a common harmony.

The remarkably un-selfconscious individuality which we see in this poem is surely the quality that makes Blake a great and seminal poet. Here it appears as a headlong sense of drama, of the moral and psychological life of man as a place of strikingly dramatic conflict. It is the very antithesis of the subdued and rather static charm of *Innocence*. At its core is an exultation which is not quite joy, exemplified by the pace of 'Into the dangerous world I leapt'. One feels that Blake's own emotional life is more responsive to such problems, such drama, such energies, to the infant piping loud like a fiend, than to the sight of lambs with bright wool, whose piping is tender and submissive rather than challenging or prophetic.

The words 'drama' and 'dramatic' are, of course, among the approving noises most typical of modern criticism. Whether unfortunately or not, the critic of Blake can hardly avoid them. Not that their meaning is simple, for if in 'The Sick Rose' and 'Infant Sorrow' the word 'drama' points to a clash between opposing forces or interests, it also points both to the instantaneous energy (something more savage than abruptness) with which the sense of that opposition is created and to the way in which the intensity of action and emotion is heightened towards completion. Each force comes to seem necessary to the very existence of the forces that oppose it. In 'The Tiger', rhythmic intensification is almost a structural principle. Here the word 'deepened' may be more appropriate than 'heightened', for Blake drives his sense of the tiger's extraordinary power as it were backward, towards its source in the creator; and the more he does so, the more the sense of present *created* power is enhanced. The first stanza masterfully creates the sense of a being, a force, both immediate and mysteriously remote, both 'burning' and 'bright', a mystery alive and challenging: so much so that there is nothing further the poet can do than to show that force in action:

> Tiger! Tiger! burning bright
> In the forests of the night,
> What immortal hand or eye
> Could frame thy fearful symmetry?

So masterful a force, by being so confronted, *demands* to be explained; yet the only possible 'explanation' is the sight of its creation:

> And what shoulder, and what art,
> Could twist the sinews of thy heart?
> And when thy heart began to beat,
> What dread hand? And what dread feet?

This remarkable effect is more than rhythmic; the final sentence has no object, and this grammatical oddity leads us to see, in the one instantaneous creative *coup*, 'shoulder' and 'art' as belonging to the creature as well as to the creator. The logic of Blake's emotionally-charged method has led him to a virtual identification of the two; the dramatising quality of his poetry has resulted in fusing what had previously been glimpsed in a tense relationship. And, by the final stanza, he has certainly earned the right—indeed, the necessity—to replace 'could' with 'dare'; some daring is required even of the reader who will contemplate the poem fully.

So fine a poem is almost defiant in its self-defining, self-enclosing energy. Yet I do suspect that its cumulative power is attained at the risk of a certain relentlessness in the images and rhythms. The frequently elided first feet may give a sense of violently measured pace, just as they do in 'London', but their total effect is slightly mechanical, where that of the latter poem is not; and the images, though magnificently physical in their suggestions, do not have the metaphorical subtlety which is perhaps the greatest virtue of 'London'.

In 'London', which I regard as the crown of his achievement and the consummation of his 'method', the emotional force and the creative pressure (though perhaps more unobtrusive) are much greater still, and take us into a unique world of feeling. It is of course what it appears, a brief vision of an actual city as a hell of contradictions, a vision which becomes an indictment of a whole set of values.

I wander thro' each charter'd street,
Near where the charter'd Thames does flow,
And mark in every face I meet
Marks of weakness, marks of woe.

In every cry of every Man,
In every Infant's cry of fear,
In every voice, in every ban,
The mind-forg'd manacles I hear.

How the chimney-sweeper's cry
Every black'ning church appals;
And the hapless soldier's sigh
Runs in blood down palace walls.

But most thro' midnight streets I hear
How the youthful harlot's curse
Blasts the new-born infant's tear
And blights with plagues the marriage hearse.

This poem is a living paradox; it is very brief, and in a way
very simple; there is no sense at all of the poet's engaging in a
creative strategy or calculating effects. But that extraordinary
simplicity and directness of perception go together with an
extraordinary concentration and even complexity of poetic
means. Indeed, the simplicity is expressed in the concentration;
the two things are inseparable. It is as though Blake's simple
and direct perception were a perception of a whole cultural
situation, the salient points of which he perceived together
and in a firm relationship. This concentrated simplicity shows
one of the ways in which poetry can deal in the subject-matter
of the novel without losing power or sweep; it provides one
proof of the necessity of poetry. It can be demonstrated by
examining the compressed logic of the poem's development
and showing, in the process, the remarkable compression of
its metaphorical usage.

The poem is an attack on a society which has in fact inverted
the values which it says it lives by. The first two lines are

pregnant with the contradiction that is perceived:

> I wander thro' each charter'd street
> Near where the charter'd Thames does flow.

There is a fierce complexity of reference here. The Royal
Charter which had once been given to the merchants of London
to bestow certain rights on them has now become a symbol of
repression: as, indeed, Blake would have expected, for, to him,
the actions of categorising and regulating contain the inevitability of repression: the city is under the rule of 'Thou shalt
not . . .', commandments voiced by commerce, the law, the
church, the army, and all in fact who consent to be agents of
this self-satisfied corruption. Men are alienated from one
another; every sound that comes to the wanderer's ear comes
as a sound of protest or woe: the results of 'charter' are universal unhappiness and oppression.

This sense of the direct perception of a society's contradictions is transferred to us by the heavy repetitive stresses in the
verse, which come to have an effect both measured and urgent,
culminating in the longer and more menacing line: 'The mind-
forg'd manacles I hear'. At this exact centre of the poem, the
nature of the attack changes: we are now to have particular
examples of the results to which repression leads. But again,
these particular examples gather a cumulative force as they
follow one another; one reason is that their presentation
becomes increasingly concentrated.

> How the chimney-sweeper's cry
> Every black'ning church appals.

The cry is one of deprivation but also one for help. The
churches seem to be both physical buildings and social institutions; and it is in this dual suggestion that the poetic complexity and concentration lie. For the notion of the Church
presented in this image is a strongly physical one. The building
growing blacker with fumes or soot merges with the institution

becoming darkened with moral cowardice and indifference. So when we have the boy's cry 'appalling' the Church, we have it appalling something the two senses of which have been merged; and we get a strongly, indeed unexpectedly, physical sense of the relation between the needy poor and the indifferent Christian bourgeoisie; it is as though the darkening building winced and shrank away from the sound of a human voice in need.

The next two lines are even more concentrated in their effect—this time not because two significances are blended in the one reference but because the logic of the action depicted is so powerfully telescoped:

> And the hapless soldier's sigh
> Runs in blood down palace walls.

What a complexity of relations is enacted here by the intense physicality of the lines, in which it is as though we saw things happening simultaneously, a logic of events short-cut, an action immensely compressed. The concentration is carried on to the last stanza, which is more expansive in its movement and yet more savage in its effect. Here the complexity comes from the fact that seemingly diverse moral and psychological conditions are seen as producing each other, and forces, values, institutions stretch out through a web of sensed inter-relationships to become their own opposites. The 'most' announces the culmination of a process of inversion the whole poem has been charting. Harlot and bride belong to each other, and the infant belongs to both. The effect is to indict a number of institutions together.

In this poem, Blake successfully suggests an almost mystic inter-relationship of lives and events of the sort given an abrupt and epigrammatic form in 'Auguries of Innocence'.

> A Skylark wounded in the wing,
> A Cherubim does cease to sing.

Such a vision of the interaction of lives deserves an adjective like 'mystical' or 'visionary', because it is a vision of lives interacting at a level at which they are decisive for one another's corruption; yet this quality does not detract from but rather establishes the sense of observed social fact. Social fact is *seen* at its mystical root; we are given an immediate vision of mystical inter-relations perceived in the world of actuality. And Blake's view of this inter-relationship has nothing of the careful and in a way calculated balance that we would get from a more sophisticated and self-aware great poet. The directness is achieved through the complexity of the poetry; the complexity of the situation is perceived with savage directness; this is the 'naked honesty' of which Eliot speaks. It is as 'inspirational' a poetry as has ever existed; yet it is also as controlled and earthy a poetry as has ever existed. It is a remarkably paradoxical creation, and its definitiveness makes us aware that Blake's originality is a matter not just of 'vision' but of method, if I may use a word which seems hardly to apply to Blake at all. I do not mean to imply that our attention is caught at any stage by matters of technique as such. What I have been pointing to may seem a considerable technical originality; but it will be depreciated and cheapened if it is thought of in merely technical terms. The flesh of this poetry is formed and warmed by a visionary spirit, not by any poetic habit, however accomplished. If Blake is a great poetic innovator, it is not because he has made technical experiments which can be used by his successors; it is because originality of vision and originality of method are in him not only inseparable (as they are in all great poets) but quite indistinguishable, so that his poetry comes to us as an instantaneous creative act.

The earthiness and concentration of 'London' may seem rather strange coming as they do from a man who claimed to see 'not *with*, but *through*, his bodily eyes', and to see not the body but the spirit behind it. Yet such gnostic conceptions are only part of the real Blake, and they are transcended, if not positively denied, by his greatest short poems, whose greatness consists not in any disembodiment or any vision of metaphysical essences, but in their own powerful and radiant actuality, a quality which goes with a mysterious exultation.

There is a concentrated buoyancy about the whole poem, similar in some ways to the exultation which animates 'The Sick Rose' and which is also present, though perhaps more intermittently, in 'Introduction' and 'The Tiger'. But in those poems it is explicable; it is an exulting in energy, however destructive. In 'London' it appears strange, the very last attitude the facts of the city's life, as presented, would seem to warrant; and its nature is as mysterious as its motivation. Yet it seems to me unmistakably there, throughout the poem, from the elevated tone of the first line, through the first two stanzas, with their chanting rhythm, to the vision of inverted energies presented in the last stanza. One might characterise it best by saying that it has more in common with the Old Testament prophets than with any other English poet. Perhaps it is the exultation of a man exalted by the exercise of his own prophetic mission (as by his need and capacity to reach into his own deepest feelings to confront such a world), and it transforms the feelings of disgust and protest into something quite other. Yet it remains anomalous.

In a sense, then, Blake at his best is not only a prophetic, but also a fleshly, an incarnational poet. Poets often represent qualities antithetical to those they claim to admire. Yeats too thought of himself as an esoteric poet, re-presenting both ancient insights into experience and the ancient myths which express them, but he was in fact a poet of dramatic situations, in which a modern world is brought to its apotheosis. One of the striking things about Blake's great lyrics is the strength and humanness of the feeling expressed in them. It is only in his poems of the second class that he is a calm, limpid poet who has won beyond (or has not yet managed to attain) strength of feeling. Nor does his greatest poetry have the transparency we might expect; it has an unusual density of texture, and an unusually dramatic structure. This is as true of 'The Tiger' and 'The Sick Rose' as it is of 'London'. Their power comes from the dramatic starkness with which conflicting tendencies are brought into relationship.

IV

The tension which we feel recurrently in Blake's poetry, and which in his greatest poems he triumphantly resolves, is a tension between the creation of a quite new vision and the presentation of allegory, parable, or thesis, none of which as a method enables him to form the vision fully. 'A Poison Tree' shows this tension in, so to speak, a pure state; 'London', 'The Sick Rose', and 'The Tiger' transcend it. In yet another poem, however, 'The Little Girl Lost and Found', it is seen not precisely as a tension between conflicting poetic concerns but as an alternation between different poetic methods. In this lies the poem's strength and its weakness; if some parts of it are stiffly expository, others present with clairvoyant power the vision which, one senses, is the original motive-power of the whole. It is not surprising that this strength should co-exist with that weakness; for I take it that, here as perhaps nowhere else among his lyrics, Blake is aiming to present a state which is neither that of 'Innocence' nor that of 'Experience', but a third one which, echoing Yeats, we may call 'radical innocence'. His task will be, therefore, the almost impossible one of presenting, or at least suggesting, three states in the one poem, and showing the third as the resolution of the tension between the other two. And he undertakes it in a way which invites misunderstanding.

We do not have to agree with Kathleen Raine's contention that the wanderings of Lyca are Blake's 'version' of a neo-Platonist myth of generation to see that the pattern of her wanderings does have a close similarity to other myths of the lost girl who is finally found and who, when found, revivifies those around her. Shakespeare also deals with this theme, notably in his last plays; and indeed it a recurring theme throughout our literature, one which seems to have a great suggestive power for people concerned with the religious bases of life.

In this case, we do not have to apply to neo-Platonist or alchemical explanations of the poem; although there is some possibility that Blake had such references in mind, the symbolism has an overt significance which must be taken seriously. The poem seems to be about a girl entering puberty, and, because she ignores conventional fears and repressive taboos, coming to terms spontaneously with the powers of adult passion which are also 'Energy', the holy forces of life (we can take her 'seven summers' as having merely a symbolic meaning); coming to terms with these passions, and by her example leading her parents out of the wasteland of their conventional fears and into a greater harmony with her, with their own natures, and with the basic forces of life. That, in simplest terms, is what the poem seems to be 'about'; we can see that there is an archetypal quality in the theme, which is one of mutual redemption (not, as Kathleen Raine, relying on Blake's supposed 'sources', suggests, one of a 'descent into generation').

But it is in narrative form, and the symbolism works to elucidate a sequence of events. In a way, the focus of attention is on the parents rather than Lyca. It is their hard-won innocence, an innocence through and of experience, that the poem finally establishes. They recover innocence because they consent to have the gates of their perception cleansed, and to see with a double vision; and they consent to this because of the moral courage of the father (a figure whom Kathleen Raine's analysis virtually excludes from the poem).

> Rising from unrest,
> The trembling woman prest
> With feet of weary woe:
> She could no further go.

In his arms he bore
Her, arm'd with sorrow sore;
Till before their way
A couching lion lay.

Turning back was vain:
Soon his heavy mane
Bore them to the ground.
Then he stalk'd around,

Smelling to his prey;
But their fears allay
When he licks their hands,
And silent by them stands.

They look upon his eyes
Fill'd with deep surprise,
And wondering behold
A spirit arm'd in gold.

On his head a crown,
On his shoulders down
Flow'd his golden hair.
Gone was all their care.

Here are the typically Blakean themes concentrated into one moment or phase of a narrated action. And if the symbolism works to elucidate the narrative, the narrative works, equally, to elucidate the themes: human lives are radically intertwined, for good or for ill, for mutual corruption or mutual salvation; and only an acceptance of the forces of life and a direct vision of their holiness can lead to salvation. The symbols have a certain radiance about them, a certain primitive brightness. But they also have a certain solidity. There is nothing merely fanciful or illusory about that lion who, to the cleansed eyes of vision, is a 'spirit arm'd in gold', the holy and royal power of life; he is unmistakably there, solidly created and relevant. There are momentary crudities, but they cannot destroy the impression of radiant solidity which the poem as a whole creates.

Such themes, treated in such a way, do force us to ask whether or not they point to a third stage or condition in the conflict of the soul. This poem was among the four which Blake transferred from *Innocence* to *Experience*; and Stanley Gardiner argues that it shows experience encroaching on innocence, and therefore demanded to be placed among the poems of repression. Whatever Blake's reasons were for transplanting it, and whatever traditional symbols lie behind his symbols, Gardiner's interpretation seems to me quite wrong. The major theme of the poem is rejuvenation, regeneration. Lyca never wavers from the state of innocence; and her parents win through experience to a renewed innocence—or, to put it another way, are enabled to see the things of experience with the eyes of innocence, an adult and elevated innocence. The poem is most valuable in providing (what none of *Innocence* provides) a graphic account of the conflict between two ways of seeing the world. It is, in a way very different from 'The Sick Rose' or 'London', a dramatic poem; it enacts a conflict in a narrative, and the conflict ends in a state of reconciliation, harmony, the restoration of health and vision. The parallel with the last plays of Shakespeare is again remarkable.

This poem is, then, an extremely interesting one. It does not have the economy or the almost savage concentration of the other great poems in *Experience*; compared with them, it is leisurely and expansive, having a quality of exposition or of the thesis. Yet I think that, for the reasons I gave earlier, it is a great poem in its own way. That is a very different way from the way of 'London' or 'The Tiger'; and it is a way that may not evoke much sympathy from a contemporary audience. The poem may seem a melodramatic allegory, rather too repetitive and obvious. I do not think it is obvious, and I do not think that the symbolism is merely allegorical at all; at crucial parts of the narrative it concentrates poetic power in a way which the narrative structure itself does not seem to demand:

> Sleeping Lyca lay
> While the beasts of prey,
> Come from caverns deep,
> View'd the maid asleep.
>
> The kingly lion stood
> And the virgin view'd,
> Then he gamboll'd round
> O'er the hallow'd ground.
>
> Leopards, tigers, play
> Round her as she lay,
> While the lion old
> Bow'd his mane of gold
>
> And her bosom lick,
> And upon her neck
> From his eyes of flame
> Ruby tears there came . . .

The poems I have looked at, and two or three others I have merely mentioned, seem to me to cast the most light on Blake's unique genius, and to be, in fact, the core of his poetic achievement. Blake criticism and research being what they are, one must take care to forget Blake the seer, and Blake the Messiah, and Blake the disembodied spirit, and Blake the grown-up child; the first step in coming to terms with Blake is to restore his humanity to him, and to learn to see that the remarkable revolution which he caused in poetry is a revolution in ways of seeing and feeling the situation of human beings rather than in the notion of a poetic symbology. When we see that, we will hardly be surprised that his poetry has a drama and a density for which a mere recounting of his 'doctrines' could not have prepared us. His way of presenting his vision of the world is a poet's way; it is poetry he offers us, and not abstract wisdom. As a poet, he is a great innovator. This innovation is not just a matter of 'techniques'; but it is true that Blake at his finest shows a splendid tact in the moulding of his perceptions into poetic form. One can see this very clearly if one looks at the variant readings of 'The Tiger', and notices that the present enormously dramatic effect at the end of stanza 3 (so paradoxically right) is the result of a fourth stanza's having been left out. Blake comes to us as a great visionary poet because he is a great maker.

His many faults as a poet are of minor significance. Admittedly, the concentration and intensity of his poetry seem to result in the creation of a poetic world that is perhaps too narrow and exclusive. He is a comparable case to Eliot; he gives us a constant suggestion of breadth, but not the breadth itself. His greatness is not of a discursive or an inclusive kind; it is a matter of an extraordinary intensity of seeing and of acting-out. He does not explain, describe, or even evoke; he reveals. As he said himself to a correspondent, 'I live by miracle'; so does his poetry.

CHAPTER VII

Melville: The White Whale as Hero

I

MOBY DICK has gripped the imaginations of very different men, liberating some and half-strangling others. The adequacy of the response in each case seems to have something to do with the book's mythic nature and stature; for, if it creates a myth, it may also be said to propagate one, and to have become, in fact, something of a myth itself. Is one right, for example, to get the uneasy feeling that several of its best critics think its ultimate importance is in its capacity to dredge up and to display in violent movement not only the secret of an historical moment in the 'American experience' but the essentially American psyche itself? Personally, I do not believe in the essential psyches of peoples, and I feel ill-at-ease with a literary criticism which undertakes the large task of associating a specific literary work with an historical movement deep within one such psyche. Yet it is obvious that the best American critics have a freedom with *Moby Dick* that the rest of us cannot equal. So abundantly and well have they written of it that a non-American could be pardoned for thinking that there are mysteries in it which only they ought to approach. Certainly, if a non-American elects to deal with it, he will be wise to avoid talk of historical moments and essential psyches; for some of us cannot *help* being un-American. But I think it necessary for non-Americans to write of it because, in the first place, its historical placement or its psychological representativeness can hardly be the deepest source of its greatness (even though they both reflect that greatness), and because, in the second place, the myths it does create and make accessible to men of a different culture have an enormous significance for the psychic life of each of us. My interest will be in two matters: in asking a question about the sense in which it is an heroic work, a question which leads me to offer a different suggestion about its 'hero' from any I have seen advanced elsewhere; and in raising certain questions about the very various poetic qualities of its prose. The two questions are, ultimately, one; for the profound and barely conceivable imaginative pressure which led Melville to throw Ahab and the white whale against each other, and both of them, seemingly, against common humanity, leads him also to dramatise and to expound those conflicts in just such language as this: language that reverberates in a myriad ways with the pressures to which it answers.

Inured as one may be to the large talk about mythopoeic significances, one may still be struck by the fact that both *Moby Dick* and *The Scarlet Letter* which influenced it come at the mid-point of the nineteenth century; for it is probably true, as many writers have suggested, that they also come at the mid-point of the historical process by which a Calvinist theology and a Calvinist imagination became converted into a Transcendentalist philosophy and sensibility. But it is just as likely true, as other critics have suggested, that in *Moby Dick* Melville entered the debate about the Transcendentalism which had become dominant in New England literary circles at the time of its writing. At any rate, no-one is in danger of forgetting that it is a New England novel, a novel dramatising and questioning aspects of New England religion. And when one thinks of nineteenth-century New England and of the amazing literary growth which it nurtured, one reflects that if that growth shows in its chief representatives a radical psychic disturbance, it also shows an even more important psychic courage in dealing with it. No doubt so radical a disturbance can never be fully defined in works of literature, but it can be partly objectified and dramatised; and this both Melville and Hawthorne do.

Immediately after the novel's completion, Melville con-
fided to his new hero, Hawthorne: 'A sense of unspeakable
security is in me this moment, on account of your having
understood the book. I have written a wicked book, and feel
spotless as the lamb.' This confidence has fathered many critical
misunderstandings or puzzles, as it was bound to do. Most
critics, in the end, find themselves having to decide whether
to take it with solemn literalness as the key to the book's
nature or to reject it with a certain resentment. For *Moby Dick*
presents with unusual sharpness problems not merely of deciding its 'meaning' but also of discovering the terms appropriate
to discussing it at all. The better the critics the more funda-
mental their differences are likely to be on both scores; it is
largely temperament and habit which decide the discovery of
terms, and, so many and various are the 'meanings' which the
book itself offers to us, it is largely chance which leads a critic
to emphasise one rather than another.

The three greatest New England writers—Melville, Hawthorne, and Emily Dickinson—do have certain pre-occupa-
tions in common. They are much possessed by the problem of
personal salvation and damnation; they are aware of (fascinated
and terrified by) dark and threatening forces both in the human
individual and in that natural environment which is to be seen
as the *milieu* of his fate; they struggle to create images of a
paradise which becomes ambiguous even as they touch it and
of which, in *Moby Dick*, the superbly extended image is Chapter
LXXXVII, 'The Grand Armada'; seemingly guilt-ridden (for
they come, in Auden's term, from a society of guilt rather
than one of shame) they turn about the questions of the
identity of God (if there *is* a God), and of themselves as striving
to create an identity for themselves in the light (or is it, they
seem to ask, the darkness?) of God; their writing is inclined
to move rather feverishly between a kind of sensuality and a
kind of abstractness; they grow rhetorical and exclamatory in
the manner of a preacher even as they try to maintain a tone

of irony towards what the preacher in their bones exhorts on them; they have difficulty with their inherited literary forms, and in the end have to create their own, accepting as they do so the danger of formlessness (as Melville says, with evident application to *Moby Dick*, 'there are some enterprises in which a careful disorderliness is the true method'). And in all this, while there is sometimes an unpleasant quality of chewing the spiritual fat, or of lapsing with a sort of guilty relief into the blackness of their own imaginations, there is also that quality, in part stoic, in part exultant, which I have called psychic courage. The demon with which they wrestle is not only the daimon of art.

It is not surprising, then, if the critical judgments of *Moby Dick's* critics are as diverse as their approaches. Alfred Kazin is most concerned to ask about the extraordinary nature of the literary *phenomenon* which confronts him, and to give to his own writing a texture in some way correlative to its own; his interest will not be primarily of the sort that is most readily called 'moral'. Richard Chase is interested in its literary affinities and psychological sources; he too is more concerned with it as a phenomenon than as a dramatisation of moral conflicts and meanings. Leslie Fiedler is interested in its hidden metaphysic, as an example of the ways in which 'the American experience' has been an experience, in the depths of the psyche, of certain metaphysical and emotional contradictions. And Marius Bewley shows an interest which is chiefly ethical; his analysis of the book's significance is done not in terms of the confusion or interchange of good and evil, as Fiedler's is, but in terms of their clear opposition. He sees Melville, threatened by the ideological maelstrom of his America, in perpetual danger of confusing good and evil, making 'a tremendous effort' to overcome that danger and 'to introduce order into his moral universe'.

For my part, I can only say that all these approaches and judgments have illuminated the book for me; and if I think that ethical considerations must be raised, for the book forces them on us, I do not think that they have to be formulated in terms of clear options. The book's logic tends to subvert an 'Either-Or' mentality in its critics. It does not seem to me silly to argue either that the book is, in total effect, a Christian novel or that it is, in total effect, an anti-Christian one; but such simple oppositions are likely to thwart one's sense of the exploratory and even esoteric nature of its dealing with religious forces; and when, later in this essay, I argue for an affinity between the white whale and the God of the Old Testament, I do not intend to give a typological reading of that affinity or to load it either with Christian or with anti-Christian preferences; for, as I shall also argue, it is neither 'a wicked book' in any intelligible sense nor a covert proof of the existence of the Christian God. Its 'argument' is in its drama, and that drama is not clearly one thing or the other.

II

'A careful disorderliness' almost, but not quite, expresses the book's extraordinary structure. Our first questions about it are questions about the function of the cetological chapters, but they are also questions about the function of Ishmael as narrator. In raising them together, in effect I am committed to raising the questions, Who is the book's hero? and In what does the heroism consist? In Part III of his fascinating book, *The Enchaféd Flood*, W. H. Auden gives the most telling account I know of the novel's dramatic logic; and since that is in itself a sort of paraphrase, lasting twenty pages, it would be otiose to try to paraphrase it here. But even Auden begs certain important questions about the identity of the narrator, or, perhaps more accurately, about how consistently his identity is maintained.

This is a matter of the recounting voice, and of the ways in which that voice crosses, harmonises with, or is subdued to other voices. My own view is that the first twenty or so chapters establish both the personality and the voice of Ishmael as narrator; but from that point onward we are generally unable either to read the narrative tone as continuing the characterisation of Ishmael or to identify the narrator at all, at least as one of the characters *within* the narration.

No such difficulty arises in the first 23 chapters. We might describe them as the Ishmael section in much the way we describe the first part of *Ulysses* as the Telemachus section. The narrative is unmistakably in his voice, the pace of transition from scene to scene and interest to interest is governed by his temperament, and the interest is chiefly in what will happen to him and to the *Pequod*, on which he has chosen to sail. They are plainly preparatory chapters, and what they seem chiefly to prepare us for is the account of Ishmael's destiny at sea, that element which, so Auden says, is 'the real situation . . . of man'. But the expectation quite deliberately aroused by them is falsified from Chapter XXIV onwards. From then, it is *not* Ishmael's destiny that is paramount in the prose and in the reader's interest; still less is it that relationship between him and Queegueg which, so the early chapters suggested, was to be as portentous as it is peculiar. Of the later chapters, some are monologues spoken by one or other of the characters, some (like XXXV, 'The Mast-Head') are musings by Ishmael, but most are spoken in a voice which, whether it is expatiating on the mysteries of whaling or dramatising an action, is both definite and anonymous. More than one critic says that the personality of Ishmael as narrator here becomes 'a Mask for the author'; I should prefer to say that, in a sense, these chapters have *no* narrator.

It is interesting that the first of these post-Ishmael chapters, XXIV and XXV, discourse on whaling in such a way as to suggest that the enterprise and acts of whaling are themselves to be given an epic stature, and only then are the chief crew-members introduced. When they are, it is in such terms that, as both narrative and voyage proceed, whales and whalers and whaling all take on an epic stature in the shadow of one another. Whaling is an empire, whalers are empire-builders, and whales are themselves an imperial breed; so the logic of these chapters insists. And, as they succeed one another, one is driven to ask whether or not the white whale, Moby Dick, as the crown and consummation of that imperial breed, the mysterious entity determining this very voyage and fixing the imaginations of those who take it, is the book's hero.

Certainly whales and whaling are its central myth, if that is not too odd a word for what we actually get. As Yvor Winters justly says:

> The description of the (whale's) skeleton follows a great many other chapters in which the anatomy of the whale is treated part by part: one is familiarized in great detail with the structure, size, and functions of the animal, as well as with his habits, and with the stupendous medium in which he moves. Probably no other book exists which so impresses us at once with the vastness of the physical universe and with the vastness of the idea of the universe. The allegory is incalculably strengthened by this sense of vastness and power, and by the detailed reality through which it is established. Ultimately we are shown the extent of time which the whale inhabits, as well as of space; we meet the fossil whale; and we see how the idea of the whale is imbedded in all nature, for his physical form is repeatedly suggested in rocks, in mountains, and in stars.

I do not read the novel as an 'allegory', and in other respects I disagree with Winters' ethical assessment of Ahab's quest; but this statement seems to me admirably succinct and clear. The purpose of the cetological chapters is plainly to establish just such a sense as Winters describes. Or, rather, that is one of its purposes. The other, it seems to me, is to mock man's metaphysical certainty about whales and about the signs they give of the structure of the universe by the very means, the

'scientific' exactitude and careful confidence, which establish
its actual existence. The more we know of the morphology of
the whale, the less certain we grow of our ability to construct
a morphology of the universe to which it provides so marvellous a correspondence and analogy. To know the whale is both
to know and not to know God; naturalism both creates and
undermines a metaphysic. It would be a great pity to see the
cetological chapters as constituting a difficulty for the reader
to cope with, or even to see them in a more positive way as
providing a prosaic framework in which a poetic drama may
grow. They are integral to the book's meaning, and hence to
its drama; they are the matrix in which Melville casts his image
of heroism. For it is out of the seemingly pedantic though far
from tedious cetology that the metaphysical questions arise,
later to be dramatised in the confrontations between man and
man, man and whale. And it is in relation to these accounts that
we begin to see this ship and this crew as doomed; in a way,
the very calmness, the very pedantry of the accounts dooms
them; for who could ever stand against a majesty and a
power given such an imprint in the very contours of visible
reality?

III

Ishmael and Ahab have each been proposed as the novel's
hero. It may seem odd to argue the case for either, because
there is a sense in which the book clearly has no hero at all;
but it does have an aura of heroism, and critics understandably
feel the need to locate its source and identify it. In my view,
its source is to be found in neither of them, and in fact is not
to be defined in terms of a human individual at all.

The case of Ishmael is the simpler, yet the more elusive. No
doubt our democratic predilections tempt us to see him as the
hero, since he is everyman, the man who 'suffered and was
there', the sole survivor and witness to the meaning of the
drama he has suffered. Yet he has nothing of the *heroic* about

him. I agree that he is the most interesting human actor in the drama; but that is largely because of the great variety of tones and attitudes in which we sense the unconfessed volatility of his nature. It is a volatility which could never make him a hero in such a confrontation as this, because it is too merely boyish as well as too obviously unsettled. In any case, it is established through the use of his voice as narrator, and I have already stated my conviction that that ceases to be *his* voice, a voice created and identified as belonging specifically to him, quite early in the piece.

The book begins with the words, 'Call me Ishmael': not 'My name is Ishmael', but '*Call* me Ishmael'. In this formula he is not telling his name but announcing his office: he is the outcast, the wanderer on the waste places, the man tested and tempted by solitude and the hunt, the mighty yet vague desert hunter of the Old Testament. It is possible that Melville, with his Calvinist upbringing (attributed also to the Ishmael of the narrative) here intends a private allegorical reference to his own alienation from Christianity (among the seed of Abraham, yet unacknowledged by his father); if so, it remains a private one. And the ambiguous nature of his office, the Ishmael-role, is felt in the half-jocular tone, involving as it does a certain refusal of responsibility, of the pages which follow the opening:

> But wherefore it was that after having repeatedly smelt the sea as a merchant sailor, I should now take it into my head to go on a whaling voyage; this the invisible police officer of the Fates, who has the constant surveillance of me, and secretly dogs me, and influences me in some unaccountable way—he can better answer than any one else. And, doubtless, my going on this whaling voyage, formed part of the grand programme of Providence that was drawn up a long time ago. It came as a sort of brief interlude and solo between more extensive perform-ances. I take it that this part of the bill must have run something like this:

'Grand Contested Election for the Presidency
of the United States

WHALING VOYAGE BY ONE ISHMAEL
BLOODY BATTLE IN AFGHANISTAN.'

It is a refusal of responsibility, yet also an uneasy awareness
that responsibility exists, looms, may be forced on one: guilt
whistling in the dark, and self-mockery groping down to its
dark roots. In all of Ishmael's accounts in these first chapters,
there is a mixture of accents and an uneasy movement among
emotional stresses. Three paragraphs after the passage I have
quoted, the great image emerges, as though out of a dream, of
what the responsibility may mean:

> By reason of these things, then, the whaling voyage was
> welcome; the great flood-gates of the wonder-world swung
> open, and in the wild conceits that swayed me to my purpose,
> two and two there floated into my inmost soul, endless pro-
> cessions of the whale, and, mid most of them all, one grand
> hooded phantom, like a snow hill in the air.

Ishmael, then, is representative man, just like each of us,
except that he is wittier and more volatile and has actually done
battle with the grand demon of the sea. To call him the book's
hero, however, would be to hold out a pretty attenuated sense
of what its heroism amounts to. Not that he is at all despicable;
but he is passive, overshadowed and overwhelmed by the
forces which he confronts.

Ahab is 'heroic', certainly, but perhaps too much so; he
does not entirely persuade us that, to use Matthew Arnold's
terms, he is the 'grand thing' that matches the 'grand name'.
His diabolism is impressive at the risk of making his desolation
unconvincing, or, at any rate, of placing it in an emotional
scale much smaller than that of Lear. Is he, as Yvor Winters
suggests, the blighted hero confronting the destructive forces
of the universe in such a way as to pervert his heroism into
blasphemy? Or is he, as Marius Bewley argues, the man so

L   153

displaced within a moral universe as to become an agent of
evil? Ahab seems to see himself alternately in these lights; and
so, possibly, does Melville. Yet, whatever Melville intended
(and his intentions do not seem to me unambiguously translated into art) I do think Ahab is presented overwhelmingly as
an antagonist of the forces of life, not as their protagonist.
To Captain Peleg, he is a 'grand, ungodly, god-like man',
reminiscent of that Ahab in the Old Testament whose blood
was licked by dogs, yet for all that 'a crowned king'. To the
'prophet' Elijah, he is blighted, a blasphemer, an evil force
seeking the destruction of ships and of souls; and in Chapter
XXVIII he is presented as follows:

> There seemed no sign of common bodily illness about him,
> nor of the recovery from any. He looked like a man cut away
> from the stake, when the fire has overrunningly wasted all the
> limbs without consuming them, or taking away one particle
> from their compacted aged robustness. His whole high, broad
> form, seemed made of solid bronze, and shaped in an unalterable
> mould, like Cellini's cast Perseus. Threading its way out from
> among his grey hairs, and continuing right down one side of his
> tawny scorched face and neck, till it disappeared in his clothing,
> you saw a slender rod-like mark, lividly whitish. It resembled
> that perpendicular seam sometimes made in the straight, lofty
> trunk of a great tree, when the upper lightning tearingly darts
> down it, and without wrenching a single twig, peels and
> grooves out the bark from top to bottom ere running off into
> the soil, leaving the tree still greenly alive, but branded.
> whether that mark was born with him, or whether it was the
> scar left by some desperate wound, no one could certainly say.
> By some tacit consent, throughout the voyage little or no
> allusion was made to it, especially by the mates. But once
> Tashtego's senior, an old Gay-Head Indian among the crew,
> superstitiously asserted that not till he was full forty years old
> did Ahab become that way branded, and then it came upon him,
> not in the fury of any mortal fray, but in an elemental strife at
> sea. Yet, this wild hint seemed inferentially negatived, by what

a grey Manxman insinuated, an old sepulchral man, who, having never before sailed out of Nantucket, had never ere this laid eye upon wild Ahab. Nevertheless, the old sea-traditions, the immemorial credulities, popularly invested this old Manxman with preternatural powers of discernment. So that no white sailor seriously contradicted him when he said that if ever Captain Ahab should be tranquilly laid out—which might hardly come to pass, so he muttered—then, whoever should do that last office for the dead, would find a birth-mark on him from crown to sole.

This fine and famous passage, compounded as it is of an opposition between suggestions of life and those of death, of carefully composed description of the man's presence, of rumour, superstition, and surmise, gives the essential introduction to Ahab's spiritual nature and to his dramatic role. It is a physical description plainly suggestive of a spiritual one; Ahab carries not only his fate, but his spiritual nature, branded on his body. One cannot suppose that the account ought to be read, as it were, retrospectively; Ahab is not doomed because he bears this mark; he bears this mark because he is doomed. And we must note that his behaviour in Chapter XXXVI ('The Quarter-Deck') is presented as not only maniacal but demoniacal.

But it is in the comparison between the description in Chapter XXVIII and the events in Chapter XXXVI that our doubts arise about Ahab's heroic stature. He is heroic until he acts or speaks; he is grand in the perceptions others have of him, but in his behaviour he is melodramatic. I do not say that his behaviour is entirely lacking in magnificence, but it is a magnificence partly vitiated by the terms in which it finds utterance. 'Death to Moby Dick!' he shrieks, and we see before us a soul not damned but merely distraught. The demoniac lapses back towards the maniacal.

One cannot, I think, see him as a figure of pure evil, as a figure of the devil. In the first place, no sooner have the demoniacal suggestions been made than another note enters:

> But Ahab, my Captain, still moves before me in all his Nantucket grimness and shagginess; and in this episode touching Emperors and Kings, I must not conceal that I have only to do with a poor old whale-hunter like him; and, therefore, all outward majestical trappings and housings are denied me. Oh, Ahab! what shall be grand in thee, it must needs be plucked at from the skies, and dived for in the deep, and featured in the unbodied air.

Once again, the voice is that of Ishmael, or of Ishmael-Melville; and the powerful compassion gives us a valuable qualifying stress to the suggestion that we are to enter fully into Ahab's spiritual drama. We cannot enter fully into it, because it is not fully created. The Luciferian stature created for him at one point is threatened at another, so that he often appears grotesque or merely silly; but he never does so in Ishmael's or Starbuck's perceptions of him.

For the first, he is mysteriously doomed, for the second he is clearly damned; and both perceptions seem accurate to the reader's experience of his quest. But his actions are, after all, taken under the influence of Fedallah, his harpooner, who seems to me unmistakably a figure of the devil, though Yvor Winters suggests that he may be an 'emanation' from Ahab himself. If I am right, Ahab is less evil than possessed, less a Beelzebub than a Faust: a fact which would in itself prejudice his heroic stature. And as the quest draws to its close, to become an actual hunt, the emotions we are in danger of feeling for him are pity and impatience. His impiety and his crazed inhumanity are felt, finally, as ebbings of his own vital force.

Compared with him, Ishmael is a focus of human value *and* of human interest; and, for the reasons I gave earlier, the white whale takes on the heroic and mythic stature from which Ahab declines.

I have already mentioned that Moby Dick is presented as the

crown and consummation of the imperial breed of whales, and that the logic of the book as a whole works to give whales in general, and him in particular, a mythic and heroic stature. He gains this stature only by having whalers and whaling share it; but because they do, he gains it more triumphantly. I will now suggest that Moby Dick *is*, in the most relevant sense, the book's protagonist; that it is only to Ahab that he appears the enemy of life, and that in the book as a whole he embodies and represents certain awe-invoking forces of life which Ahab in *his* being denies and Ishmael in *his* wanderings has not yet found, but in relation to which he feels guilt. Those forces have sexual and historical expressions, and they are the forces of *natura naturans*, working in the depths not only of the sea but of the psyche; they are forces which link sea and psyche, they demand awe and reverence, and they are therefore religious forces.

This is the polar opposite of the reading given by Yvor Winters, for whom the white whale is 'the chief symbol and spirit of evil'. Certainly, one is tempted back from time to time to some such reassuringly clearcut plan of the novel's morality. In this reading there is no disturbing central paradox of the creative imagination, no wicked book whose creation leaves its author spotless as the lamb. And if one *is* tempted towards such a clearcut anatomy, it may be because one does *not* feel the book to be in any radical or compelling sense a wicked one. Yet as a reading it clearly will not do. By creating the whale so powerfully as an antagonist for Ahab, Melville creates him as a protagonist for what Ahab denies, in himself, in society, and in nature. Ahab may not be pure evil; but, for myself, I can see no possibility of associating the white whale with evil at all.

One cannot argue the case at much length; but I may state the considerations which have become decisive for me. The first is, that the one really compelling image of a paradisal state is created in Chapter LXXXVII ('The Grand Armada'), on which Marius Bewley properly places such importance, and to which I shall return. The second is, that in all the introductory material on the white whale, the narrative tone is not only admiring but reverential. It seems inescapable that he both is and represents a force which is to be reverenced. We read in one place, in a quite casual suggestion, of a whale 'brushing with its flanks all the coasts of Africa'; we hear of the white whale presenting himself to the sailors' imaginations as 'the gliding great demon of the seas of life'; and, to give one extended example of the many offering, we read at the end of Chapter LXXIX ('The Prairie'):

But in the great Sperm whale, this high and mighty god-like dignity inherent in the brow is so immensely amplified, that gazing on it, in that full front view, you feel the Deity and the dread powers more forcibly than in beholding any other object in living nature. For you see no one point precisely; not one distinct feature is revealed; no nose, eyes, ears, or mouth; no face; he has none, proper; nothing but that one broad firmament of a forehead, pleated with riddles; dumbly lowering with the doom of boats, and ships, and men. Nor, in profile, does this wondrous brow diminish; though that way viewed its grandeur does not domineer upon you so. In profile, you plainly perceive that horizontal, semi-crescentic depression in the forehead's middle, which, in a man, is Lavater's mark of genius.

But how? Genius in the Sperm Whale? Has the Sperm Whale ever written a book, spoken a speech? No, his great genius is declared in his doing nothing particular to prove it. It is moreover declared in his pyramidical silence. And this reminds me that had the great Sperm Whale been known to the young Orient World, he would have been deified by their child-magian thoughts. They deified the crocodile of the Nile, because the crocodile is tongueless; and the Sperm Whale has no tongue, or at least it is so exceedingly small, as to be incapable of protrusion. If hereafter any highly cultured, poetical nation shall lure back to their birth-right, the merry May-day gods of old; and livingly enthrone them again in the now egotistical sky; in the now

unhaunted hill; then be sure, exalted to Jove's high seat, the
great Sperm Whale shall lord it.

I do not exclude the possibility that there is a certain irony
in all this; but if there is, I think it would be rash to conclude
that it is directed against the majesty of the whale or his associations with religion, both Hebraic and Pagan. The over-
whelming impact of the passage is one of reverence and wonder,
and it presents the whale as a being to be feared and reverenced. As is typical of Melville, the reverencing is ambiguous;
but it is also characteristically deep-felt and forceful. I do not
want to be dogmatic, for, after all, as Auden has pointed out,
the white whale means different things to different members
of the crew. But when we reflect that the accounts of Moby
Dick grow longer and more religious in those very parts of the
book where the personality of Ishmael has been most fully
subsumed under the voice of his author, we must conclude
that there is, as it were, a *total* presentation of him and of his
significance which transcends, though it incorporates, the
perceptions of Ishmael, or Starbuck, or Flask, or Ahab, or the
Manxman. I know that, however definitely Moby Dick is one
thing, one significance, he is not that thing simply. He is a
dramatised presence created at the centre of a tissue of analogies, summation of a whole order of beings and powers, who
re-presents analogically all the questions about God that the
world by its very constitution poses. Perhaps that is the reason
why Melville thought it a wicked book, and not because Ahab
was permitted to howl delirious blasphemies to delirious stage
effects. When we follow out very closely the way in which
whales are talked about in the expository chapters, we see that
at one moment an analysis of whaleness is used to stress the
immutability of natural processes, at another it is used to
stress the inscrutability of the human heart, and at another it
suggests the opaqueness of the divine action in and through the
world. But the reverence we feel for Moby Dick, for what he

is and re-presents, is Melville's reverence.

Daniel Hoffman says, 'But neither is Moby Dick God; he is God's whale—and Job's whale'. I think the analogical process on which Melville is embarked is more tangled, more mysterious, and less pious than that would suggest. While recognising the ambiguities, I would venture the suggestion that at more than one point the whale is associated so directly with the God of the Old Testament that he comes to seem not God's creature or even agent, but an analogy for God, and one who has the force within nature that the creator might be supposed to have. *That* God was not to be named, he presented himself to Moses as a burning bush or a cloud, and he appeared always as a non-appearance, showing himself 'from the hind-parts'. So with the whale:

> For all these reasons, then, any way you may look at it, you must needs conclude that the great Leviathan is that one creature in the world which must remain unpainted to the last. . . . And the only mode in which you can derive even a tolerable idea of his living contour, is by going a whaling yourself; but by so doing, you run no small risk of being eternally stove and sunk by him.

And, in a still more daring passage:

> The more I consider this mighty tail, the more do I deplore my inability to express it. At times there are gestures in it, which, though they would well grace the hand of man, remain wholly inexplicable. In an extensive herd, so remarkable, occasionally, are these mystic gestures, that I have heard hunters who have declared them akin to Freemason signs and symbols; that the whale, indeed, by these methods intelligently conversed with the world. Nor are there wanting other motions of the whale in his general body, full of strangeness, and unaccountable to his most experienced assailant. Dissect him how I may, then, I but go skin deep. I know him not, and never will. But if I know not even the tail of this whale, how understand his head? much more, how comprehend his face, when face he has none?

Thou shalt see my back parts, my tail, he seems to say, but my
face shall not be seen. But I cannot completely make out his back
parts; and hint what he will about his face, I say again he has no
face.

Moby Dick is not God; but he is not simply 'God's whale'
either; he is God's analogy. The problems associated with
coming to know him are metaphysical ones; and the course of
hunting him is a religious course. To make out my case about
the way in which Moby Dick himself is the protagonist of life's
deepest forces and the hero of the novel, I would point, finally,
to the passages in which Melville eventually shows him in
action, in the book's last three chapters. The magnificence of
his action there cancels out all earlier ironies, if they exist at
all.

IV

The uniqueness of *Moby Dick* is partly in the prose by which
these heroic dimensions are created. Critics have found
affinities for it with *Paradise Lost*, *The Divine Comedy*, and
Faust; but there seems general agreement that the strongest
influences are Hawthorne and Shakespeare, both of whom
Melville was reading at the time of the book's composition.
The affinities with Hawthorne are obvious; and the influence
of Shakespeare's tragedies can be clearly seen both in the
conception of Ahab and in the melodramatic qualities in his
speeches. To say this is to suggest that something has gone
wrong between influence and creation; for Ahab does not strike
us as a 'hero' created and controlled with Shakespeare's authority, and the total effect of the book is very different from that
either of *The Scarlet Letter* or *King Lear*. Its marked unevenness
of tone and unpredictability of accent have led many readers to
dismiss it as, in total effect, manic or fantastic. I do not think
it is either, because there is a sufficiently characteristic expository method to allow us to speak of a staple prose, and there is
a frequent magnificence which quite transcends the fantastic or

grotesque elements that we find, for example, in much of Ahab's behaviour. That magnificence, I have suggested, comes generally from the accounts of whalers, whaling, and whales, and is triumphantly consummated both in the preparatory accounts of the white whale and in the descriptions of him in action in the last three chapters. And it is not separate from, but integral to what I have called the staple expository method. In fact, we might say that the relation between them is very similar to the relation between the creation of an heroic stature for the whale and the scientific circlings of the cetological chapters: the more prosaic is a matrix for, the creative condition for, the more poetic, in such a way that we must say that the total conception of the work is a poetic one.

The distinctiveness, the poetic amplitude, of Melville's prose has the following features, which I may perhaps mention briefly before dealing with the two chief of them: The capacity to reach, in the middle of a most levelheaded passage, a sudden *coup* of poetic realisation in an image or set of images; the rapid and astonishing heightening of 'ordinary' reality gained by such means; a lingering-out quality created by the meditative and even pedantic convention of exposition, in which the images stretch out towards several dimensions; the undeniable magnificence with which the finest passages move towards an heroic vision; and a quality of innocence, of grand yet quaint innocence, associated with that.

Of the first, I may give an example (though there are a myriad available) which will be particularly convincing because of the grotesqueness of its context. After the chapter in which Ahab swears his crew to a maniacal covenant with him, there is a chapter (XL: 'Harpooneers and Sailors') in which the crew, apparently drunk, is singing and talking to itself. This is a quite ridiculous chapter, inevitably unsuccessful; yet in the middle of it, the old Manx sailor, who is credited with second sight, muses

I'll dance over your grave, I will—that's the bitterest threat
of your night-women, that beat head-winds round corners. O
Christ! to think of the green navies and the green-skulled crews!

which is a sudden *coup* of the most spine-chilling poetry,
realising in a single cadence the fate that awaits this ship and
this crew.

Of the second and third together, the following passage is
perhaps an example:

> At last, passage paid, and luggage safe, we stood on board the
> schooner. Hoisting sail, it glided down the Acushnet river. On
> one side, New Bedford rose in terraces of streets, their ice-
> covered trees all glittering in the clear, cold air. Huge hills and
> mountains of casks on casks were piled upon her wharves, and
> side by side the world-wandering whale ships lay silent and
> safely moored at last; while from others came a sound of car-
> penters and coopers, with blended noises of fires and forges to
> melt the pitch, all betokening that new cruises were on the
> start; that one most perilous and long voyage ended, only begins
> a second; and a second ended, only begins a third,—and so on,
> for ever and for aye. Such is the endlessness, yea, the intolerable-
> ness of all earthly effort.

Here is surely an instance of that 'felt reality' whose existence
in the book is denied by hostile critics, and particularly by
critics brought up on a more 'social' kind of novel, on Dickens
or George Eliot. But it is a reality felt with an intensity we are
justified in calling poetic; for the feeling goes beyond that
usually produced by or invested in passages of social observa-
tion. It is a feeling, among other things, for the mysteriousness
of what to most men would seem merely ordinary, a feeling
for the metaphysical dimension of what most men would take
as no more than observed fact. Are those 'ice-covered trees'
the masts of ships or living trees? The preternatural clarity of
the prose prompts the question even while it makes any
answer irrelevant. What is created at that point in the paragraph, in the 'terraces of streets', in the 'huge hills and

mountains of casks', in the silence of the 'world-wandering whale ships', is a sense of a quite mysterious and awe-inspiring suspension of energies, in which natural and social forces merge with each other. Growing from this perception of energies suspended through a whole town come the 'blended noises of fires and forges', the possibility of the town's moving; and it is only then that the presentation of an observed yet heightened reality becomes a musing on the unremitting insecurity of all human effort. As we see here, it is characteristic of Melville's prose that a sense of the solid world should move powerfully towards and against a volatile emotional habit, so that the prose rhythms have to accommodate two or more conflicting elements in his temperament as well as in his themes. The more successfully it does accommodate them, the more we grow aware of the mysterious nature, the poetic potency, if I may call it that, in the world which his imagination creates and broods within. And that world, *as prose*, has great variety:

> He paused a little; then kneeling in the pulpit's bows, folded his large brown hands across his chest, uplifted his closed eyes, and offered a prayer so deeply devout that he seemed kneeling and praying at the bottom of the sea.

That gives the controlledly surrealist nature of his sensibility, as this, from Fr. Mapple's sermon, gives the eccentrically homely,

> Oh! most contemptible and worthy of all scorn; with slouched hat and guilty eye, skulking from his God.

or as this gives the capacity to uncover within a jocular tone the shiver of dreadful reality,

> . . . actual cannibals stand chatting at street corners; many of whom yet carry on their bones unholy flesh.

No doubt these strengths in the prose have to contend with encroaching weaknesses: with the *Boys Own Paper* prose into which Ishmael sometimes lapses, with real as distinct from feigned pedantry, with the suffocating 'richness' of the imagery in the scene where Tashtego falls into the Sperm whale's head, with excessively exclamatory gestures and pointless raisings of emotional pressure, and with the habits revealed in Ahab's speeches, which Melville seems to have regarded highly, but which, if they develop a certain strength, also produce a certain taint in it:

> If man will strike, strike through the mask! How can the prisoner reach outside except by thrusting through the wall? To me, the white whale is that wall, shoved near to me. Sometimes I think there's naught beyond. But 'tis enough. He tasks me; he heaps me; I see in him outrageous strength, with an inscrutable malice sinewing it. That inscrutable thing is chiefly what I hate; and be the white whale agent, or be the white whale principal, I will wreak that hate upon him. Talk not to me of blasphemy, man; I'd strike the sun if it insulted me. For could the sun do that, then could I do the other; since there is ever a sort of fair play herein, jealousy presiding over all creations. But not my master, man, is even that fair play. Who's over me? Truth has no confines.

This is the strongest part of one of Ahab's few strong speeches. Obviously, it is modelled on Shakespearean blank verse just as the chapter in which it appears (XXXVI: 'The Quarter-Deck') is modelled on the form of a Shakespearean scene. The language has a feverish and exotic abstractness, in which a metaphor is no sooner established than it is cast aside; yet its elevation is uneasy; and whereas it does reach the condition of blank verse, it holds that condition only for a few lines. In the short term, it is extremely impressive; but in the long term it bores us as none of Lear's or Antony's speeches do. Its elevation demands too much strain.

It is arguable that there is a sense in which Melville was not a 'natural novelist' at all, and that he has his greatest difficulty in those scenes where emotion has to be translated into alienated behaviour in a social setting and in those where social behaviour demands to be realistically observed in its own terms, as in many of the opening chapters. But, while this may account for the unevenness in the prose, it does not really reduce the scale of his achievement, which exists in quite other terms.

I have already indicated those terms by speaking of the heroic in connection with an unusual kind of innocence; and of course these qualities are blended most splendidly in his feeling for the sea and its inhabitants. It is created quite early; Chapter XIV: 'Nantucket' is a good example:

> The Nantucketer, he alone resides and riots on the sea; he alone, in Bible language, goes down to it in ships; to and fro ploughing it as his own special plantation. *There* is his home; *there* lies his business, which a Noah's flood would not interrupt, though it overwhelmed all the millions in China. He lives on the sea, as Prairie cocks in the prairie; he hides among the waves, he climbs them as chamois hunters climb the Alps. For years he knows not the land; so that when he comes to it at last, it smells like another world, more strangely than the moon would to an Earthman. With the landless gull, that at sunset folds her wings and is rocked to sleep between billows; so at nightfall, the Nantucketer, out of sight of land, furls his sails, and lays him to his rest, while under his very pillow rush herds of walruses and whales.

What is distinctive about this is not so much the ardent, repetitive, fast-moving quality which, after all, Melville has in common with other writers, like Dickens. It is so affecting because it is so affectionate; and its affection is a quality of its innocence. If there is quaintness here, it is not dominant; and and it is even less in evidence when we come to a chapter like 'The Grand Armada', in which the innocence is nearly cosmic in its scope, and much more powerful in its sense of the innocent *acting*. In the earlier chapters, of which the passage above is a good and far from unique example, the prose works rhythmically in something like the way poetry does, conveying that wonderstruck quality, that childlike amplitude and affection for the unusual going quite intriguingly with the tendency to a sceptical and self-mocking philosophising which could not be anything but adult. But in 'The Grand Armada' we are given the full scope of innocence:

> But far beneath this wondrous world upon the surface, another and still stranger world met our eyes as we gazed over the side. For, suspended in those watery vaults, floated the forms of the nursing mothers of the whales, and those that by their enormous girth seemed shortly to become mothers. The lake, as I have hinted, was to a considerable depth exceedingly transparent; and as human infants while suckling will calmly and fixedly gaze away from the breast, as if leading two different lives at the time; and while yet drawing mortal nourishment, be still spiritually feasting upon some unearthly reminiscence;— even so did the young of these whales seem looking up towards us, but not at us, as if we were but a bit of Gulf-weed in their new-born sight.

and:

> Some of the subtlest secrets of the seas seemed divulged to us in this enchanted pond. We saw young Leviathan amours in the deep.
>
> And thus, though surrounded by circle upon circle of consternations and affrights, did these inscrutable creatures at the centre freely and fearlessly indulge in all peaceful concernments; yes, serenely revelled in dalliance and delight. But even so, amid the tornadoed Atlantic of my being, do I myself still for ever centrally disport in mute calm; and while ponderous planets of unwaning woe revolve around me, deep down and deep inland there I still bathe me in eternal mildness of joy.

The astounding quality revealed by these brief passages is in fact created with much greater scope than they can represent. It is a quality of magnanimity, created in a large-souled prose which is capable of suggesting in the one movement a distinctive intensity of seeing and feeling and a certain eccentricity of action which, nevertheless, does not ever become grotesque and is too grand to be called quaint. The magnanimous quality is achieved largely through the leisurely, bending, wondering pace of the narration; and its innocence is quite remarkable; I can think of no other writer who has seen his world in such terms, and a world of 'monsters' at that. We are persuaded that they *are* 'inscrutable creatures at the centre', but at the centre of our potential beings as well as of their own order; the analogical habit is once more powerfully at work. Whimsy, over-familiarity with the great, are quite explicitly fended off by the predominant tone, which is one of reverence and wonder: reverence for an innocence which, both in its largeness of scope and in its intensity of seeing and feeling, quite transcends the usual conceptions of that virtue, and which, far from reducing or patronising, enlarges and celebrates the objects of its attention.

Yet even in this chapter enters that dark component of Melville's imagination which all the critics emphasise, that brooding on destructiveness, that sense of fatedness. A wounded whale runs amok in his death-agonies:

> So that tormented to madness, he was now churning through the water, violently flailing with his flexible tail, and tossing the keen spade about him, wounding and murdering his own comrades.

Even so superbly imaged an Eden produces its example of pain and destruction. And the wonder, the innocence, are all the greater because the sense of the whale's destructive potency becomes so powerful when we finally meet the white whale not in speculation, but in action:

> Then the whole world was the whale's; and, king of creation, he left his wake along the present lines of the Andes and the Himmalehs. Who can show a pedigree like Leviathan? Ahab's harpoon has shed older blood than the Pharaoh's.

It is the white whale seen in that perspective, and under that aspect, and not, or not primarily, as the King of the nearly cosmic harmony imaged in 'The Grand Armada', that Ahab is hunting, and that consents to be sighted at the end of the book. He is seen with dramatic suddenness, and immediately the boats are put down after him. As they approach him, the paradisal note returns, even more powerfully than in the earlier chapter, and one feels for a long moment that they are indeed hunting God:

> Like noiseless nautilus shells, their light prows sped through the sea; but only slowly they neared the foe. As they neared him, the ocean grew still more smooth; seemed drawing a carpet over its waves; seemed a noon-meadow, so serenely it spread. At length the breathless hunter came so nigh his seemingly unsuspecting prey, that his entire dazzling hump was distinctly visible, sliding along the sea as if an isolated thing, and continually set in a revolving ring of finest, fleecy, greenish foam. He saw the vast, involved wrinkles of the slightly projecting head beyond. Before it, far out on the soft Turkish-rugged waters, went the glistening white shadow from his broad, milky forehead, a musical rippling playfully accompanying the shade.

But the initiative belongs to the whale, not the hunter; and as this chapter proceeds, 'the grand god' plays with his pursuers, to their ultimate destruction. And, as the action proceeds towards that destruction, while the prose keeps up its strong, unhurried attention to movement and perspective, there comes almost imperceptibly a change in the quality of the wonder, now awestruck rather than reverential.

> Through and through; through every plank and each rib, it thrilled for an instant, the whale obliquely lying on his back, in the manner of a biting shark slowly and feelingly taking its bows full within his mouth, so that the long, narrow, scrolled lower jaw curled high up into the open air, and one of the teeth caught in a row-lock.

M   169

The magnificence of such prose (which can be seen only at the length of these three chapters) consists not simply in the creation of a sense of the whale's greatness and even inviolability, or of the human feelings appropriate to those qualities, but in the fact that they are created in action. The very slowness and attentiveness of the prose through the relevant pages dramatise the whale as the chief actor, act out his paradoxical taking of the initiative. Of course that perception carries with it the appearance of a certain malignancy; but once again it is a question of Eden's capacity to seem destructive. The unusual satisfaction that the prose seems to carry comes, I think, from the very qualities of inviolability and self-sufficiency in the whale which terrify the whalers. Having as it were seen *this* whale act out his nature, we could not possibly expect that he would ever be captured by mere men; we could not expect that he would be comprehended by them; we could not expect that he would even be approached by them if he did not want to be. What certain passages in the expository chapters had created in one mode is recreated now in another: the mythic and heroic stature of Moby Dick not only as an object of speculative or even contemplative attention but also as the chief actor in the human drama concerned with his pursuit, and therefore, inescapably so it seems to me, agent and analogy of those life-forces which the pursuit, in effect, denies:

> For not by any calm and indolent spoutings; not by the peaceable gush of that mystic fountain in his head, did the White Whale now reveal his vicinity; but by the far more wondrous phenomenon of breaching. Rising with his utmost velocity from the furthest depths, the Sperm Whale thus booms his entire bulk into the pure element of air, and piling up a mountain of dazzling foam, shows his place to the distance of seven miles and more. In those moments, the torn, enraged waves he shakes off, seem his mane; in some cases, this breaching is his act of defiance.

It is a being rising with 'utmost velocity from the furthest depths' of life that the *Pequod* hunts; it is the sense of him as contemplated being and as actor that the prose establishes. It is no wonder that the hunter should come to his own destruction; and it is no wonder that Ishmael, the sole survivor, should have a coffin for his life-buoy.

So grandly conceived a tale and so grandly active a prose have little trouble in surviving their author's incidental grandiosities. And the achievement to which they lead is as religious in nature as it is extraordinary in scope. In so tirelessly scrutinising the white whale's power and mystery, Melville makes it clear that he is, by analogy, scrutinising God, and man, and the natural world, all three; to the extent that Ahab's emotions are endorsed (and I think that they are endorsed only momentarily, if at all) what is endorsed is an assault upon the metaphysical order composed of those three. We may certainly say that Melville creates a set of mythic terms, centred on the whale's power and majesty, in which to raise a set of metaphysical questions, centred on the whale's mystery and inscrutability. We may even say that he is on the verge of creating a new image of God, but one which leads so unmistakably to a re-definition of God's presence in the created universe that a nineteenth-century Presbyterian, even a lapsed one, might well find 'wicked' the book in which it was done. No doubt at many points of the novel we may wonder whether we are in the ambience of religious mystery or the arena of religious mania; but for the most part Melville triumphantly creates an enduring feeling which I think we must call religious, and which bears him, sustains him, through a questioning which is certainly metaphysical. It is in the white whale that it comes to fullest and most fearful definition.

CHAPTER VIII

W. B. Yeats and the Sacred Company

But the passions, when we know that they cannot find fulfilment,
become vision; and a vision, whether we wake or sleep, prolongs
its power by rhythm and pattern, the wheel where the world is
butterfly.—*Mythologies*
If we would create a great community—and what other game is
so worth the labour?—we must recreate the old foundations of
life.—*Explorations*

I

YEATS' reputation since his death seems impregnable, and
his stature that of a great master. The movement of criticism has, as every one notes, become a spate; and the very
solidity of some of it, combined with the very brilliance of
other parts, may have had the effect of confusing the reader
whose access to the poetry is much more direct and pleasurable
than many a critic suspects. In a way, too much has been dis-
cussed and explained. Yeats' rhetorical power has called out
the half-buried poet in many critics; and someone like myself
who has read a great deal of the critical work finds in himself
an odd reluctance to go back to any of it when he is actually
reading Yeats or proposing to write about him. Then, too,
there is the sense, which a great many people seem to share,
that Yeats' poetic achievement, though great, has had to
emerge by conflict from a world-view itself unusual to the
point of absurdity. Auden's 'You were silly like us . . .' for a
time may have seemd a just, even a charitable estimate; there
would always be the double unspoken suggestion, 'a damn
sight sillier', and 'not really quite like us at all'.

I think it dangerous to assume that Yeats' world-view was
absurd, or that his silliness was greater than our own. Both

172

Moore and Leavis judged him to have a magnificent intelligence; writers so dissimilar as Sean O'Casey and Frank O'Connor both loved him for reasons partly to do with his grasp of issues and affairs; his humour is so evident that nobody ever seems to notice it; and I cannot help agreeing with Allen Tate's remark that 'Yeats had a more inclusive mind than any of his critics has had'. All this would be good enough for me even if my own reading of his works were not; and frankly I have never been able to see how anyone could read twenty consecutive pages of his mature prose, much less twenty of his mature poems, and still think 'silly' an appropriate word. What we find in both poetry and prose is a combination of wisdom, innocence, and shrewdness, with a generous and noble kindliness to set beside, and beneath, the bitterness and the posturing. Yet the strain of misguided admiration persists: '*though* you were silly, not quite like us . . .'; and sometimes it becomes the opposite of admiration, as when, for example, Yvor Winters belabours his poetry in defence of reason. As though Yeats ever did *it* much harm.

There is another, and more tempting way of praising him which is also likely to mislead; it is that perhaps suggested by, though not represented in, A. D. Hope's line

To have found at last that noble, candid speech.

Like everyone else, I have my head filled, if not stuffed, with quotations from Yeats, in much the way people used to have couplets from Pope to suit every occasion, or lines from Browning to divert every question. And I notice that we tend to bring them out with an air, an air which shows that our hidden purpose is not merely to make a comment or to illuminate a situation, but also to remind ourselves that a human being *could* talk like that, habitually, naturally, and as though by right. Yeats Chrysostom, the poet for whom speech was utterance and a perception a symbol. Yet there are two things wrong with leaving one's sense of him at the level suggested by this friendly habit. First, we may bring his reputation to seem something like that of Tennyson in the last years of his life, the reputation of someone valued for the quality of his voice and for that alone. Second, we will forget that he is a master of rhythm, and that the special quality of his utterance is created not merely by a tone but by a rhythm.

No doubt most people will agree about that, but I still think it dangerous to assume that we know in what his rhythmic mastery consists, and what his characteristic rhythm *is*. Certainly, it is not just a habit which sweetens the rhetoric or gives conviction to a feat of tone; it is a movement which, however nobly overt it sounds, is as complex and delicate as it can be. No-one can be a master of rhythm in Yeats' way who is not also a master of the organisation of impulse and form by rhythmic means. To quote even a relatively uncompelling passage:

> When long ago I saw her ride
> Under Ben Bulben to the meet,
> The beauty of her country-side
> With all youth's lonely wildness stirred,
> She seemed to have grown clean and sweet
> Like any rock-bred, sea-borne bird:
>
> Sea-borne, or balanced on the air
> When first it sprang out of the nest
> Upon some lofty rock to stare
> Upon the cloudy canopy,
> While under its storm-beaten breast
> Cried out the hollows of the sea.

It is tempting to think that the rhythmic quality which delights us here is a plangent simplicity made purposive. For my part, I think that what holds us is the delicate checks and balances which create a sense that Yeats is obeying a ceremony of the mind by attention to which the spirit and the bodily poise of the mind's object can be not only indicated but realised. And I think that an analysis of 'rhythm' would come to take in so many details of phrasing, pace, of gently dramatic juxtaposition, that we would find the word 'drama' inescapable; in raising the considerations suggested by that word, we would find that we were touching on the centre of Yeats' whole creative impulse: there is no separation in him between the impulse to sing and the impulse to speak. The rhythm, delicately organised as it is, itself organises a world of momentary perception; and yet the achievement certainly seems 'a moment's thought'.

He is a *dramatic* poet, whose poetic form is usually lyric in scope and resonance. But the dramatic emphasis is put on two things: on so presenting and heightening the details of human lives, including his own, that they come to seem representative; and on enclosing, in order to define, a notion and a movement of the *sacred*. It is when these two interests become one that his best work is likely to emerge, although of course his great poem 'Meditations in Time of Civil War' invites a different reading. He looks often into a period of history as an arena of conflict in which, following the doctrinal hints given in such works as *A Vision*, he can discern the sacred at work in the large; one example is 'The Second Coming'; another is 'At Parnell's Funeral'. But perhaps more often he looks towards his own friends, his family, his loves, his political commitments, in order to find in them some grounds for and some means of specifying the sacred. I shall argue that, when he does, he characteristically ends by declaring *them* sacred. In a few poems (and personally I think this is what really happens in 'Meditations')[1] he goes beyond such a task of specification to dramatise the personal tensions which, in a given historical situation, may open within his idea of the sacred even at the risk of threatening that very idea. But generally one can say that he is concerned to dramatise lyrical experience, and that

[1] For an excellent analysis of this poem see Penelope Curtis: 'Yeats: The Tower in Time of Civil War', *Melbourne Critical Review*, No. 6, 1963.

the terms in which he tends to dramatise it are the terms of its potentiality to sacredness.

I offer these remarks as something more than a procedural aid. We have to ask, after all, *why* Yeats so insistently goes back in time, in a way so different from Eliot's, to call upon the past for his images and examplars. This is not simply a habit of his 'bitter' last years, that period which Vivienne Koch calls 'the tragic phase', but is a feature of his poetry throughout. The early volumes, understandably enough, call on a communal or racial past, and one which it is pretty hard to be convinced had any poetic future; yet the harking-back to a *personal* past begins surprisingly early in his development. *In The Seven Woods*, which appeared in 1904, is full of it, and the poems there in which it is most marked, like 'The Arrow' and 'Adam's Curse', are more memorable than such flights of fancy as 'Red Hanrahan's Song about Ireland'. The next volume, *The Green Helmet*, is even more noticeably affected, and *Responsibilities*, the volume of 1914 which many critics speak of as signalling his leap into creative maturity, may be said to be alternately directed by and evasive of the challenge presented by the past.

> Pardon, old fathers, if you still remain
> Somewhere in ear-shot for the story's end. . . .

Anyone who thinks of the Yeats of the 1930s, with his Reinach operation and his 'lust and rage', may find the 'still' and the 'end' amusing. But they are moving as well as amusing, and the end which they promise is as great and terrible as it is prolonged.

This habit of reminiscence and re-creation is a matter of mood, certainly, but it is not created from mood, does not get its strength and persistence from any habit of moodiness. It does not come from disappointment or nostalgia, though there are disappointment and nostalgia in it; at any rate, they appear with plangent force in the volume of 1904, but after that they are increasingly subsumed under a more powerful movement of the spirit. It does not bring the old world to redress the balance of the new, or the heroic past to reproach the ignoble present; for he is capable of crying out with great conviction, 'When Pearse summoned Cuchulain to his side . . .'. Nor does it, by a more subtle reading, bring the promise of the past to endorse the decisions of the present, though Yeats in his senatorial chair evidently saw himself as in a long line of champions. Its aim becomes increasingly to mourn and to celebrate in one; yet again one senses that the impulse goes deeper still, and that no tone of elegaic nobility, however heroic its subject, could satisfy it.

As we try to find a reading and a guiding formulation more or less adequate to the poetry, we are forced to see that he is basically concerned to recover, affirm, and recreate something which is sacred: that is, his heroic friends are valuable to him not *only* because they are heroic and friends, but because they represent more than they accomplished. And *that* in itself is a possibility not just for human living but also for a cosmic order realised in history: an 'opening toward the transcendent', as Mircea Eliade calls it, which testifies to the possibility of a completion not merely in humanity but of humanity. These lives, recovered in the poetry, represent the 'old foundations of life' on which a unified society might be built.

At its strongest, then, this poetry so completely transcends whatever element of regressiveness was in its initial impulse that we are conscious only of an affirmation in the present, an affirmation of the past as bearing on the future. In other words, Yeats' concern with the past, racial or personal, gay or bitter, was at every stage religious in nature. When one notices that, one notices how often, and with what verve, he associates hero, fool, and saint:

> The greatest art symbolises not those things that we have observed so much as those things that we have experienced, and when the imaginary saint or lover or hero moves us most deeply, it is the moment when he awakens within us for an instant our own heroism, our own sanctity, our own desire.

II

It may be valuable, in testing these contentions, to ignore many of the obvious cases and to take up one of the indubitably great poems which would seem to offer us a case to the contrary. I refer to 'The Man and the Echo'. This poem comes from just before his death, is bitter in many of its emphases and clearly so non-ritualistic in its method that the word 'stark' has often been used of it; as well as this, there has been a certain amount of debate about the orientation of its closing lines ('despairing' or 'life-affirming'?) But we are fortunate in having two versions of this poem, the completed version which appears in *Collected Poems*, and a version which he sent to Lady Dorothy Wellesley in July 1938. The latter I take to be a relatively advanced draft, yet the differences between it and the finished version are important enough to be crucial to my argument. I think that a comparison of the two would show how comprehensive a term 'rhythm' must be if we are to deal at all adequately with Yeats, how it concerns the shaping of experience towards drama, and the shaping of drama towards a sacred re-presentation of lived reality. That is, Yeats' movement as we see it in his revisions is away from the documentary to the numinous quality which fact may have and, in Yeats' view, *must* have if poetry is to be a fully representative art. Consequently, it is, however delicately, a movement away from statement to expressive utterance in which the quality of statement is both completed and transcended.

The earlier version reads:

MAN AND ECHO

The Man

In the broken stone of the Alt
Where sky's a narrow slit I halt
And shout a secret to the stone:
All that I have said or done,

Now that I am old and ill,
Seems to have done but harm, until
I lie awake night after night.
I never get the answers right.
Did that play of mine send out
Certain men the English shot?
Or did my spoken words perplex
That man, that woman now a wreck?
I say that I have done some good
As well as evil, but in this mood
I see but evil until I
Sleepless would lie down and die.

Echo

Lie down and die.

The Man

That were to shirk
The spiritual intellect's great work
And shirk it in vain. There's no release
In a bodkin or disease,
Nor can there be work so great
As that which cleans man's dirty slate.
While man can still his body keep
Wine or love drugs him to sleep;
Waking he thanks the Lord that he
Has body and its stupidity,
But body gone he sleeps no more,
And he unless his mind is sure
That its vision of life is true
Pursues the thoughts that I pursue;
Then he being satisfied blots all
Human existence from his sight
And sinks at last into the night.

Echo

Into the night.

179

The Man

O rocky void
Shall we in this great night rejoice?
What do we know but that we face
One another in this place?
Up there some hawk or owl has struck
Dropping out of sky or rock.
A stricken rabbit is crying out
And its cry distracts my thought.

The second version shows even a change in title:

THE MAN AND THE ECHO

Man

In a cleft that's christened Alt
Under broken stone I halt
At the bottom of a pit
That broad noon has never lit,
And shout a secret to the stone.
All that I have said or done,
Now that I am old and ill,
Turns into a question till
I lie awake night after night
And never get the answers right.
Did that play of mine send out
Certain men the English shot?
Did words of mine put too great strain
On that woman's reeling brain?
Could my spoken words have checked
That whereby a house lay wrecked?
And all seems evil until I
Sleepless would lie down and die.

Echo

Lie down and die.

Man

That were to shirk
The spiritual intellect's great work,

And shirk it in vain. There is no release
In a bodkin or disease,
Nor can there be work so great
As that which cleans man's dirty slate.
While man can still his body keep
Wine or love drug him to sleep,
Waking he thanks the Lord that he
Has body and its stupidity,
But body gone he sleeps no more,
And till his intellect grows sure
That all's arranged in one clear view,
Pursues the thoughts that I pursue,
Then stands in judgment on his soul,
And, all work done, dismisses all
Out of intellect and sight
And sinks at last into the night.

Echo

Into the night.

Man

   O Rocky Voice,
Shall we in that great night rejoice?
What do we know but that we face
One another in this place?
But hush, for I have lost the theme,
Its joy or night seem but a dream;
Up there some hawk or owl has struck,
Dropping out of sky or rock,
A stricken rabbit is crying out,
And its cry distracts my thought.

The completed version is longer by a mere 2½ couplets than
the earlier; and the similarities between the two versions
would seem obvious enough: the logic of the poem remains
unchanged, the *mise-en-scène* is the same for both, the echoes
come at the same places in the argument and echo the same
crucial rhyme-words, the response on each occasion called

forth from the man is, or seems, the same, and the much-debated final couplet is in fact reprinted without change. Yet more has been added than 2½ couplets. It is tempting to say that what has happened is a tightening-up of the verse and the argument which it carries. In a sense this is true; but in a more important sense there has been a loosening-up of attitudes and rhythms sufficient to convert into prolonged cadences what had before been mere statements. The total effect of the final version is *triumphant* in a way one would simply not postulate of the earlier.

It would be a fascinating exercise to compare the two in moment-to-moment detail; but it would also be distracting to my present argument. The differences might briefly be expressed as follows: The first version is lacking in variety of mood or accent, and although there are a couple of weak movements towards balancing the initial perceptions with others, they come in lines like 'I say that I have done some good', in which the prosaic language and lax rhythm actually count against the effect intended. The couplets are presented as self-enclosed accusations or claims, generally lacking that rhythmic force and variety which, in the final version, move and mould them to seem whole cadenced paragraphs, not moments, of feeling. In consequence, while the Echo's interruptions are there, and at much the same 'dramatic' moments as in the later version, they do not have the effect of climaxing a movement of the spirit. At the most, they provide a comment on what has been said; they do not climax it, and in fact hardly seem part of its movement. No drama of understanding turns on them, because they have not the force, or the relevance, to turn the psychological into poetic drama.

But the differences of that sort, however marked and important they are, point to and express a difference of another sort, which is still more crucial and from which they are inseparable. Quite simply, the sense of a personally important *mystery* in things is missing from the draft; and with it is missing that ambience of the sacred which, however lightly established it is, in the completed poem gives a fresh and refreshing weight of significance to the final cry. Between the two versions, 'The broken stone of the Alt' becomes 'a cleft that's christened Alt', and the 'broken stone' becomes transferred to the second line; now, too, it is 'under' broken stone that the speaker halts. The *mise-en-scène* becomes something more than that, a spiritual condition charged with the mysterious and possibly threatening quality of the place. One is justified in feeling that this change has something to do with the new freedom of movement in the self questioning, which gains at once a ritual quality in the questions posed and a quality of spontaneous force in their juxtaposing. So we gain a sense of a movement both free and purposive, of a whole verbal body moving together: poetic unity of being.

No doubt even the final version may seem to many readers a poem naturalistic in conception and dramatic in shape if we compare it with a poem such as 'Sailing to Byzantium', symbolic in conception and dialectical in shape. I do not think the differences ought to be stated in such terms. In fact, 'The Man and the Echo' seems to me a poem enclosed or framed in an almost religious frame, in which the facts with which it begins and ends are charged with a 'symbolic' awareness of them as bearers of extra-human forces affecting human destiny. For if the poem begins with an undeclared yet esoteric sense of some sacred importance in the *milieu* which calls forth the self-scrutiny, it ends with a stoic sense of a relation between a death in nature and the cessation of a human thought-process. And it is interesting to note that the sound of the dying creature comes with a soft, self-recollecting 'hush' at that point where, the meditation having opened out once more with that wonderful cry 'O Rocky Voice', the poet asks

> What do we know but that we face
> One another in this place?

Yeats does not answer his own question except in action; it is nature's action, and the answer is ambiguous. We are not to hold easy opinions on the extent to which rejoicing is presented as possible or on that to which distraction is inescapable. We may, however, hold that, given its themes, the poem itself rejoices to an astonishing degree. For it is also interesting that, whereas in the first version it was a 'rocky void' that is addressed, and 'this' dark night (of present incomprehension?) that is in question, in the final version it is a 'Rocky Voice' (an active power) that is addressed and 'that' dark night that is in question: the night, presumably, of death, a great and terrible rather than a merely restricting night, of which the question asks itself whether rejoicing is possible there. These changes of emphasis do not simply add a tone to the questioning or a dimension to the whole experience, they crucially change the relation between Man and Echo. At this point of the poem the ultimate nature of the earlier changes, which may have seemed by themselves little more than matters of the management of a rhetoric, becomes clear, and they are seen as changes towards giving the poetic experience, *from within*, a sacred orientation and fact a numinous significance. I stress 'from within', for the changes in rhythm have in fact accomplished this end.

III

Part of my reason for concentrating on these aspects of Yeats' art is a belief that much critical commentary (though little of the best) has been wrong in seeking to account for his greatness by appealing either to the role which his esoteric system plays in his poetry or to his achievement as a love-poet or a nationalist poet. As to the first, I have no doubt that the working-out of such a system, which effectively began while he was entering on the first of his great periods, *is* relevant to his achievement; but it was more relevant to Yeats as poet than to ourselves as readers; and while I do not deny that it provided an important impulse towards the greater complexity which his poetry came to have, acting as a formative agent as well as a scheme of easy reference, I cannot see that its presence in or to particular poems goes any distance towards helping us to assess their greatness. As I have suggested, the famous 'view of life' is nothing so simple, monolithic and analysable as some critics have insisted; poetically, it is in fact remarkably protean; and I cannot help agreeing with Allen Tate when he says that it will be unfortunate if Yeats scholarship results in 'the occultation of a poetry which I believe is nearer to the center of our main traditions of sensibility and thought than the poetry of Eliot or of Pound'. That centrality is a matter not only of the humanity with which he deals with human problems but also of the sacred potentialities which he shows humanity to have.

As to the second, it is true that one of the interests of reading Yeats is to trace changes in his conceptions of his task as a love poet and as a poet of nationalist aspiration, while tracing, too, those changes in his conception of poetic *body* which enable him to flesh those attitudes. But it has seldom been remarked that he is not in fact, by comparison with Chaucer and Shakespeare, Wyatt and Donne, much of a love poet at all, and that few among his finest poems have as their chief motive-power the desire simply to *celebrate* national aspirations. These aspirations are a constant preoccupation with him rather than a consistent attitude. Measured, therefore, against the scale of his own highest achievement, his poems of love and of patriotism are bound to seem rather disappointing.

Nevertheless, even in tracing out changes in his attitudes to the national problem, we might find evidence for the case which I have been urging: that one of his chief impulses is to specify the sacred in human affairs, whether in personal relationships, observed human stances, or political situations. If, for example, one compared 'To Ireland in the Coming Times' with 'September 1913' and 'Easter 1916', one would surely be struck by the greatness of the progress from the first to the second and the quickness of the progress from the second to the third. And if one then, following out the hints gained by such an examination, went on to consider (say) 'The Curse of Cromwell' and 'Under Ben Bulben' as the *terminus ad quem* of this process, one might be forced to see how the process had involved a progressive reaching for images of the sacred, and by what means Yeats had developed sacral ideas. In other words, one would see his development as less a development from 'symbolism' to 'realism' than one from a fanciful and intermittent to a purposive and blood-laden dealing with religious forces.

To take only two of these poems. 'Easter 1916' is something of a test case for anyone seeking to analyse Yeats' development in any terms whatsoever. As compared even with the rousing 'September 1913', it obviously marks a new conception of the *dramatic* possibilities of the lyric measures; and there has been much illuminating discussion of the nature of that drama. But it is necessary to ask also what is the nature of the new and more heart-felt *piety* which the poem declares and which, indeed, permeates it:

> Hearts with one purpose alone
> Through summer and winter seem
> Enchanted to a stone
> To trouble the living stream.
> The horse that comes from the road,
> The rider, the birds that range
> From cloud to tumbling cloud,
> Minute by minute they change.

The accent of this is an emotional world away from

> Was it for this the wild geese spread
> The grey wing upon every tide;
> For this that all that blood was shed,
> For this Edward Fitzgerald died . . . .

It is not that a new composure has been gained, but that the very grounds of the national *pietas* have shifted. Unless we take the rubric, 'Transformed utterly', to be a piece of melo-dramatic arm-waving, we may indeed judge the weight of the poem to suggest that the sixteen dead men have passed over to a different order of being, from which they have the power to both startle and sanctify the imaginations of those who celebrate them.

I do not really want to argue that this is in any easily identi-fiable way a 'religious' poem; but I am certain that it is some-thing more than a kind of secular hymn devoted to recording a change of poetic mind or even an access of perceptiveness and sympathy. Yeats seems to insist that their heroic act has shaped a world nearer to the sacred possibilities which are now coming to be his chief concern. The poem is, at any rate, whether it was produced by shock or not, a marked change from the elevated complaint of 'September 1913'; it is equally far from the more simply celebrant attitude expressed in 'In Memory of Major Robert Gregory'. There, it is the variety and completeness of his subject's endowments, virtues, that make him 'as it were all life's epitome'. But in 'Easter 1916' what individual qualities are mentioned are either discreditable or treated with a certain aristocratic patronage; *they* are not the point; yet the mentioning of them as it were demonstrates that there was much to be transformed; and the transformation, which has been effected by their translation to a new order of being, is one which the poet must strive to represent.

Much had happened in Yeats and in Ireland between 1916 and the year which produced 'The Curse of Cromwell'. This poem seems to me never to have been given its critical due; critics intent on psychological realism have no doubt been diverted by its rhythm of a ballad or come-all-ye. It offers, in my opinion, a supernatural-seeming apotheosis of national feeling. And it is a fascinating poem, not only because of its roots in the Gaelic poetry of earlier centuries or because of the urgency of that national feeling, charged as it is with a certain hatred of England, but also for the abrupt and compelling shifts in attention from stanza to stanza:

> That the swordsmen and the ladies can still keep company,
> Can pay the poet for a verse and hear the fiddle sound,
> That I am still their servant though all are underground.
> > *O what of that, O what of that,*
> > *What is there left to say?*
>
> I came on a great house in the middle of the night,
> Its open lighted doorway and its windows all alight,
> And all my friends were there and made me welcome too;
> But I woke in an old ruin that the winds howled through;

The house is both a reminiscence of the great houses of the Catholic gentry whose fall was mourned by the old Gaelic poet quoted in the poem's opening stanza, and a visionary house, a symbol of Yeats' own vision of life's possibilities and defeats. The poem obviously should not be considered with the ballads and marching-tunes more or less contemporary with it, but with his greatest works. A surprising number of his customary themes come strongly into its seemingly jaunty rhythms. I would not call the result complexity, for the rhythms forbid that, but I would insist on a certain multiplicity of interests and a certain wholeness of statement together. In the passage which I have quoted, for example, we notice the strength of the insistence, 'That I am still their servant . . .', reversing yet echoing the statements of the opening stanza; and we notice how it leads, without warning but without fuss either, into the visionary power of the last stanza, so reminiscent of that in 'Crazy Jane on God'. The interest of the whole is in something much more powerful than nationalism.

It is of a piece, however, with his resorting to the past, personal and historical, for figures who would help him specify in the present his sense of the sacred and of sacred areas or dimensions in his life. These figures include heroes from the Irish mythology, of whom Cuchulain is the most noticeable, examples of the artist, of whom there are many, and champions of cultural unity, like Duke Ercole or Guidobaldo. They include also the anonymous ones who, whether in individual or in communal activity, can provide images of the desired unity of being, with its ambience of the sacred. Among the poems which call up these latter figures are two delightful poems, which are seldom included among his greatest but which never fail to move me, and for the reaons, I think, that Yeats intended; they are 'The Fisherman' and 'At Galway Races'.

In both of these Yeats has, so to speak, generalised and concentrated his sympathy for a whole people and for his friends among that people. 'The Fisherman' seems to me remarkable for the effectiveness of its rhythms, and all the more so since they are so unobtrusively developed. Its end repeats and extends its beginning, most strongly because the evocation of this figure who combines in his solitary stance the virtues of action and those of contemplation provides the context for a powerful indictment of those forces in society which tell against the virtues represented in him:

> The beating down of the wise
> And great Art beaten down.

But the evocation of the figure himself is perhaps the chief virtue of the poem:

> Maybe a twelvemonth since
> Suddenly I began
> In scorn of this audience,
> Imagining a man,
> And his sun-freckled face,
> And grey Connemara cloth,
> Climbing up to a place
> Where stone is dark under froth,
> And the down-turn of his wrist
> When the flies drop in the stream;
> A man who does not exist,
> A man who is but a dream;

> And cried, 'Before I am old
> I shall have written him one
> Poem maybe as cold
> And passionate as the dawn!

It is perhaps less 'dream' than memory concentrated into vision; and the tribute which is actually written is hardly 'cold'; it is, on the contrary, a triumph of a particularly urgent sort of sympathy.

What is presented in an individual in this poem is a very similar awareness of the possibilities of life to that created in communal terms in 'At Galway Races':

> There where the course is,
> Delight makes all of the one mind,
> The riders upon the galloping horses,
> The crowd that closes in behind:
> We, too, had good attendance once,
> Hearers and hearteners of the work;
> Aye, horsemen for companions,
> Before the merchant and the clerk
> Breathed on the world with timid breath.
> Sing on: somewhere at some new moon,
> We'll learn that sleeping is not death,
> Hearing the whole earth change its tune,
> Its flesh being wild, and it again
> Crying aloud as the racecourse is,
> And we find hearteners among men
> That ride upon horses.

It is, of course, something of a sport in Yeats' *œuvre*; one does not associate him with the Silver Ring; but it is a lovely, innocent invocation, from which, interestingly enough, all sense of horse-racing as a *contest* has disappeared, to be replaced by a sense of communal joy in action, and in which even the 'timid breath' seems harmless. Its rhythm is to a degree mimetic, horses and crowd move in its lines, but with the sort of weightless unemphatic movement they might take in a child's story.

I make this remark in no critical spirit, but to suggest that the 'radical innocence' Yeats wanted the soul to recover can be recovered in his own poetry by more ways than one; if it is got sometimes by great labour, it can also be got, as here, by letting the world sing itself. And again that rhythm is more delicate than its mimetic function would suggest; there is a certain genius, for example, in the choice of 'upon' in the third line in preference to 'on'.

But anonymity of the subject rules here, and is in part responsible for the active presence of that innocence. And such anonymity is not characteristic of his invocation of the past. On the contrary, when he calls up friends and heroes, enemies and anti-heroes, the point of his dramatic method of treatment is precisely to deny them anonymity. They must be specific, they must be named, they must be given particular associations and powers, in order that, in attaining the status of symbol or representative image they may become more than they were. No other poet (not even Pound) has this fascination with and need for actual names. Not that Yeats always names his subjects; but he usually does; and he almost always identifies them in such a way as to enable us to name them, if we want to. As in the famous ending to 'Friends', the function of this identification becomes plain; it is to enable him to specify the powers (sacral and life-giving) with which he associates them in the unending drama of his own life:

> And what of her that took
> All till my youth was gone
> With scarce a pitying look?
> How could I praise that one?
> When day begins to break
> I count my good and bad,
> Being wakeful for her sake,
> Remembering what she had,
> What eagle look still shows,
> While up from my heart's root

So great a sweetness flows
I shake from head to foot.

The end is sacred: the memory of friendship, and still more of love, is an opening on to the transcendent, but one which moves from within the whole body and being of the poet; and once more we are forced to notice the rhythm, here seemingly so curt, which creates this sense by prolonging statement into a cadence of finality.

Of the more formal or ceremonial callings-up of named figures, perhaps the two most obvious are 'In Memory of Major Robert Gregory' and 'All Souls Night', the first a ritual of praise for a dead 'hero' and 'perfect man', the second a ceremony of actual conjuring of ghosts which, I think it not unfair to say, are those of anti-heroes. The first has always seemed to me harmed by the relative simple-mindedness, the good-hearted absolutism, of its celebration; and certainly the terms in which Gregory is praised fall far short of any viable concept of the sacred. The second, which is as preternatural as Old Nick, seems, though a much more interesting and moving poem, to have the complementary fault. There is something perverse and willed about the drama of preternatural forces in it; and unfortunately MacGregor Mather (oddly like Robert Gregory in this, if in nothing else) comes to seem a quite uninteresting individual. What *is* interesting is the melodramatic deliberateness of Yeats' own posture as a ghost-raiser, his half-ironical conviction of his own powers.

These two poems are instructive in suggesting that it is not when he most deliberately adopts the bard's or conjurer's role that Yeats achieves the most compelling note of celebration. In a way, he is both too dramatic and too lyrical a poet to start anywhere but *in medias res*, the *res* being his own personal situation and feelings. And the poems in which we can most helpfully locate his sense of the sacredness of his friends and their associations are probably 'Coole Park 1929', 'Coole and

Ballylee, 1931', and 'The Municipal Gallery Revisited'.

I mention these poems not because I want to give any formal analysis of them but because I think it illuminating to juxtapose them as a group with 'Sailing to Byzantium', a poem in which a quite different sense of and concern for the sacred are evident. I may add, a much more valuable sense and concern, for the two Coole Park poems are threatened by sentimentality, and 'The Municipal Gallery Revisited' by the violence of an attempt to do that impossible thing, to *describe* an emotion.

'Coole Park, 1929', which seems to me much the lesser poem, has a greater smoothness, and its motive-power seems, in fact, to say an *Ave atque Vale* to Lady Gregory in her role specifically of hostess. Of course, it is no simple nostalgia that produces

> Thoughts long knitted into a single thought,
> A dance-like glory that those walls begot,

or

> Back turned upon the brightness of the sun
> And all the sensuality of the shade—

but the spirit that moves with a brooding lightness through the poem is one of enclosure: this place, this past, this company, these people are seen as self-enclosed. It is not until the second poem that their importance is recognised, as it were, in the context of an action not theirs; it is not loss, but foundered promise, that animates the lines, and loveliness becomes associated with sanctity.[1] In fact, the basic suggestions of the opening and closing stanzas enforce the feeling that what has

---

[1] It is interesting that the note quoted by Thomas Parkinson as a 'prose summary' to guide Yeats in his writing of 'Coole Park, 1929' actually has a more forceful relevance to the second poem. V. Parkinson: Vestiges of Creation: *The Sewanee Review*, Vol. LXIX, Winter 1961, p. 84. Indeed, the whole of this important article is relevant to my argument.

gone is not just friendship—but communal power and capability. What is at stake is history: the stress on unity of being, and on its sacredness, is less domestic. And of course it is this process of generalising and sacralising which is extended in the third of the poems, 'The Municipal Gallery Revisited'. The portraits seen in the Dublin gallery remind us that 'that self-same excellence' cannot come again; but for all that, the gallery is a 'hallowed place'; the gestures it establishes in paint are sacred ones, an attempt to achieve that sacred condition 'Unity of Being':

> You that would judge me, do not judge alone
> This book or that, come to this hallowed place
> Where my friends' portraits hang and look thereon;
> Ireland's history in their lineaments trace;
> Think where man's glory most begins and ends,
> And say my glory was I had such friends.

The magnificence of this is in its noble and heartfelt directness; yet one notices the intensity of its concern with beginnings and endings, and is brought to consider how far that is a concern for something deeper than is exemplified in Major Robert Gregory, for something which invites the imagination, of reader as of poet, to open on to the transcendent.

IV

But Yeats' greatness as a religious poet is not seen fully even in poems of that kind. Personally, I consider any one of them much less great than 'The Man and the Echo' or 'Meditations in Time of Civil War'. And they do not allow for the immediacy or power of religious feeling which we get in poems of a different kind, and most markedly in 'Sailing to Byzantium'. I am referring to poems in which, whether by emphasis on Yeats himself or by invocation of an imagined figure like Crazy Jane, the visionary faculty itself is affirmed as sacred. I put the matter in these terms because I do not want to encourage the notion of Yeats-as-bard; in these poems, in 'Among School Children', 'Lapis Lazuli', 'Crazy Jane and Jack the Journeyman', 'Crazy Jane on God', and in several others besides 'Sailing to Byzantium', we have not bardic utterance, the excitement of noble speech, but a creation of the process of visionary perception in the act of affirming its possibility or necessity.

This quality can perhaps be shown by comparing 'Crazy Jane on God' with an effective and moving lyric which is not far removed from it in time, 'Quarrel in Old Age':

> Where had her sweetness gone?
> What fanatics invent
> In this blind bitter town,
> Fantasy or incident
> Not worth thinking of,
> Put her in a rage.
> I had forgiven enough
> That had forgiven old age.
>
> All lives that has lived;
> So much is certain;
> Old sages were not deceived:
> Somewhere beyond the curtain
> Of distorting days
> Lives that lonely thing
> That shone before these eyes
> Targeted, trod like Spring.

It is a finely shaped poem, and the first stanza is more subtle than at first appears. But it is also a poem which seeks to lead statement to culminate in religious or visionary suggestion; and since that is so, its very logic invites one to scrutinise the language in which the suggestion is introduced. One's conclusion might well be that the second, visionary stanza is too smooth for its own good, and that the affirmations made in it are no more than a momentary 'comforter'. In a way, the failure, inoffensive as it is, is reinforced by the loveliness of the two final lines, for, though they refer to a life lived in another world, their force comes from their reminding us only of this world. With 'Crazy Jane on God', the process is of a quite different sort, and the success complementary to the other poem's failure:

> That lover of a night
> Came when he would,
> Went in the dawning light
> Whether I would or no;
> Men come, men go;
> *All things remain in God.*
>
> Banners choke the sky;
> Men-at-arms tread;
> Armoured horses neigh
> Where the great battle was
> In the narrow pass:
> *All things remain in God.*
>
> Before their eyes a house
> That from childhood stood
> Uninhabited, ruinous,
> Suddenly lit up
> From door to top:
> *All things remain in God.*
>
> I had wild Jack for a lover;
> Though like a road
> That men pass over
> My body makes no moan
> But sings on:
> *All things remain in God.*

This marvellous poem has evaded praise, probably because of its obscurity; there is little here that could be 'explained' where it does not explain itself. As I earlier suggested, it has an affinity with 'The Curse of Cromwell' in more than one respect. Yet it differs from that poem in substituting for a certain historical romanticism a carnality which is doubly compelling in its power to suggest an order of being that is distinguishable, though not necessarily separable, from the bodily. It mixes modes of apprehension in a seemingly arbitrary way, but is actually directed to establishing a hair-raising complexity of instantaneous perceptions. In feigning a 'mad' and dissociated vision, it in fact creates a vision whose elements fuse by a sort of immediacy of indirection. The strangeness of that 'lover of a night' leads as though naturally to other strangenesses, all of them associated in the evocation of God as Great Memory. No doubt it leaves questions with us: *whose* eyes, for example, are referred to in the third stanza? Yet there seems no need of answers, when the refrain so tightly binds the moments of vision together. However brief the lines, the movement of the poem is really one of expansion, an expansion of sexual into religious feeling by rapidity of associations; the movement of 'Quarrel in Old Age' is one of problem and answer, and it is jeopardised by the relative weakness of the answer. Yet the metaphysical affirmation is, abstractly speaking, the same in both cases.

The achievement of poems such as this one is particularly interesting when it is put in the context of 'Sailing to Byzantium'. Thanks to the work of Curtis Bradford, we now know through what changes of conception this poem passed before reaching its final splendid version. And we now have the evidence to suggest what Yeats meant *in this poem* by Byzantium: evidence which makes it clear that, in asserting the necessity for a new way of imaginative life, Yeats is not merely opting for 'art' over 'life'. In his questing imagination, sixth-century Byzantium and the Ravenna mosaics come together to create a total image of a new life; as two scholars say:

> The whole city, with its great dome and its mosaics which defy nature and assert transcendence, and its theologically rooted and synthetic culture, can serve the poet as an image of

the Heavenly City and the state of the soul when it is 'out of nature'.[1]

This seems to me to indicate the point at which we may start; Byzantium in this poem provides a dual reference to a state of living blessedness, of which one artistic tradition is a representative and symbol. From many passages in his prose works, we know how Yeats pretty consistently conceived Byzantium:

> I think that in early Byzantium, maybe never before or since in recorded history, religious, aesthetic and practical life were one, that architect and artificers—though not, it may be, poets, for language had been the instrument of controversy and must have grown abstract—spoke to the multitude and the few alike. The painter, the mosaic worker, the worker in gold and silver, the illuminator of sacred books, were almost impersonal, almost perhaps without the consciousness of individual design, absorbed in their subject-matter and that the vision of a whole people.

One must emphasise that the poem is not to be taken as a versifying, a verse-endorsement, of this prose judgment. Nor is this judgment to be taken as a gloss on the poem. But if we need a comment which casts a bright passing light on certain emphases in the poem, then this is it. Poems like 'A Prayer for My Daughter' are ritualistic in a fairly obvious sense, and moral in a fairly obvious sense. They recommend goals in terms which are unequivocally ethical. 'Sailing to Byzantium' cannot be accounted for in those terms; its dialectic is less overt because it comes from a deeper source of energies. But its dramatic quality is much more powerful, largely because it is so much more compressed. Here is Yeats facing with his poetic powers at their highest pitch the agonising realisation that the physical energies he has come increasingly to rely on must inevitably be abandoned, and that the labour of replacing them with higher energies must be immediate and intense.

[1] D. J. Gordon and Ian Fletcher: Byzantium: reprinted in the Twentieth Century Views *Yeats* (ed. John Unterecker). Prentice-Hall, 1963, p. 136.

Consequently, the opening gesture of rejection is quite violent, and the dialectic between physical and spiritual energies is expressed in an almost hypnotic pace and rhythm:

> That is no country for old men. The young
> In one another's arms, birds in the trees,
> —Those dying generations—at their song,
> The salmon-falls, the mackerel-crowded seas,
> Fish, flesh, or fowl, commend all summer long
> Whatever is begotten, born, and dies.
> Caught in that sensual music all neglect
> Monuments of unageing intellect.

Anyone who yields himself, however self-critically, to the power of the opening gesture, 'That is no country for old men . . .', will see that it is sudden, almost desperate, in its force. The unexplained 'That' is a sign of the completeness of the renunciation; it is a renunciation not of a single real country of Ireland, not of an idea either, but of a commitment to a way of seeing, living, and feeling. And the interesting thing is that, after the renunciatory gesture of these few words, the verse becomes not bitter or explanatory but celebrant. It is the flux of physical passion which the first stanza celebrates, even while it is announcing the need for a renunciation of it. 'The young/In one another's arms, birds in the trees' is higher in pitch than the opening words, and more expansive in its movement. In the third line, the essential ambivalence of the whole poem is represented at a quite simple level, in the breaking up of the expansive celebration by 'Those dying generations'. Yeats would be false to his own sense of the issues if he allowed the note of celebration to sound unchecked; but it must be sounded. After this intervention, as though in answer to his self-dramatising doubt of it, the whole power of natural life is presented: life at its moments of physical realisation. The poetry here is about flux, but it presents that flux as a sort of ceremony. For the tone rises again after 'song', and the next three lines flow to a climax, and ebb to the lingering regret of

'Whatever is begotten, born, and dies'.

In the recurrence of the note of regret at the end of this stanza, it seems to me that Yeats is urging a depreciated case. The best he can for the moment say about the intellect is that it is 'unageing'; and it has only 'monuments' to set against the passion of physical living. The superb half-stop rhythm—Neglect/Monuments'—enforces this sense of ambivalence in his case for intellect. Throughout the poem's first six lines, it is a 'sensual music' that predominates. It is the early supremacy of that music which establishes the dialectical movement and brings a note of celebration and of generalisation out of the very personal drama which has been so immediately presented; for Yeats has now to espouse and enact a much fuller sense of 'intellect' than he has so far shown. The rest of the poem is devoted to this. In the next three stanzas, the claims of intellect are pressed; and intellect itself is presented to us in a way which makes us see it as transcending any mere process of logic, of 'thinking things out', or of 'coming to terms with old age'.

The bridge between the celebration of what must be renounced and the celebration of what must be discovered or created is, of course, the very understandable bitterness of the second stanza. But we find a hint there of the real nature of the thing he is to espouse:

. . . unless
Soul clap its hands and sing, and louder sing
For every tatter in its mortal dress. . . .

Not logic, but the soul's singing; the echo from Blake shows that Yeats is aiming at a superior awareness of life, and the joy which springs from that awareness. And fully mature song, for him, arises only from an order lapped in self-contemplation, from a Unity of Being. So 'sailing the seas' is an image not merely of rejection, or even of mental pilgrimage, but of commitment to a new order, a new state of the soul and imagination.

In the third stanza the celebration of spirit and imagination reaches its height; and what had earlier appeared as a lively order appears as a sacred one:

> O sages standing in God's holy fire
> As in the gold mosaic of a wall,
> Come from the holy fire, perne in a gyre,
> And be the singing-masters of my soul.
> Consume my heart away. . . .

It is the artist-saints, the sanctified artificers of historic Byzantium, who alone will teach the soul to sing. Here Yeats' prose statement becomes most relevant. Byzantium was for him a civilisation in which all activities—religious, philosophical, artistic, and practical—were unified in the one sacred order. An achieved Unity of Being is the real singing-master; perhaps it is the only master that a modern poet can usefully know.

It is important to recognise that Yeats is not seeking refuge in the contemplation of Byzantine art at the safe distance of a thousand years from the passion that went to achieve it. He is not rejecting life in favour of art at all. It is not escape from being that he seeks, but fullness of being. The ambiguity of the stanza's opening is very significant. He cries out not to the painted saints but to the real ones '. . . standing in God's holy fire/*As in* the gold mosaic of a wall'. And he cries out to them not for consolation, but for release, self-transcendence; their fire will purge him, not warm him. It is not artistic modes or surfaces that concern him, but the unified and sacred energies which Byzantine art fixes and expresses. His concern is for the discovering, or the creating in himself, of a unified sacred energy: not historical Byzantium, which is irrecoverable, but a personal imaginative equivalent to it, fed by Byzantium. So, to purge him, the artist-saints must 'perne in a gyre', come down the long winding cone of history. The rapidity and force of this phrase express the urgency with which he calls on them to do so. At the end of the stanza, the sudden savage personalising of the issues serves, too, to make the question of self-commitment an urgent one:

> . . . sick with desire
> And fastened to a dying animal,
> It knows not what it is.

This savagery of self-disgust is part of the dialectical answer to the first stanza. But it is not the whole answer; that is to be sought in a state 'out of nature', in the 'artifice of eternity'.

The stress of these phrases provides a difficulty. What is meant by 'out of nature'? In what sense is eternity an 'artifice'? The release from bodily flux ('out of nature') may mean actual death, or it may mean the attainment of a state of being ruled by the sanctified imagination. What is more interesting is the almost playful way in which the final stanza opens, and the comparatively relaxed tone of the poem's closing movement. 'When I'm at last released from the body's tyranny, I'd like to be an artificial bird'. There is something of subtle irony about this, something almost of an Irish joke which has provided, and still provides, a stumbling-block to the earnest reader. The problem is one of poise in reading. We must take the suggestion seriously, but the poem makes it difficult for us to do so, since it invites us to take it literally. And obviously it would be absurd to take it too literally; even believers in reincarnation seldom envisage themselves in a future life as being not so much reborn as remade. But perhaps it is Yeats' way of insisting that sacred poets *are* made and not born: self-created in and through the discipline of the imagination. He may be seeking, in a half-serious half-joking way, to define the terms on which, in his old age, he can enter his Byzantium. And the bird's function is more important than its artificiality; it is the created artifact which stimulates, even prophesies, while it seems only to entertain. It is thus a symbol of the poet freed from the stress of his personal tensions.

This last stanza is, despite its relatively relaxed tone, cele-brant as well. It is in some ways not immediately satisfying, because we are presented with an image of life so stylised and hierarchical that the stylisation threatens to negate the life. Yeats barely avoids the danger; and his emphasis on artificiality is probably a weakness in the poem. But, while a brittle gold-ness does dominate the stanza, it does so chiefly as a visual and tactile impression. The rhythm remains both flexible and vital, affirming a quality of living. Gold is, after all, the tradi-tional colour of eternity; and the poet does create something of this sense of it. And the poem closes, after all, with the stress on prophecy. The sanctified imagination does not reject temporal life, the process of flux and change; it simply adopts a different and superior role towards it. The poet is released; he is not emasculated.

Again we see that the note of 'custom and ceremony', which it would be dangerously easy to take as an anti-life quality in poetry, is present in this poem, and contributes to its value. True, its force is of a rather different sort from that in lesser poems; for here it is balanced by a re-presentation of unthinking pulsing life, as well as by the notes of sudden over-whelming exasperation and self-contempt which occur in stanzas II and III.

The greatness of the poem is that it sets both cases so powerfully, and establishes so real a tension between stanza I and stanzas III and IV. It resolves the conflict between passion-ate bodily life and the imagination not so much by statement as by the authority of its rhythm which, in establishing the dialectic, transcends its terms. The 'sensual music' does not die after the first stanza; it echoes throughout the poem. Both cases are powerfully enacted; the poem is not 'moral' in the sense that it contrasts one way of life to another in such terms as to make a choice between them inevitable. The life of the body is by no means deliberately depreciated; it is deliberately celebrated. Yet, both cases set, Yeats opts for one of them; his choice is enhanced by its necessity, and by the near-desperation with which he recognises it. It is a tribute to the poem that the final effect which we take from it is not desperation but a sense of a purposive fullness of life, which the subdued and varied exultation of stanzas III and IV helps to establish. Above all, we take away the sense of a completed movement of the spirit and the senses affirming a sacred possibility which the facts of living would seem to deny.

It is, of course, an appeal to the past quite different from that in any of the other poems I have dealt with; for *this* past is to be created in the personal future. Its creation of a sense of the sacred is also different, in ways which I hope I have indicated. In the other poems, it was not that he could not distinguish between ancient heroes, Renaissance men, contemporary acquaintances, and old friends or loves. Of course he could; but they all perform a similar function for his poetry, even if they do not play the same roles in it or in his life. He saw them as leading his imagination outward to the completion whose possibility they all represent. They are, in short, witnesses. And the completion which they represent as possibility is precisely that which, in 'Sailing to Byzantium', he makes such an heroic attempt to create as present imaginative fact. We may remember also that, in more than one place, he takes his own body as a witness, or a sign of the sacred: 'I shake from head to foot', 'My body on a sudden blazed'. That, too, gets its equivalent in the rapid, powerful dialectic of 'Sailing to Byzantium'. Hopkins saw the world as stressed with God's presence, 'charged with the grandeur of God'. Yeats saw it as uncovering God, whether by the long process of meditation or by the sudden blaze of an imagination stretched to its uttermost yet strong with bodily presence. In uncovering God, he is himself within the sacred company that his poetry creates and celebrates.

CHAPTER IX

T. S. Eliot: The Growth of Vision

'Like all of Valery's poetry, it is impersonal in the sense that personal emotion, personal experience, is extended and completed in something impersonal—not in the sense of something divorced from personal experience and passion. . . .'—T. S. Eliot: Introduction to *Le Serpent*

I

THE death of T. S. Eliot agitated a thousand complacencies; and a hundred writers of obituaries must have quietly wondered why their tributes sounded a faint note of irrelevance. The truth is that many whose self-imposed duty it was to remind the public had forgotten in what ways Eliot was great, and many others had never learnt it. Certainly, if we compare his case with that of Yeats, we can see an interesting lack of agreement. Almost everyone agrees on the broad lines of an account of Yeats' development; but many critics of Eliot would seem to deny that he had developed at all, in any sense that we might admire. Yet, reading even those obituaries, one is struck afresh by the sense that he haunts English poetry and criticism, indeed he haunts European culture, like some benevolent yet disturbing spectre of its own *raison d'etre*; and anyone who offers to try and arrive at some sensible, albeit personal, account of his greatness has to take up directly the question of his development, its phases, its ambiguities, and its profundity. Personally, I think we are confronted with the most ambitiously experimental religious poet since Wordsworth. For, if it was 'J. Alfred Prufrock' and 'The Waste Land' that accomplished the revolution in the sensibility of a generation, it is *Four Quartets* that is the peak of his personal achievement as a poet.

Four quartets, and 'Little Gidding' in particular. It has been clear for many years to what extent the spirit, and even the nervous system, of European man vibrates not only with the themes but with the harmonies, the very phrasing, of 'The Waste Land'; so I find it all the more heartening to see, from the special Eliot issues of *The Sewanee Review* and *The Review*, how deeply the Quartets have entered that same consciousness to become acclimatised and naturalised there, though no doubt with less emphasis on the nervous system. I shall be arguing that the Quartets are the culmination of a poetic process which took a whole creative lifetime to develop; and in doing so, I shall argue also that there is a development within *Four Quartets* paralleling or answering to a development in his poetic *œuvre*: a development, in each case, if not from the problem to the answer (for such terms seem to get us nowhere in the discussion of poetry), at any rate from the pilot project to the full experiment, or from the hypothesis to the synthesis.

As with most great poets, there is both a continuity and a discontinuity between the various stages of that development. *Four Quartets* are much less 'religious' in any limiting sense than the earlier poems, and it is true that many people spontaneously use the word 'philosophical' rather than the word 'religious' about them; yet as a religious expression and exploration they seem to me much the most satisfying of his poems. Not that they are insistently religious at all; in fact, they are less so than most of the earlier poems because they are much less the expression of a need for the consolations of religious self-commitment. At the same time, they are more fully the product of a self-questioning and hence, presumably, of some personal need, a need which the great authority of the rhythms declares as a need less to console than to know and to place the self.

At every important stage of Eliot's growth, it is as though he were troubled by a double thought, strained at the depths of his being by a double question: What *must* this poetry be?

and How *may* this poetry be religious? Freedom and the recognition of necessity work together in every poet's psyche; in
Eliot's the struggle was Antaeus-like. At first sight he would
seem to have been luckier than Yeats, for he knew, or was
convinced that he knew, precisely what the sacred is and
where it is to be found. In a sense this is true; we are in no
doubt of his allegiances or of his theology. But in another and
deeper sense, I think the truth is precisely the opposite: he
had a mind too scrupulous, senses too palpitant, a spirit too
aware of intangibles, to assume anything very much for very
long about his own access to the sacred; and the doubt, the
self-doubt, seems to be particularly intense when he is actually
forming a poem in which the sense of that access, and of its
object, may itself be created. In his prose there are many
examples of smugness; in his poetry there are almost none.
Certainly, he did not have, as Yeats to his great benefit came
to have, the reassuring challenge of believing that the poet
himself is a *vates*, and that his creative acts or sayings are themselves sacred. Both Eliot's faith and his doubt were of a quite
different order, indeed of a quite different psychological cast.
His faith was in the presence of an ultimate pattern, however
hard that is to apprehend, much less to comprehend; and his
doubt was in the integrity of the human venture as it took
shape under the shadow and towards the composition of that
pattern. Faith and doubt are, in Eliot's poetry, the bright
misty outline of each other; and, since it is *pattern*, not instantaneous revelation, that is in question, there is a dialectic in
each of his major works between form and fragmentation, the
establishment of pattern and the capture of the elusive moment.
In other words, to echo what he himself said of 'In Memoriam',
his faith has a much deeper dimension of doubt than Yeats';
so his religious poetry is much more a matter of self-scrutiny,
and his development within it much more a matter of adapta-
tion to the pressures of self-scrutiny. It is not surprising that he
developed seemingly by fits and starts, frightening advances

and tentative withdrawals, yet actually with an underlying logic which is daunting in its force, and perhaps in its uniqueness.

II

The questions which we must ask about *Four Quartets* teem with paradoxes. We note, for example, that the thinking and feeling in them are much more Eliot's own than previously; he does not rely on other people's sense of horror and deprivation to get a result which is little more than a set of religio-poetic 'effects', as he does recurrently in *Murder in the Cathedral*; nor does he rely on the Church's liturgy to produce what is little more than a set of institutional stock-responses, as he does in parts of *Ash-Wednesday*. We have the sense of a man thrown back to a surprising degree on his own resources, speaking (and sometimes intoning) in his own voice, confronting with a profound honesty the question posed by his whole being; yet the total effect of this confrontation, as we witness it in the poems, is much less subjective than in *Ash-Wednesday*, more vibrant with a certain communal experience which is sensed in or behind it.

For the first time, Eliot brings himself unequivocally into his poetry, dramatises his presence there and analyses his own stance. His work is religious in that it is a creation of a sense of the religious *subject*, of the self as actively subject to the forces which it tries to answer and apprehend. The meditation is both prolonged and expansive; it both arises from philosophical questionings and is rooted in individual circumstance; it is theological in its orientation yet non-proselytising in its spirit. Here, more than anywhere else in his poetry, we find the evidence for Michael Hamburger's contention that 'he was a mystic before he was an orthodox Christian', and that whatever discarnational quality we find in his poetry is the result of *that*: not of an orthodoxy or even of a temperament but of a belief and a mental habit which cannot be fully expressed in terms of either. At the same time, it is obvious that

Eliot is the crucial case in our era of a poet who has tried to solve the general religious dilemma from within the patterns of Christian orthodoxy, not by reducing the problems to fit the pattern but by expanding the pattern to comprehend the problems. That expansion of the orthodox pattern is not an addition of doctrines but an expansion and examination of sensibility; and it is not seen fully, it is not even seen clearly as such, until 'Little Gidding' completes the tentative patterns of *Four Quartets*. To that extent, it is an unusual work within his *œuvre*, and it cannot help making us conscious of the discontinuities in his development.

At the same time, there are continuities too. Northrop Frye has pointed out that in 'The Waste Land' as in *Four Quartets* 'there is an elaborate imagery of the four elements', and that in fact there is throughout his work a recurring preoccupation with seasonal and other cycles. Stephen Spender, noting the dates of their composition, sees a close relation between the cultural circumstances of 'The Waste Land' and those of at least the last three of the Quartets; and he suggests that 'the objectivization of his poetry towards which Eliot strove came nearest to realization when the poetry was concerned with an actual crisis of civilization'. For my part, I would add that both are religious poems, in a sense yet to be defined, and that the continuity between them is of a sort which is unusual in a poet's *œuvre*, in that the later poem partly inverts and partly completes the former, yet in a mode so different that it is hard for the casual reader to accept that they have anything to do with each other.

Many people would agree with this contention; the problem is not to make it but to do the analysis which will support it. In other circumstances, one might feel obliged to consider *Four Quartets* in the total pattern which they compose, deliberate, diversified, and complex as it is; for the pattern is that provided by the asking and defining, the repeating and expanding and re-defining, of certain questions about the possibility that there is a pattern in human life. As with his *œuvre* as a whole, so with *Four Quartets*: without the tentative formulations and the provisional answers on which he rests at different moments, there could be no culmination at all, and therefore no possibility of a satisfying final definition. One would like to trace out in detail the logic of this process. Yet it is usually possible to say something useful without trying to say everything possible. Many of the questions I want to raise about the Quartets are better asked at the local level, where the answers will not be jeopardised by the sheer complexity of the achievement and the sheer strain of the critical task. And they are best asked of 'Little Gidding', whose greatness can be most clearly seen, I think, by comparing it with 'The Waste Land' and 'Ash-Wednesday'.

From the beginning we see in his poetry a careful avoidance of personal emotion, and an interesting failure to ward off subjectivity. For that reason, if for no other, I feel it is quite false to judge that his strength lies in social diagnosis. Some of his poetry in that kind is undoubtedly strong, but for one thing there is usually a note of self-disgust in the attack on social *mores*, and for another the attack is usually developed in a context whose resonances are of quite a different sort, sometimes warranting the adjective 'lyrical', sometimes even suggesting the word 'heroic'. Certainly this is not the case in such highly accomplished apprentice work as 'Prufrock' and 'Portrait of a Lady'. Both of these are poems which present and analyse an emotional condition, significantly one either of emotional paralysis or of emotional confusion. But they both exist not to 'express' any emotion of the author's but to analyse an emotion of their characters'; and they do even that indirectly, by analysing the social manners, the tone, the pitch, the rhythm of the world in which the characters are both native and alienated.

It is only in that limited sense that their concern is 'social': they are concerned with emotional privation experienced in a world defined by a manner. And if they have not the social breadth of 'The Waste Land', they have little, either, of that resonance which I have called sometimes lyrical, sometimes almost heroic, and of which one splendid example will be found in the following:

> The time is now propitious, as he guesses,
> The meal is ended, she is bored and tired,
> Endeavours to engage her in caresses
> Which still are unreproved, if undesired.
> Flushed and decided, he assaults at once;
> Exploring hands encounter no defence;
> His vanity requires no response,
> And makes a welcome of indifference.
> (And I Tiresias have foresuffered all
> Enacted on this same divan or bed;
> I who have sat by Thebes below the wall
> And walked among the lowest of the dead).

It could be said that there is a certain snobbery in this whole episode of the typist, that the 'situation' is rigged to produce too pat a judgment and too easy a disgust, that the rhymes fall with a curtness at once proselytising and overbred, that the relevance of the *voyeur* Tiresias to the required judgment is not established, and that what called for compassion has been answered with cynicism. But it could not, I think, be said that the episode is merely constricting to the emotions, or that the note, at once heroic and haunting, struck by the surely liberating movement of Tiresias' voice, has been imported only to reinforce the social diagnosis or to justify the disgust. In fact, it is not only the 'lowest' dead that are in question, or *these* dead, of this living Hades, but the dead of Thebes. In other words, a question is posed as much as a judgment is invited; it is a question about the relations of orders of experience which seem antithetical; and it is posed in the very resonance which I have called at once haunting and heroic.

The fact is that the preoccupations which we see as social

or psychological are, in 'The Waste Land', religious as well; and their religious character is seen not only in what we can extrapolate of the poem's 'themes' but also in what we respond to in the great, albeit confusing, variety of its resonances. In this section, for example, there is Tiresias with his evocation of Thebes; but there is also the *milieu*

> where the walls
> Of Magnus Martyr hold
> Inexplicable splendour of Ionian white and gold.

The question posed by the poem has to do, among many other things, with the nature and the possibility of that splendour.

Admittedly, in one sense the poem seems to answer its own question or, rather, to give two conflicting answers to it: that splendour is impossible, and that it is possible only in the Sanskrit invocations of the poem's close: which is to say, that it is not 'really' possible. But I think its quality of questioning is more important than any answers it suggests. The religious concern is of an unusual sort, and it is partly concealed by the heavy overlay of technical devices. Certainly the poem is much more than the representative voicing of a common disillusionment which it was once taken to be; but neither is it chiefly the 'symbolic' acting-out of a subjective sexual dilemma which one or two rather prurient critics have read into it. It is, in an extremely restricted sense, a religious poem, which binds its sections together by a theme of religious search, and seeks to affirm religious meaning by negation, by showing the dreariness associated with its absence. And it disguises the religious nature of the search by using anthropological and sociological terms to analyse the malaise of the civilisation in which it was produced.

I think it could be shown that 'The Waste Land' is not the splendidly impersonal analysis of the state of a civilisation which people have often taken it to be; the poet's personal preoccupations do intrude, and the poem becomes a releasing, an acting-out, of tensions; its seeming impersonality is the result of a strategy undertaken to conceal, from Eliot himself as much as from his readers, the personal nature of those preoccupations. One can give a half-hearted assent to the claim that its parts work together organically to achieve a structural unity, and yet be nagged by the sense that that unity is pretty mechanical in its total effect. And I think it could be shown that those people are wrong who maintain that it is a religious poem of a remarkably positive sort, full of subtle religious affirmations; on the contrary, its great vigour and scope come not from any affirmation or from the power of values affirmed, but from the force with which a scarified and searching sensibility feels the emptiness of modern life. It *is* a search, but its vigour is the vigour of its rejections. It is not regeneration that is dramatically presented in its final section, but a compulsive clinging to the words like 'water' which might be able to give some poetic reality to the idea or hope of regeneration. The positive quality represented by water is felt more in the stressing of water's absence than in the force with which the coming of rain is presented. That rain, after all, cannot be imagined as bringing fruitfulness to the 'young man carbuncular', to Phlebas the Phoenician, or to Mr. Eugenides; the images of release, and their religious overtones, are offered to us as though for their own sake; and the author's voice, or that of his *persona*, dwindles and lapses at last into the distracting noises of a civilisation which his Hindu exhortations cannot, in the last resort, enliven or control. In other words (and I invoke words which have lately been used pretty liberally about Eliot's early work) 'The Waste Land' seems to be neither an anti-Christian poem wearing its frustration on its sleeve nor a Christian poem in heavy disguise, but a compulsive yet still *pre*-Christian one.

But the problem of Eliot's religious poetry arises most acutely with the explicitly Christian poems, and especially with the first of them, 'Ash-Wednesday'. Between 'The Waste

Land' and this poem a new quality enters his poetry as unmistakably as it enters his prose—a quality suggesting that he has identified himself thoroughly with the Church of England as a cultural institution, and has invested a lot of emotional capital in the identification. He becomes for a while a religious poet whose note is more ecclesiastical than Christian; he relies on the Church to give him the impersonality, the imperviousness to the ebb-and-flow of emotion, that he so badly wants. Anglo-Catholicism becomes less a vision of the world than an institution and an ideology; one is less conscious of the life it gives him than of the loyalties which he feels it exacts from him. In *Murder in the Cathedral*, he subdues his voice not to the sexless yet occasionally very moving tone of Tiresias the eclectic observer but to the tone of Anglican ritual. To impersonalise here means to institutionalise. There is something in common between *Murder in the Cathedral* and 'Thoughts after Lambeth'.

This is not true of 'Ash-Wednesday' in the same way or to the same degree. But that poem is, if anything, an institutional work in an even more disturbing way, if only because the emotional effort of producing it is obviously so much more intense and anguished. It is very far from being what its title suggests, a devout meditation on the place and significance of Lent in the procession of the liturgical seasons. On the contrary, it is in a way the most explicitly personal, the most openly emotional, of all Eliot's poems. It is the exploration of a personal condition which he sees as a period of emotional aridity, the beginning of a *subjective* Lent. It is an emotional cry of emotional deprivation and of a hope for release from it. The trouble is that the personal nature of the emotion is not declared, but is disguised as the traditional cry of the Christian people beseeching its God. 'Impersonality' now becomes a poaching on the stored-up experience of the Church: a poaching, not because he is not entitled to draw on that experience and these perspectives but because he uses them to disguise rather than to define his own plight.

The treating of a personal situation in terms of institutionalised religious experience is nothing new, of course; Eliot did
not invent it. Nor was he the first to use it too glibly. What I
mean by 'disguise' can be seen in the fragmentary nature of the
treatment, and the unmistakable tendency to resort to scriptural and liturgical terms whenever the stress of emotion becomes acute, so that Eliot seems to be not so much creating or
discovering impersonal objective correlatives for his personal
feeling as drawing freely on those more remote and inevitably
depersonalised objective correlatives which the Church makes
available to him in her texts for public worship. I cannot help
feeling that this is one more example of his attempt or tendency to follow out his own critical dictum that poetry should
provide not an expression of emotion but an escape from it.
The net effect is a certain fragmentation both in the experience
recorded and in the verse-form that records it:

> Will the veiled sister pray for
> Those who walk in darkness, who chose thee and
> oppose thee,
> Those who are torn on the horn between season and
> season, time and time, between
> Hour and hour, word and word, power and power,
> those who wait
> In darkness? Will the veiled sister pray
> For children at the gate
> Who will not go away and cannot pray:
> Pray for those who chose and oppose
>
> O my people, what have I done unto thee.

I hope no-one would regard this as among the best passages
in 'Ash-Wednesday'; yet it is, I think, verbose and mannered
as it is, characteristic and crucial. The whole of Section V,
from which this extract comes, seems to aim at the effect of a
broken, passionate succession of religious petitions, of a pas-
sionately improvised prayer of petition; and the liturgical and
scriptural echoes are there to give stability to the broken

meditation. In fact, they succeed only in enhancing the hypnotic quality of the rhythms and disguising the intellectual and emotional vacancy behind. In converting these ecclesiastical offerings to his own creative use, Eliot is not only refusing the challenge to integrate his beliefs with his personal dilemma but is also failing to define his personal dilemma with any clarity at all. Not that we want a confessional poetry, but if there *are* large problems at the centre of the poem we would be helped in reading it by having some idea of what they are.

It is most noticeable that recourse to the Church for a virtual smokescreen happens least in the first section. There, the feeling of loss, renunciation, desolation is poignantly evoked and placed in a context of Christian acceptance of the will of God. But at this stage there is no attempt at and no need for any more specific definition of the personal situation that the poet is dealing with. It is only later, when specific definition is necessary (and, so far as we can see, attempted), that the heavy liturgical reinforcements are called up: they are called up to *strengthen* the personal feeling, but end in disguising and diverting it. There is pretty obviously a strong sense of personal desolation established in Section 1:

> Because I cannot hope to turn again
> Consequently I rejoice, having to construct something
> Upon which to rejoice
> And pray to God to have mercy upon us
> And I pray that I may forget
> These matters that with myself I too much discuss
> Too much explain. . . .

The ritual circlings and repetitions of the verse, mannered as they are at times, help to present this sense of personal desolation successfully. Yet the forcing of the soul to recognise its own aridity also forces upon it a sense of the possibility of a realistic, unsentimental, unillusioned hope, which keeps in check the tendencies to self-laceration evident earlier in the section.

But it cannot keep in check the evasive rococo ornamenta-
tion, the wordy circlings round an undefined crisis, the preten-
tious conversion of Christian tradition into a private mythology,
and the posturing stoicism, of the next four sections. In these
central sections, the vacuity of the approach can be neither
disguised nor redeemed by the occasional superb cadence, or
glittering reminiscence, or richly evocative passage, like the
second half of Section III. For two-thirds of the poem we are
invited not into our own world defined and freshened by a
Christian vision but into a fanciful world in which Christian
references provide the props and into which a sense of personally apprehended reality breaks only at isolated moments.

This is a harsh judgment to make on a poem so obviously
written with effort and concern; but the more one studies
'Ash-Wednesday' the more bafflement and irritation set in.
The fine last section, after all, returns us to the general desolation and groping for acceptance recorded in the first section:
but the sections that intervene between the first and last
movements have not really defined either the dilemma or the
poet's stance; so the last movement does not strike us as having
won from anything that precedes it the right to adopt the
freed and heightened consciousness which it seems to record:

> And the lost heart stiffens and rejoices
> In the lost lilac and the lost sea voices
> And the weak spirit quickens to rebel
> For the bent golden-rod and the lost sea smell
> Quickens to recover
> The cry of quail and the whirling plover
> And the blind eye creates
> The empty forms between the ivory gates
> And smell renews the salt savour of the sandy earth.

Taut and suggestive, confident and free-moving though this is,
its strength once more comes from the strength of what it
rejects. That is fitting enough, but it has the effect of making
us feel that the elaborations which take up so much space in

the preceding sections are, in the end, elaborations of nothing-very-definite and nothing-very-relevant.

The whole poem, then, is dominated by a sense of the need for positive release, but not by any immediate promise or even hope of it. That is an additional reason for suspecting that the reliance on liturgical language, liturgical rhythms, and the dialectical form of versicle and response, becomes a device for diverting both Eliot and his reader from a definition of his dilemma. A careful probing of the poem uncovers more questions than the poem answers: *whose*, for example, are the 'lilac and brown hair' of Section III? The way they are presented does not enable us even to ask with any confidence whether or not it matters whose they are. But it *is* obvious that Eliot is facing with intense and almost desperate determination a personal situation which could be defined in other than religious terms; he and God and the Virgin Mary are plainly not the only actors in this vaguely defined interior drama. And we have to conclude that his approach to it, an approach at once insistent and elusive, repetitive and evasive, uses liturgical echoes as a way of providing an emotional strength and resolution which he either cannot or will not provide by more usual means. Even in the last section, repentance, beseeching, and nostalgia are more in evidence than any immediate sense of the presence of God or of any other person. The emotional force is provided at the expense of self-understanding or a more general human relevance.

I do not want to advance a case at the expense of a poem which was, after all, very obviously written with great emotional pressure and which in its finest moments gives us cadences of breathtaking power:

> Blown hair is sweet, brown hair over the mouth blown,
> Lilac and brown hair;
> Distraction, music of the flute, stops and steps
>   of the mind over the third stair,
> Fading, fading . . .

But I have been arguing that the critic's puzzlement comes partly from the difficulty of seeing the relevance of those cadences to the poem's avowed themes. Allen Tate says that 'the form of the poems in *Ash-Wednesday* is lyrical and solitary'; and I would agree that they are so despite their author's sustained attempt to make them something other, to give them a force and a dimension not personal but institutional. In fact, I think that my reading accounts for that other quality which Tate notes, 'the regular yet halting rhythm, the smooth uncertainty of movement'. The addition of 'smooth' to 'uncertainty' shows what is damaged in the poem's achievement; it is to some extent a mimed or pretended uncertainty, so that the unmistakable distress and nostalgia become covered over by something which both resembles them and distracts attention from them. For that reason, I feel that we must take 'Ash-Wednesday' as a transitional poem in the development of a great religious poet, and its faults as cautionary. Perhaps they were cautionary for Eliot himself, for by the time he comes to *Four Quartets* he has nearly eliminated them.

III

I may perhaps raise the question of how this is done by recalling a famous remark by D. W. Harding and by returning to one of my own. Of 'Burnt Norton' Harding said that its method involved the 'creation of concepts': that is, that it creates its questions in a philosophical mode which was simply not available to the poet at the time of 'Ash-Wednesday'. I think this is true, and that it gives a clue to the certainty with which Eliot there approaches his chief creative problem, what I earlier called the tension between form and fragmentation, pattern and momentary perception. For the problem which *Four Quartets* pose, and pose quite deliberately, is that of the relation between moment and continuity, perception and pattern, shaft of sunlight and crowned knot of fire. Broadly, it is true that 'Burnt Norton' is dominated by the momentary vision, and 'Little Gidding' by the awareness of pattern. In the first, the problem is to be able even to conceive of a pattern, so that the reference to 'the form, the pattern' in Part V seems not so much unconvincing as unconvinced; in the second, the problem is to avoid glibness in speaking of the pattern which has now been apprehended. There has therefore been a development from one to the other, so that the moments become a mosaic of meaning, and this is reflected in the movement and patterning of the poem itself.

The development did not happen without strain; Donald Davie has argued, to my mind quite convincingly, that 'The Dry Salvages' is 'the odd one out in all sorts of ways', and Hugh Kenner has suggested that in this quartet is advanced a 'false' solution, an arbitrary and somewhat sterile patterning, which has to be transcended before the 'true' patterning of 'Little Gidding' can be arrived at. Personally, I sometimes feel that Kenner writes about such matters in a way that suggests something like a conspiracy-theory of poetic composition; and I think it likely that the failure of 'The Dry Salvages' is a good deal less deliberate and schematic than Kenner's analysis seems to suggest.[1] But failure I take it to be, and I think that an examination of the role of the sestina in Part II would show it quite clearly. In considering the development within *Four Quartets*, one finds oneself tempted to slide over 'The Dry Salvages' completely; for its presence tends to blur the advance which undoubtedly takes place, an advance from perspective to perspective, but also in the achievement of the pattern whose absence from human lives has caused so much distress, in, for example, the train imagery which forms the centre of Part III in each of the first three quarters, and so, in at least a geographical sense, the centre of each quartet itself.

Actually, the question of pattern had been Eliot's problem

[1] In fact, Davie takes up Kenner's suggestion and extends it, in a surely unprofitable way. See 'T. S. Eliot: The End of an Era', in *T. S. Eliot* (Twentieth Century Views Series: Hugh Kenner, Ed.), p. 197 ff.

all along: not just conceptually but procedurally. So, if his art shows a progress in the explicitness with which he formulates this as the question which each poem has existentially to answer, it shows also a progress in the firmness with which a *poetic* pattern is in fact established. This seems to me obvious if we compare either 'The Waste Land' or 'Ash-Wednesday' with 'Little Gidding'; but it is also true if instead of 'Little Gidding' we think of 'East Coker' or even of 'Burnt Norton', a poem devoted almost entirely to posing the problem by evoking moments of awareness without pattern. The early poems are momentaneous, non-discursive, in method; 'Prufrock' makes a comedy and a half-success of its own fragmentary nature, 'Portrait of a Lady' makes a half-diagnosis of it. But there are three chief stages in which the fact of disjunction, of fragmentariness, and the possibility of pattern are played against each other; they are 'The Waste Land', 'Ash-Wednesday', and *Four Quartets*. The first in effect yields to the disjunction, is built of fragments, sometimes great and glowing but nevertheless confusing ones; and what pattern it asserts (if, indeed, it can accurately be said to assert any) is arbitrary and in a way a confession of despair because the name of the pattern is necessity. The second has a clearer sense of pattern but, as I have argued, it is one imposed on the emotions and failing in any case actually to order or even to cover them. The third, as a whole, achieves the pattern which is its subject; but it does so only by fighting out interiorly, and with great courage and resource, the problem involved of realising the possibility of pattern at each stage. This is perhaps the deepest sense in which it is an exploratory work; the 'concepts' it creates have to do with its own procedures as much as with any philosophical or theological mysteries; and one can see how profoundly right F. R. Leavis is when he says that this poetry is 'a searching of experience, a spiritual discipline, a technique for sincerity—for giving "sincerity" a meaning'. Nothing could be further from the truth than Herbert Read's claim that Eliot 'stultified his speech' for the 'unspoken law' of the spiritual life. On the contrary, he made that unspoken law and that life his subject, and probed it with as much freedom and stamina as one could hope for.

Four Quartets are, of course, as openly Christian poems as 'Ash-Wednesday', but not so insistently. They are indeed concerned with 'sincerity', and chiefly with the sincerity of their author. When he asks,

> 'Had they deceived us
> Or deceived themselves, the quiet-voiced elders',

one is conscious of the aspect of 'elder' in the *persona* which he had deliberately created, and one is conscious also of the quietness of the voice which addresses this question both to us and to himself. Christian man is not man declaring, or man puzzling, but man wondering; and in his wonder capable of torment as much as of joy. Therefore, even a statement of the poems' themes (although it could be given) would inevitably appear jejune; for the themes are both stated, as themes are in music, and asked as questions, as themes are in philosophy: questions about time and eternity, history and the Incarnation, sanctity and poetry, the whole and the now, the opaqueness and the transparency of personal experience. The musical themes receive a philosophical extension, and the philosophical questions receive a musical elaboration; however varied the poetry is in *Four Quartets*, it is not ultimately possible to separate these two aspects of Eliot's procedure. He states them as themes and poses them as questions in the one poetic activity; and they are not asked as a set of separate questions either, but uncovered as though by a slow-moving organic exploration.

It is also true that, if the presuppositions of the poem are Christian, so are the terms in which exploration is made. As Leavis has suggested, *Four Quartets* live out a paradox: they presuppose certain values as necessary for their very structure as poems yet devote that structure to questioning their meaning and relevance. The whole work is, in fact, the most authentic example I know in modern poetry of a satisfying religio-poetic meditation. We sense throughout it not merely a building-up of an intricate poetic form on the foundation of experiences already over and done with, but a constant energy, an ever-present activity, of thinking and feeling. The fact that some of the most crucial experiences which engage that activity are childhood ones, and that the poet genuinely re-creates them in questioning their significance, makes the comparison with Wordsworth an apt one. The first impression one gets is of deliberate precision, a prose-like recollectedness in the pace and the language; the second impression is of the complex spiritual and emotional energies which the precision is directed to clarifying and bringing to a point of balance.

And to expanding. The most remarkable feature of *Four Quartets* (and again the reference to *The Prelude* has some point) is the way the terms of reference, and hence, in effect, the subject-matter, widen from one quartet to another. I have already suggested that what began as a seemingly philosophical concern ends as a religious one. It is also necessary to stress that this change is not a simple process, and is not in fact anything that one would be content to call a 'change'. There is a gradual widening of perspective as each standpoint taken up by the author is provisionally established, so that he is enabled to move outwards to others. This is the most important structural fact about the poems, more telling, for example, than their imitation of musical form. The meditation not merely becomes more subtle, it also becomes more complete; and it becomes more inward, more recollected, more intense, more contemplative.

This judgment needs more demonstration than is possible here. But I may point to the fact that, if 'Burnt Norton' is domestic in its range of suggestion, 'Little Gidding' is familial and monastic; if the first concentrates on a question of individual memory, the last concentrates on that of historical memory. In doing so, it not only provides a summation of certain themes and basic images which have been explored and synthesised under different aspects in the earlier quartets, but also raises new considerations, and creates a whole new pattern of images in which to synthesise them with earlier ones as a way of drawing the whole meditation to a close.

We can begin to see the distinctive achievement of 'Little Gidding' by tracing the way in which the relation of concrete to abstract methods of presentation changes and develops from one quartet to another. The development certainly results from the expansion of the themes, but also from a growth in the stability with which Eliot manages his world. And it is a very noticeable development. In 'Burnt Norton', which begins with a laborious, repetitive, and difficult statement in abstract terms on the problem of time, its tyranny over the individual consciousness, and its possible redemption, and goes on immediately to present a personal experience in which ecstatic memory and present contemplation are blended, the concrete seems to be offered as an *example* of what is postulated in the abstract. 'Little Gidding' evades the problems raised by such a relatively primitive conception of philosophical poetry; and it approaches the question from the opposite direction. It begins with a splendidly realised evocation of the poet, or a closely related *persona*, entering the deserted grounds of Nicholas Ferrar's community-house and then, after observing, noting, and responding in spirit to this place 'where prayer has been valid', questioning himself on the significance of his prayer, the meaning this past has for him, and the nature of his allegiances. In this case, the questioning arises naturally out of a presented personal reality, and is stabilised by the sense we already have of a definite figure placed at a particular time in a specific place with a definable history.

The result of this, and of the developing logic of *Four Quartets* as a whole, is that 'Little Gidding' is a superb essay in self-definition. It has nothing of the self-indulgently confessional about it; it defines the self by defining the context and content of its allegiances. Its characteristic 'element' is fire, the fire at once of revelation and of purgation; and its tone is not one of desperation or disturbance (as too much of 'The Dry Salvages' is), but one of composed achievement which does not try to conceal, but rather builds on, the strenuous spiritual effort which we can sense in or behind it.

The place with which it opens is the deserted centre of Ferrar's community, the time is not the heavy summer morning of 'East Coker' or the vibrant autumn afternoon of 'Burnt Norton' but that strangely arresting time, 'midwinter spring'. In this paradoxical place at this paradoxical time, charged as they both are with subtle symbolic meanings, moves the figure of the poet, presented as a seeker trying to define the purpose which has brought him here. The rest of the section, and in a way the rest of the poem, is concerned with asking what are the real motives of his quest:

> You are not here to verify,
> Instruct yourself, or inform curiosity
> Or carry report. You are here to kneel
> Where prayer has been valid. And prayer is more
> Than an order of words, the conscious occupation
> Of the praying mind, or the sound of the voice praying.
> And what the dead had no speech for, when living,
> They can tell you, being dead: the communication
> Of the dead is tongued with fire beyond the language
> of the living.

To be here, though, is to be in history, and is to invite a questioning of the history to which one is, as it were, committed. The poem proceeds to query its author's sense of his own commitments.

The second section performs the same function as in the earlier quartets. It does not elaborate something already established, but swings off seemingly at a tangent, to an impersonal, objective, formal lyric which provides a setting for a futher stage of the meditation. Once again, the meditation is on the theme of old age, its wisdom and its folly, language and the depredations that time makes on it, and the spiritual potentialities of the ageing poet. But though it does not elaborate something already established, it has been prepared for by that earlier dramatic establishment of the poet meditating on his experience. We see no incongruity in the abrupt presentation of this new and extraordinary portrait of Eliot as an air-raid warden during a London air-raid, a calm figure in an apocalypse questioning and being questioned by a figure which apparently represents at the same time a humanism which must be renounced and poetry and the spiritual labour that poetry entails. This remarkable passage indicates a change, however, in his habits of composition; it has nothing of the resemblance to circling expository prose which its counterparts had in the earlier quartets. Now prose-meaning is assimilated to a grave and distinctive poetry, instinct with rhythmic force and emotional assurance:

> First, the cold friction of expiring sense
> Without enchantment, offering no promise
> But bitter tastelessness of shadow fruit
> As body and soul begin to fall asunder.
> Second, the conscious impotence of rage
> At human folly, and the laceration
> Of laughter at what ceases to amuse.
> And last, the rending pain of re-enactment
> Of all that you have done, and been; the shame
> Of motives late revealed, and the awareness
> Of things ill done and done to others' harm
> Which once you took for exercise of virtue.
> Then fools' approval stings, and honour stains.
> From wrong to wrong the exasperated spirit
> Proceeds, unless restored by that refining fire
> Where you must move in measure, like a dancer.

If ever there was a great passage of explicit moral wisdom in modern poetry, here it is; the gravity of the speaking voice is too exalted for us to use the word 'didactic'; the impersonality is almost that of some annunciation. Yet it is an impersonality won from grappling with the obviously tormenting elements in the poet's personal situation; a note of fierce pain persists, a note almost of violence, perfectly controlled by the conventions of meditation which Eliot has himself created. The meditative conventions which can contain such a fruitful and exalted ambiguity are flexible ones indeed, and the intensely close relation which is established between Eliot and a compound ghost so familiar as to be almost an *alter ego* shows that it is not merely the renunciation of a world-view that is in question.

Part III is as abrupt in its taking of a new direction as was the section before it. Now we have a personal meditation on alternative spiritual possibilities, weighed with a composure very noticeable after the nightmare London of Part II. As in the earlier quartets, a personal concern broadens to become a general one; and here as before Eliot analyses the ambiguities of words, motives, and spiritual states. This time the specific problem is that of one's attitude to the past, a problem which has, under different aspects, been central to each of the preceding sections: should one adopt an attitude of partisanship towards the parties in an ancient feud; or should one aim at a detachment that enables us to reach compassion and understanding? For

> History may be servitude,
> History may be freedom.

This section shows the struggle to recognise such alternative possibilities truly and to find the inner strength to opt for the right one. Its assured tone, its noble movement, present Eliot as *deciding*, not merely as meditating on the need for decision. And in the quotation from a medieval mystic, with which it ends, we can see the temporary end of such self-questioning in a calmly stated reliance on the providence of God, Who is 'the ground of our beseeching'. The thematic movement at this point may be called 'dramatic', in the sense that tensions worked out and frightening alternatives faced in the earlier sections are here subsumed under a prolonged cadence: a movement in the liberation of a personality which has faced 'very much reality', very much of the darker reality of itself.

In this context, the lyric which comprises Section IV seems almost jaunty. Certainly, it is gravely joyful in its treatment of its purgatorial theme. One begins to see more clearly the logic of the poem: the fire of purging leads to, or actually becomes, the fire of pentecost; the fire of separation and fear becomes that of the enlightened and liberated spirit. The dove of Part II and that of Part IV have the same apparent action, but different uses. The Holy Ghost comes as comforter, but bringing a terrible comfort, for

> We only live, only suspire
> Consumed by either fire or fire.

Each section, then, has its paradoxes, and they are central to the poetic working. Each paradox arises out of the resolution of a preceding one. But with the pentecostal paradox we are close to the end of Eliot's meditative pilgrimage. Part V provides a resolution to the whole quartet and the whole poem. Since 'Little Gidding' is not a noticeably disturbed or anguished meditation, as 'East Coker' and 'The Dry Salvages' are, each in its way, the function of this section is not to dissolve tension, as the lyric of Part IV would quite adequately have done, in any case, but to sum up, draw together, and consummate. It is marked by the unusually exalted confidence and control which are characteristic of the whole quartet. Its first few lines briefly recall questions, themes and phrases from all the earlier quartets, but do not now elaborate any problem; it is too late in the development of the poem for that. Instead of an involved posing of alternatives, we get simple and direct statements which, by repeating the words in which the questions were put earlier, and placing them in a new and expanded context, as it were, answer the questions themselves.

As it develops, the passage evokes a sense of communion with the experience of those now dead and the efforts of the living, restating the importance and even the holiness of the time-process, even though the importance and the holiness have to be seen through the dangers, fears, and losses which it inevitably brings. But the tone is not one of nostalgia or regret but one of consummation. There is now no question of opposing the 'timeless moments', so eloquently presented in 'Burnt Norton' and 'East Coker', to the temporal flux. The sustained and dialectical meditation of *Four Quartets* has poetically established the conviction that history is not just process but also pattern,

> history is a pattern
> Of timeless moments. . . .

and that the painful growth involved in the realisation of this difficult truth can be accomplished only by submission to the providence of God. In retrospect, we can see that this realisation is what *Four Quartets* is all about; and their development records the struggle towards it. So it is not unfitting that the whole work should end with a Dantesque vision of the unity of all things in holiness.

Such an account of the thematic development of 'Little Gidding' has, I think, an important bearing on the sense in which we may regard it as a religious poem. Certainly, it is a much more searching and critical exploration of the poet's beliefs, feelings, and environment than any of the earlier poems, Christian or otherwise. It is plainly neither a piece of propaganda nor a work of 'self-expression', but a self-exploration: an exploration, conducted in Christian terms, of one man's stance as a Christian. Its logic is that of exploration rather than exposition; and its elaborate structure is not designed as a shape into which the exploring meditation can comfortably run but as a way of posing to Eliot himself as well as to the reader the dilemmas, the tensions, the crucial alternatives which the meditation must face if it is to be what it claims to be. The structure is, in other words, a dialectical one.

But, to my mind, one of the biggest questions raised by *Four Quartets* as a whole is one I have already touched on in passing: the relation between concrete and 'abstract' methods of presentation; for it is here that Eliot faces his main danger as a religious poet. And it is only in 'Little Gidding' that he faces it with complete assurance.

Especially in 'Burnt Norton' and 'The Dry Salvages', too much of the exploration of significance is done in passages having a marked similarity with prose. From the way the whole work develops, it looks as though Eliot recognised this tendency and became conscious, at least by the end of 'East Coker', that an experiment was in danger of getting out of hand; for an exploration conducted too much in such explicit terms would become not a poetic exploration of the sensibility at all but an evasion of it; or, rather, the exploration would lapse into the exposition it had sought to avoid. There seems to be an attempt in 'The Dry Salvages' to change the relation of abstract comment to sensuous presentation; not by having less abstract comment but by having it less obviously separated, working it in more closely with the sensuous presentation. That attempt failed; there are more crudities and lapses in poetic tact in 'The Dry Salvages' than anywhere else in the Quartets. But it served as an experiment by which the transition could be made to the method of 'Little Gidding'. In that poem the abstraction has been transmuted into more satisfyingly poetic terms; it is the only quartet that has nothing provisional about it.

Even in Part III, the section which in the other quartets had led Eliot into disastrous failures of tone, the assurance remains.

One reason is that he has now abandoned the symbolism of trains and travelling which in the earlier quartets does such damage to his poetic composure. But another is surely that, instead of trying to assimilate concrete detail to an abstract discursive mode, he inverts the process and assimilates abstraction to the workings of a tightly controlled rhythmic pattern:

> History may be servitude,
> History may be freedom. See, now they vanish,
> The faces and places, with the self which, as it could,
>   loved them,
> To become renewed, transfigured, in another pattern.
> Sin is Behovely, but
> All shall be well, and
> All manner of thing shall be well.
> If I think, again, of this place,
> And of people, not wholly commendable,
> Of no immediate kin or kindness,
> But some of peculiar genius,
> United in the strife which divided them;
> If I think of a king at nightfall,
> Of three men, and more, on the scaffold
> And a few who died forgotten
> In other places, here and abroad,
> And of one who died blind and quiet,
> Why should we celebrate
> These dead men more than the dying?

The rhythmic pattern is here of great importance, and it is the main agent in establishing not only the tone of grave musing but the necessary sensuous suggestions. It is not a strongly sensuous poetry, full of compact images. On the contrary, its language might, under other circumstances, be considered quite 'abstract'; but its effect is one of bodily presence, and that effect is achieved largely through the rhythmic impulse that works so delicately throughout the passage. It goes, too, with an elimination of both the attitudinising that affects the comparable section of 'The Dry Salvages' and the over-charged emotionality in the two earlier quartets. This section of 'Little Gidding' seems to me an excellent example of how the process of thinking, of intellectual analysis, can be rendered or enacted in modern poetry. For it is clearly a poetry of intellectual analysis; the sinews of thought are not disguised or thickened by any attempt to render the whole process in images. It is balanced and 'charged with meaning' through a rhythmic force and subtlety that suggest the concrete rather than insist on it.

But Eliot's achievement as a modern religious poet does not consist only in his creation of a 'discursive mode' that adequately fuses abstract and concrete. It consists also in the sustained self-awareness which I have noted in my exposition of the dialectical logic of 'Little Gidding' as a whole. And it consists, most important of all, in the analogical mode created most strikingly in Part I of that poem.

The immediate power of this section goes with a delicacy and precision of a sort that we find nowhere in 'The Waste Land' or 'Ash-Wednesday':

> When the short day is brightest, with frost and fire,
> The brief sun flames the ice, on pond and ditches,
> In windless cold that is the heart's heat,
> Reflecting in a watery mirror
> A glare that is blindness in the early afternoon.
> And glow more intense than blaze of branch, or brazier,
> Stirs the dumb spirit: no wind, but pentecostal fire
> In the dark time of the year. Between melting and freezing
> The soul's sap quivers. There is no earth smell
> Or smell of living thing. This is the spring time
> But not in time's covenant.

This goes far beyond any of the techniques Eliot may be supposed to have learnt from the French Symbolists. It is patterned in such a way as to evoke with splendid accuracy the feel of one order of existence yet to evoke also another order of existence to which the first has an analogical reference. It works not by deploying a central symbol in the midst of the details of some actual situation, but by suggesting symbolic significances in the whole, and in every part, of what is sensuously presented. We may call this an analogical use of symbolism; the symbols are not things which point directly to what they stand for, but things which suggest an order of experience other than that in which they exist. There is paradox here, of course; the natural world is a 'mirror' of the supernatural world, reflecting its 'glare which is blindness'; things appear as their own opposites: snow is a kind of hedge-blossom, the stillness he speaks of has in it the vibrancy of marvellous growth. Fire, frost, sap, blossom, cold, heat are the items of a spiritual as well as a climatic condition; the pattern they compose reflects one in which Grace is co-present with nature, and in which the paradoxes of this extraordinary state of nature present the possibility of Grace.

All this could hardly have been established if the poet's perceptions had not been so precise, and if they had not been so precisely unified by the splendid control of rhythm, with its balance of expansiveness against repetition and insistence. The effect is to suggest a fine balance between concentrated attention and expansive response, between awareness of particulars and delight in the whole.

If we compare this passage with any of those already quoted from the earlier poems, we cannot help seeing what a great development has taken place in Eliot as a religious poet. Whatever the force of those earlier passages, it is not a force of this complex experimental kind. An 'impersonality' has been achieved not by escaping from or by disguising emotion but by accepting it and using it as an agent in the deployment of an analogical vision. It is significant that *Four Quartets* are the only poems where Eliot accepts his own presence and nature as basic, necessary data, and builds his poems around them. And in 'Little Gidding', he has shown us how a great religious poetry may be written in our time by accepting the self and, as it were, exploring its content.

The greatness of 'Little Gidding' is, of course, achieved at some cost: the intensity of vision is achieved at the cost of breadth of reference, the honesty is achieved at the cost of explicit human sympathy. But the self-exploration is not necessarily self-concern, and the intensity is not necessarily coldness. In the earlier quartets these limitations trouble us; in 'Little Gidding' they do not. Within the considerable limits of his temperament, Eliot has there climbed to an eminence of meditative nobility where no other contemporary poet can follow him; the fact that the ascent has been painful merely adds to the achievement.

IV

I cannot forego a couple of remarks by way of appendix. It would be dishonest, for one thing, to leave the impression that *Four Quartets* are totally exploratory; they *are* an exploration, but, as their name and their form both suggest, they are also a rather ritualised one, too much so in some ways; and that remarkable 'musical' shape which has been elaborated to reach and create such a variety of significance also has its diverting aspects, as we may see in 'The Dry Salvages' or in Part III of each of the first three quartets. For another thing, it would be unfortunate if my remarks about a certain crudity of procedure were to disguise the remarkable delicacy and distinction of the opening section of 'Burnt Norton', and still more unfortunate if my insistence on a multiple development throughout the work were to disparage 'East Coker', whose opening and closing movements strike me as hauntingly honest and greatly moving. In fact, it would be a valuable exercise, and something much more than an exercise, to make a comparative analysis of Part I of 'East Coker' and Part III of 'The Waste Land', by way of examining not only the subtlety but also the variousness of Eliot's sensibility. And, for a third, I cannot rest entirely happy in leaving the impression that Eliot's religious poetry at its greatest is only of a philosophical kind. For, if he creates 'concepts' he also creates an ambience of the sacred; and this is not always of the kind we might expect from a poet so definitely of one religious allegiance.

In saying so, I am thinking partly of that lovely poem, 'Marina', and of some remarks that have recently been made about the nature of Eliot's poetic genius and that have to do with the quality I am speaking of. The Eliot whom I value is not the Eliot whom I had pressed on me when I was an undergraduate, the ingenious seeker of effects whose comparison of the city evening with a patient etherised upon a table is in fact so sterile and absurd in its flight from any sensible reality. It is the Eliot whose cadence, resonance, instantaneous movements of feeling are so vivid and unforgettable. In fact, John Bayley is surely right to speak of him as one of 'the most passionate and spontaneous of poets', and of certain passages as having 'the absolute authority of feeling without a trace of self-consciousness or overt craft'. But he is surely wrong to think of Eliot as 'a lyricist and romantic, in the line of Burns no less than of Baudelaire'. The actual nature of the 'lyrical' impulse can be tested from a score of superb passages:

> Yet when we came back, late, from the Hyacinth garden,
> Your arms full, and your hair wet, I could not
> Speak, and my eyes failed, I was neither
> Living nor dead, and I knew nothing,
> Looking into the heart of light, the silence.

or

> My life is light, waiting for the death wind,
> Like a feather on the back of my hand.

or

> This form, this face, this life
> Living to live in a world of time beyond me; let me

Resign my life for this life, my speech for that unspoken,
The awakened, lips parted, the hope, the new ships.

or

And the pool was filled with water out of sunlight,
And the lotos rose, quietly, quietly,
And the surface glittered out of heart of light,
And they were behind us, reflected in the pool.

There is a variety among these passages, yet they are all breathtaking, and in much the same way. It is not, I think, the way
suggested by John Bayley in his invocation of Burns. What
affects us is not a directness and simplicity of any singable,
extravertable kind, but a haunting and haunted quality, the
cadence of a reminiscence from profound depths or unmeasured
spaces, the echo of a feeling that lives on as deep in the inner
ear as any words can go. Perhaps this quality, which Eliot is
alone among modern poets in possessing, comes from the fact
that so often the lyrical freedom lives alongside an odd sense
of psychological pressure, a pressure which would be restraint
and repression if the song were not capable of making it accessible for him. One notices the recurrence of the words 'life'
and 'light', coming with an intensity of interest which nevertheless has nothing desperate about it. One notices also the
repetition of phrases like 'heart of light', suggesting not a
poverty of imagination but its opposite, the recall to and in
language of an impulse which has been experienced as of truly
primal, sacral importance to the spirit. In that sense at the very
least Eliot is a world-restorer; it is by no means an attenuated
sense; and it has an important bearing on the ways in which he
is a great religious poet; he is concerned with radical innocence as well as with other dimensions of human life. Noticing
it, one finds it hard to believe, as Herbert Read and others
have said, that the English poet with whom he felt most natural
affinity was Samuel Johnson; but one finds it easier to believe

that the poet whose Waste Land struck so many of its early readers as a definitive echo of their own sense of fate should have come much later to see, with an amazing vividness of perception, the signs of a midwinter spring that is of its own season.

Index

About the House (W. H. Auden), 50

Absalom and Achitophel (John Dryden), 40

Adam's Curse (W. B. Yeats), 176

All Souls Night (W. B. Yeats), 192

Alvarez, A., 73

Among School Children (W. B. Yeats), 195

Anniversarie, The (John Donne), 106

Arnold, Matthew, 5-6, 49, 153

Arrow, The (W. B. Yeats), 176

Ash-Wednesday (T. S. Eliot), 208, 210, 212, 214-15, 217, 219, 221-2, 232

At Galway Races (W. B. Yeats), 189-90

Parnell's Funeral (W. B. Yeats), 175

Auden, W. H., 8, 49-53, 64, 66, 71, 146, 148, 159, 172

Auguries of Innocence (William Blake), 135

Autobiographies (W. B. Yeats), 9, 56

Bateson, F. W., 127

Batter my Heart (John Donne), 114

Baxter, James K., 67

Bayley, John, 235-6

Berdan, J. M., 78-9

Bewley, Marius, 147, 153, 158

Blake, William, 8, 10, 15, 30, 37, 42-3, 47-9, 53, 55-6, 66, 117-43

Blossom, The (William Blake), 122

Blossome, The (John Donne), 103

Bonhoeffer, D., 4, 19

Bradford, Curtis, 197

Bradley, A. C., 6-7

Broadbent, J. B., 5, 32, 39

Bronowski, J., 119

Browning, Robert, 173

Burns, Robert, 48, 235-6

Burnt Norton (T. S. Eliot), 219, 221, 223-5, 229-30, 234

Bush, Douglas, 5

Byron, Lord, 48

Calvinism, 29, 145, 152

Campbell, Joseph, 67

Canonization, The (John Donne), 106

Canterbuty Tales (Geoffrey Chaucer), 24

Chambers, E. K., 26

Chase, Richard, 147

Chatterton, Thomas, 48

Chaucer, Geoffrey, 24, 66, 124, 185

Coleridge, Samuel Taylor, 7, 10, 15, 47, 49, 55-6, 63, 66, 99, 118

Collar, The (George Herbert), 35

Collins, William, 48, 118

'Complaint' poems, 23, 26, 57

Coole and Ballylee, 1931 (W. B. Yeats), 192-3

Coole Park, 1929 (W. B. Yeats), 192-3

Cowley, Abraham, 37

Cox, Harvey E., 19

Crashaw, Richard, 32-3, 43, 108

Crazy Jane and Jack the Journeyman (W. B. Yeats), 195

Crazy Jane on God (W. B. Yeats), 188, 195-6

Crofts, Professor, 104, 109-10
Cromwell, Thomas, 83, 90
Cruttwell, Patrick, 106
Culture and Theology (Brian Wicker), 19
Curse of Cromwell, The (W. B. Yeats), 186-7, 196
Curtis, Penelope, 175 n.

Dante Alighieri, 66
Das Heilige (Rudolf Otto), 12
Davideis (Abraham Cowley), 37
Davie, Donald, 73-4, 220
Davies, Sir John, 29-30
Death be not Proud (John Donne), 114
Dickens, Charles, 163, 166
Dickinson, Emily, 54, 146
Divine and Moral Songs (Isaac Watts), 121
Donne, John, 15, 28-34, 36, 39, 43, 60, 66, 71, 95, 97, 99-116, 185
Dowson, Ernest, 53, 56
Dry Salvages, The (T. S. Eliot), 220, 225, 228, 230, 232, 234
Dryden, John, 37, 39-41, 65-6, 99
Dunbar, William, 26

East Coker (T. S. Eliot), 221, 225, 228-30, 234
Easter, 1916 (W. B. Yeats), 185-7
Elegie XIX : On His Mistris Going to Bed (John Donne), 104, 107
Eliade, Mircea, 7-8, 10-18, 29, 39, 57-8, 60, 74-5, 177
Eliot, George, 163
Eliot, T. S., 8, 16, 24, 34-5, 37-8, 49, 55-6, 64, 66, 71, 88, 99, 118, 121, 136, 143, 176, 185, 205-37
Empson, Professor William, 72
Enchafed Flood, The (W. H. Auden), 148

Enright, D. J., 39
Epithalamion (Edmund Spenser), 30
Erasmus, Desiderius, 82
Exequy (Henry King), 37
Experience (William Blake), 118-21, 123, 125-7, 138, 141
Explorations (W. B. Yeats), 9
Extasie, The (John Donne), 103

Faerie Queene, The (Edmund Spenser), 30
Fairchild, Hoxie N., 5, 41-4, 46
Falck, Colin, 73-4
Faust (Johann Wolfgang Goethe), 161
Fiedler, Leslie, 147
Fisherman, The (W. B. Yeats), 189
Flea, The (John Donne), 103
Flower, The (George Herbert), 35
Four Quartets (T. S. Eliot), 50, 205-6, 208-10, 219-24, 229-30, 233-4
Fraser, G. S., 62
Friends (W. B. Yeats), 191
Frye, Northrop, 209

Gardiner, Stanley, 141
Gardner, Helen, 103-4, 111, 113
Good Friday, Riding Westward (John Donne), 71, 113
Good Morrow, The (John Donne), 102
Gray, Thomas, 48, 118
Greville, Fulke, 24, 29-31, 33, 36
Grierson, Sir H. J. C., 99

Hamburger, Michael, 208
Harding, D. W., 219

Hawthorne, Nathaniel, 145-6, 161
Henley, William, 56
Henry VIII, King, 83
Herbert, George, 1, 17-18, 31, 33-
  36, 39, 43-4, 46-7, 60, 65, 86,
  108
Hind and the Panther, The (John
  Dryden), 40
Hoffman, Daniel, 160
Holy Sonnets (John Donne), 111, 113
Holy Thursday (William Blake),
  124-5
Hope, A. D., 8, 11-12, 173
Hopkins, Gerard Manley, 1, 15-16,
  30-1, 37, 49, 58-60, 64, 71, 204
Huxley, Aldous, 56
Hymne to God my God, A (John
  Donne), 108, 110, 113-14
Hymne to God the Father, A (John
  Donne), 108

In Memoriam (T. S. Eliot), 49, 207
Infant Sorrow (William Blake), 129,
  131
In Memory of Major Robert Gregory
  (W. B. Yeats), 187, 192
In Praise of Limestone (W. H. Auden),
  50, 52, 71
In the Seven Woods (W. B. Yeats),
  176
Innocence (William Blake), 119-21,
  124-5, 128, 131, 138, 141

Johnson, Lionel, 53
Johnson, Samuel, 1, 24, 40, 56, 99,
  236
Jonson, Ben, 33, 86
Jones, David, 8
Jordan (George Herbert), 35

Kazin, Alfred, 147
Keats, John, 48, 55
Kenner, Hugh, 220
Kermode, Professor Frank, 68-70,
  74
King, Henry, 33
King Lear (William Shakespeare),
  161
Knights, L. C., 39
Koch, Vivienne, 176

Lament for the Makers (William
  Dunbar), 26-7
Lapis Lazuli (W. B. Yeats), 195
Lawrence, D. H., 67
Leavis, F. R., 2, 99, 173, 221-2
Lewis, C. S., 104
Lienhardt, Godfrey, 69
Little Black Boy, The (William Blake),
  123
Little Gidding (T. S. Eliot), 71, 206,
  209-10, 220-1, 223-4, 228-30,
  232, 234
Little Girl Lost and Found, The
  (William Blake), 138
London (William Blake), 132, 136-8,
  141
Love (George Herbert), 35
Lowell, Robert, 16, 49, 70-1, 88

Mac Flecknoe (John Dryden), 40
Man (George Herbert), 45
Man and the Echo, The (W. B.
  Yeats), 178-84, 194
Marina (T. S. Eliot), 235
Marriage (William Blake), 121
Martz, L. L., 33
Marvell, Andrew, 33, 63, 115-
  116

Mason, H. A., 77-8, 82, 85, 91-2, 94
Meditations in Time of Civil War (W. B. Yeats), 175, 194
Melville, Herman, 15, 144-71
Metaphysical poetry, 31-2, 34, 36-7, 48, 65, 87
Miller, J. Hillis, 5, 58
Milton, John, 34, 37, 39
Moby Dick (Herman Melville), 6, 144-7, 149-71
Moore, Thomas, 173
More, Sir Thomas, 82
Mr. Edwards and the Spider (Robert Lowell), 70
Muir, Professor Kenneth, 67, 77-8, 88
Municipal Gallery Revisited, The (W. B. Yeats), 193-4
Murder in the Cathedral (T. S. Eliot), 208, 214

Nietzsche, Friedrich, 56
Nocturnall Upon S. Lucies Day, A (John Donne), 106
Nones (W. H. Auden), 50
Nurse's Song (William Blake), 123

O'Casey, Sean, 173
O'Connor, Frank, 173
O'Donnell, Donat, 5
On the Resurrection of Christ (William Dunbar), 26-7
Otto, Rudolf, 12-13

Paradise Lost (John Milton), 32, 161
Parkinson, Thomas, 193
Peter, Professor John, 22-3, 27, 41, 57

Poet and His Faith, The (A. S. P. Woodhouse), 5
Poetical Sketches (William Blake), 118
Poetry and Dogma (M. M. Ross), 5
Poison Tree, A (William Blake), 129-130, 138
Pope, Alexander, 40, 173
Portrait of a Lady (T. S. Eliot), 210, 221
Pound, Ezra, 48-9, 185, 191
Prayer (George Herbert), 35
Prayer for My Daughter, A (W. B. Yeats), 198
Prelude, The (William Wordsworth), 67, 223
Prime (W. H. Auden), 50-1
Prophetic Books (William Blake), 119
Prufrock (T. S. Eliot), 205, 210, 221

Quaker Graveyard in Nantucket, A (Robert Lowell), 70
Quarles, Francis, 37
Quarrel in Old Age (W. B. Yeats), 195, 197

Raine, Kathleen, 118, 125, 138-9
Raleigh, Sir Walter, 33
Ransom, John Crowe, 67
Read, Herbert, 221-2, 236
Red Hanrahan's Song about Ireland (W. B. Yeats), 176
Religious Trends in English Poetry (Hoxey N. Fairchild), 5, 41
Revaluation (F. R. Leavis), 2
Review, The, 73, 206
Robinson, Bishop John, 20
Roethke, Theodore, 11-12, 17-18, 49-53, 61, 67-9

Romantic movement, 11, 16, 41-2, 44, 47-9, 55-7, 61, 63, 68
Ross, Malcolm Mackenzie, 5, 38-9, 41

Sacred and the Profane, The (Mircea Eliade), 12
Sailing to Byzantium (W. B. Yeats), 183, 194-5, 197-8, 204
Santayana, George, 6, 58
Savage, D. S., 8
Science and English Poetry (Douglas Bush), 5
Second Anniversary, The (John Donne), 100
Second Coming, The (W. B. Yeats), 175
Secular Christianity (Ronald Gregor Smith), 19
Secular City, The (Harvey E. Cox), 19
September, 1913 (W. B. Yeats), 185-187
Sexton, Anne, 76
Shakespeare, William, 34, 37, 95, 97, 118, 139, 141, 161, 165, 185
Shelley, Percy Bysshe, 48, 55
Shepheardes Calendar, The (Edmund Spenser), 30
Sick Rose, The (William Blake), 125, 129, 131, 137-8, 141
Simplon Pass, The (William Wordsworth), 45-6
Silver Poets (Sir Thomas Wyatt), 94
Sitwell, Dame Edith, 67
Smart, Christopher, 15, 37, 40-1, 49, 60, 63, 124
Smith, James, 99
Smith, Ronald Gregor, 19
Social Anthropology (Geoffrey Lienhardt), 69

Songs and Sonets (John Donne), 107, 113
Songs of Innocence (William Blake), 119, 124
Southall, Raymond, 77n.
Southwell, Robert, 33
Spender, Stephen, 209
Spenser, Edmund, 29-30
Steiner, George, 5
Stevens, Dr. John, 77n., 89n., 91n.
Sunne Rising, The (John Donne), 106
Surrey, Earl of, 78, 82, 93
Swift, Jonathan, 40

Tate, Allen, 2, 9, 67, 185, 219
Temple, The (George Herbert), 34
Tennyson, Alfred, Lord, 47, 49, 55, 174
Thomas, Dylan, 9, 49, 53, 59-63, 67-8, 71
Thomas, R. S., 67
Thomson, James, 40, 42, 44, 48
Thomson, Patricia, 77n.
Thoughts after Lambeth (T. S. Eliot), 214
Tiger, The (William Blake), 131, 137-8, 141, 143
Tillyard, E. M. W., 81
To Ireland in the Coming Times (W. B. Yeats), 185
To Penshurst (Ben Jonson), 86
Tottel, Richard, 82
Traherne, Thomas, 33
Twicknam Garden (John Donne), 102
Tyndall, John, 56

Under Ben Bulben (W. B. Yeats), 186

Vanity of Human Wishes, The (Samuel Johnson), 40

Vaughan, Henry, 33, 37, 64-5
Vision, A (W. B. Yeats), 175

Warton, Thomas, 78
Waste Land, The (T. S. Eliot), 205-6,
    209-14, 221, 232, 234, 237
Watts, Isaac, 42, 121
Wellesley, Lady Dorothy, 178
Whitman, Walt, 49-51, 53-4, 61,
    63, 66-7
Whitsunday in Kirchstetten (W. H.
    Auden), 50
Wicker, Brian, 19
Williams, Raymond, 4
Wilson, Mona, 127

Winters, Yvor, 2, 150, 153, 156-7,
    173
Witcutt, W. P., 118
Woodhouse, A. S. P., 5, 7, 34
Wordsworth, William, 8, 10, 15, 34,
    37, 40, 42-4, 46-51, 53, 55-6, 63-
    66, 71, 118, 223
Wreck of the Deutschland, The
    (Gerard Manley Hopkins), 71
Wyatt, Sir Thomas, 1, 7, 28-30, 77-
    98, 185

Yeats, W. B., 9, 15, 37, 49, 55-6,
    66, 68-9, 99, 118, 127, 137-8,
    172-205, 207